SABINA·POPEA

NERO

Abina poppea Romana et illuftris fuit femia T. ollij nõ eq̃dem extreme nobilitatis viri filia qua̅q̃ nõ ex eo nomen fūpferit fed a materno auo poppeo fabino viro inclito Atq̃ triumphalis decoris et cõfolatu iñgni. nec illi cetere mliebres defuiffent dotes fi honeſt̃ fuiſſet anim̃. Fuit eni formofitatis inuife et matri fuis ãnis ceteras romanas pulcritudie excedenti pfimilis. Pretĕa erat illi ſ̄mo blandus et laudabili fonor̃ dulcedie ingenium eg̃giũ atq̃ ṽfatie fi eo honeſtis artib̃ fuiſſet vfa. Mos q̃ illi fuit aſſiduus pala̅ mõdeſtiam pferre clam

NERO

right: A gem showing merchant ships arriving at a harbour, perhaps Ostia.

frontispiece: A cameo showing Claudius and Agrippina (on the left) and Germanicus and Agrippina the elder, with the imperial eagle between. The heads are set in horns of abundance (*cornua copiae*).

EMPEROR IN REVOLT

NERO

MICHAEL GRANT

AMERICAN HERITAGE PRESS
NEW YORK

Library of Congress Catalog Card No.: 79-116178
07-024075-2
Printed in Italy, by LIBREX Milano

Contents

1 Nero Comes to the Throne   19

Nero's accession – Agrippina's early life – Caligula – Lucius Domitius
Ahenobarbus – Nero's childhood – Agrippina marries Claudius – Nero's
distinguished tutor – Claudius adopts Nero – Britannicus – the murder
of Claudius

2 Nero's Mother in Charge   35

'The best of Mothers' – victims of the regime – a permissive age – the
Satyricon – Agrippina's power declines – the murder of Britannicus –
Agrippina's removal from court

3 Nero and his Helpers   51

The theatre – Nero's nocturnal activities – the Greeks as imperial ministers
– the running of the empire – Burrus and Seneca – *On Clemency* – a correct
regime – tax reforms – bread and circuses – the eastern frontier

4 The Death of Agrippina   73

Nero's fear of Agrippina – her attempted murder – a successful second
attempt – the collaborators – the role of Burrus – Seneca's dilemma

5 An Emperor who Sings, Acts and Races   83

Singing, acting and chariot racing – lyre-player and tragic actor – Nero
as poet – Nero's favourite roles – the Youth Games – the emperor's stage
debut – the Circus Maximus – the Neronian Games – philhellenism –
Nero's medical advisers

List of Maps

Acknowledgments

Acknowledgments are owed to the following for translations: Cambridge University Press, F. H. Sandbach in *Cambridge Ancient History*, Vol. XI (Seneca); Doubleday and Company Inc., M. Hadas, *The Stoic Philosophy of Seneca*; Indiana University Press, W. S. Merwin, *The Satires of Persius*; International Authors' Agency, R. Graves, *Suetonius: The Twelve Caesars*; Loeb Classical Library, E. Cary, *Dio Cassius*, and J. C. Rolfe, *Suetonius*; New American Library, W. Arrowsmith, *Petronius: The Satyricon*; Penguin Books, R. Campbell, *Seneca: Letters from a Stoic*, M. Grant, *Tacitus: Annals of Imperial Rome*, P. Green, *Juvenal: The Sixteen Satires*, J. Sullivan, *Petronius: The Satyricon*, K. Wellesley, *Tacitus: Histories*; Phoenix House Ltd., J. M. Todd, *Voices from the Past* (Seneca); Routledge and Kegan Paul, G. and H. Highet, O. Kiefer's *Sexual Life in Ancient Rome* (the *Octavia*) and (with Basic Books Inc.) G. B. Townend in T. A. Dorey (ed.), *Latin Biography* (Suetonius); the Society for the Promotion of Roman Studies, M. P. Charlesworth in *Journal of Roman Studies* (Nero).

Sources of Illustrations

Alinari, 27, 28, 32, 47b, 52, 53b, 72, 73, 75, 79, 82, 89, 90, 92, 94, 95a
and b, 106, 108, 115, 139, 146, 154, 162, 174a, 177, 194, 211, 217, 220,
236, 252a and b, 253; Anderson, 134, 171, 193; Archaeological Museum,
Venice, 211; Hallam Ashley, 114a and b, 116a, b, c and d; James Austin,
66–7; British Museum, 4, 17, 18, 29, 31, 35, 37, 38, 39, 40, 42a and b,
47a, 49, 53a, 57a and b, 65, 70, 71, 86–7, 88, 91, 98–9, 100, 111a and b,
117, 119a, b and c, 121, 124, 127, 136, 140a and b, 142–3, 148b, 152a and
b, 159, 163a and b, 188, 195, 196, 199, 201, 202, 204, 206a and b, 207a
and b, 209, 212, 219, 222, 223a and b, 224a and b, 227, 228a and b, 231,
232, 238, 240, 242a and b, 243, 245, 247, 250, 251a and b; Capitoline
Museum, Rome, 79, 220; G. Cerletti, 178; Colchester and Essex Museum,
118; *The Connoisseur*, 24b; Otto Fein, 118; Françoise Foliot, 122–3,
141, 248; Werner Forman, 17, 31, 35, 37, 38, 39, 40, 42a and b, 49, 57a
and b, 65, 68, 71, 85, 88, 97, 119a and b, 121, 124, 127, 136, 148b, 152a
and b, 159, 163a and b, 165, 166–7, 168, 181, 182, 183, 184, 189, 190–1,
192, 196, 199, 201, 202, 203, 204, 206a and b, 207a and b, 209, 212, 219,
222, 223a and b, 224a and b, 227, 228a and b, 231, 232, 237, 238, 240,
242a and b, 243, 245, 247, 251a and b; Fototeca Unione, 63, 102, 164, 169,
174b; German Archaeological Institute, Rome, 69; Michael Holford, 86–7,
98–9, 142–3; A. F. Kersting, 125; Kunsthistorisches Museum, Vienna, 3;
Louvre, 122–3, 141, 248; Mainz Museum, 108, 115, 229; Mansell
Collection, 62; L. von Matt, 22, 24a, 26c, 44, 45, 54, 59, 104, 105, 150,
156a and b, 179, 208, 210, 234, 241; E. Meyer, 3; Museo Barracco, Rome,
25; Museo delle Terme, Rome, 66–7, 236; Museo della Civiltà Romana,
Rome, 175; Museo di Roma, 252b; Museum of Fine Arts, Boston, 46, 144;
National Museum, Berlin, 24c, 50; National Museum, Naples, 52, 53b,
68, 72, 82, 89, 90, 92, 95a and b, 100, 134, 154, 171, 174a, 190–1, 194, 203;
National Photographic Museum, Rome, 81, 157; Norwich Museum, 113,
114a and b, 116a, b, c and d; Ny Carlsberg Glyptothek, 21, 34, 36, 78,
148a; Olympia Museum, Greece, 73, 149; Oriental Institute, University
of Chicago, 128; Palatine Antiquarium, 94; Parma Museum, 32; Josephine
Powell, 61; Edwin Smith, 84, 186a and b; La Spezia Museum, 147; Spink
and Son, 218a and b; Uffizi Gallery, Florence, 24b, 27, 47b, 106, 139,
146, 217, 252a, 253; Vatican Library, 104, 105, 150, 156a and b; Vatican
Museums, 75, 180, 193; Vatican Palace, 162; Warburg Institute, London,
118; Worcester Art Museum, Massachusetts, 131, 205; Yigael Yadin, 226.

Table of Dates

64	Great Fire of Rome. Persecution of the Christians. Work begins on the Golden House.
65	Conspiracy of Piso. Deaths of Seneca and Lucan. Nymphidius Sabinus becomes joint Guard commander with Tigellinus. Death of Poppaea.
66	Deaths of Petronius, Thrasea Paetus and Barea Soranus. Nero marries Statilia Messalina. Jewish revolt begins. Visit of Tiridates of Armenia to Rome. Conspiracy of Vinicianus. Nero leaves for Greece.
67	Death of Corbulo. Nero takes part in Greek Games and declares Liberation of Greece.
68	Galba declares himself representative of the Senate and Roman people in Spain. Verginius Rufus defeats Vindex at Vesontio. Death of Vindex.
(9 June)	Death of Nero.

Introduction

Nero was born of murderous parents, and brought up in a murderous atmosphere. And he too was murderous. But only when frightened; though unfortunately he got frightened easily. If, however, there was a reign of terror, it was not to be compared with modern ones, since it only affected a minute section of the population. But it included the culminating horror of matricide: although his mother may well have been wanting his death, and perhaps even plotting it. Nero's dreadful act forms a curious contrast to his undoubted dislike of executions, gladiatorial massacres, and wars.

His distaste for war showed itself in a sensible foreign policy, which culminated in a mutually face-saving settlement with Parthia. Misgovernment contributed to two rebellions, in Israel and Britain. But on the whole the vast empire was governed well, if a trifle unimaginatively: quite as well as in the previous reigns, and sometimes better. Much of the day-to-day work of administration was performed unobtrusively by the freedmen who acted as Nero's ministers, Greeks or Hellenized orientals. But they worked according to the policies established by the imperial council, Nero's circle of selected friends, presided over by himself.

As the reign went on, however, he must have devoted less and less attention to the problems of empire. He was, it is true, glad to register a spectacular governmental success from time to time. But it was as a singer, actor, poet, athlete, charioteer, and connoisseur of the arts that he really wanted to shine. It is highly unusual for any monarch at any period in world history to have lavished such a vast proportion of his efforts on achieving personal artistic success. This, in the end, created an astonishing situation: Nero, ruler of the western world, virtually became a stage professional.

His sex life, even by the Roman standards of his day, was alarmingly depraved and versatile (if we can believe even a fraction of the reports). It also seemed to confirm the worst suspicions of the conservative Roman upper class about the evil effects of culture: the whole thing was altogether too Greek. They were even more alarmed by purges in their own ranks, which might easily, at any moment, be extended to themselves. By the proletariat of Rome, on the other hand, the emperor's position was not threatened. They grumbled sometimes, as was their custom. Yet on the whole, in spite of these periods of discontent, they regarded Nero as their benefactor, since he usually took great trouble to see that their free food supplies and amusements were maintained without interruption.

Owing to his lack of interest in military affairs, he ran a risk, by never showing himself to the legions on the frontiers. Yet they nearly all remained loyal to him. His end came when his personal troops in Rome itself, the Praetorian Guard, turned against him; this was, however, not through their own initiative but because one of their two generals deserted, while the other remained inactive. Both had been bad appointments, made for personal reasons – unlike the vast proportion of senior appointments during the reign, which were solid, undramatic and good.

But these were epithets which could not be applied to most aspects of Nero's life, which was so extraordinary that even the weirdest accounts of what he did and said do not seem incredible. The Greeks loved him because he was the most phil-Hellene Roman emperor that there ever was; the east admired him for his astute Parthian settlement and his grandiose style of living; and the Christians regarded him as Anti-Christ because he had made them the scapegoats for the Great Fire of Rome. And so, for these various reasons, immediately after his death he passed into legend (see Appendix 1).

This book is an attempt to tell the story of his life. The evidence is often difficult and ambiguous, and I believe that yet another attempt to make sense of it is justified, however inadequate this may be. For one thing, it is necessary to bear in mind important recent studies on various aspects of the subject. Some of these studies relate to the ancient authors who wrote about Nero. It is, no doubt, blasphemous to say so, but one of the chief reasons why the material is so tantalizing is because the principal account comes from one of the greatest historians who have ever lived, Tacitus, who has left his own powerful – too powerful – stamp on events. And Suetonius, too, though the most amusing of all biographers, sometimes hinders quite as much as he helps. Besides, they both wrote more than half a century after Nero's death; and the third historian whose account has come down to us (in abbreviated form) is Dio Cassius, who lived a century later still. Fortunately, however, there are other sources: ancient writings of a non-historical character, inscriptions, and coins (see Appendix 2).

I am grateful to Mr B.H.Warmington for showing me the proofs of his recent book *Nero: Reality and Legend*, to which I owe a number of debts; and to Mr D.E.L.Haynes and Mr G.K.Jenkins for advice. I also want to thank Miss Susan Phillpott of Messrs. Weidenfeld and Nicolson for a great deal of editorial assistance, Miss Antonia Raeburn for collecting material for the illustrations, and Mr Werner Forman for taking many of the photographs. My wife's aid has also been immensely helpful.

Gattaiola, 1970   MICHAEL GRANT

Nero's mother Agrippina, on a silver coin of Antioch, capital of the province of Syria (Antakya in S.E. Turkey), AD 56.

1 Nero Comes to the Throne

At midday on 13 October, AD 54, the doors of the imperial palace at Rome were thrown open, and the young Nero appeared on the threshold. He was accompanied by Burrus, commander of the Praetorian Guard, which was responsible for the safety of emperors; other senior officers were there too, as well as the principal Greek freedmen – former slaves who acted as imperial ministers. Claudius had died the night before, but the proclamation of his stepson Nero was delayed until the astrologers felt able to declare the moment favourable. Claudius' wife and Nero's mother, Agrippina, was accustomed to consult astrologers; and no doubt on this occasion they waited until Burrus' plans were ready. Now, therefore, the youth stood on the steps of the palace, and a crowd which had been mobilized for the occasion hailed his accession to the imperial throne.

Then he was taken to the camp of the Praetorian Guard, who duly provided their confirmation – without which no emperor could last a day. They possessed a habit of loyalty to the imperial house, and they had been prepared for this moment by Burrus, who during his three years of office had worked indefatigably in the interests of Agrippina and her son. And so Nero now delivered a brief address to the guardsmen, promising them gifts on the generous scale set by his father; and it was understood that they would receive a monthly allowance of grain free of charge.

The young emperor was not entirely prepossessing. He was shortsighted, and looked out at the world with blinking, half-closed eyes.[1] Suetonius, whose biography is full of racy details, describes his personal appearance as follows: 'He was about the average height. He suffered from spots and body odour. His hair was light blond, his features fine rather than attractive, his eyes bluish grey and rather weak, his neck too thick, his stomach protuberant and his legs very thin.'[2]

However, it was a great advantage that his mother's father had been the gallant Germanicus (d. AD 19), who never became emperor but caught the people's fancy to an unparalleled extent. It was also a tremendous asset that Nero's great-great-grandfather had been Augustus, the almost legendary founder of the imperial regime, who had died and been made a god of the Roman state just forty years earlier. His services to that state had been astonishing and unique. When he had established sole control over all its

A bronze head of
Claudius, found in the
River Alde, Suffolk,
England.

Italy

territories by defeating Antony and Cleopatra (31–30 BC), he found an empire racked by decades of disturbances and by repeated civil wars. By clever, patient, imaginative efficiency, not unmixed with an element of ruthlessness, he put an end to all this, and when he died left an empire that was peaceful, secure, and on the whole well administered. Its population amounted to many tens of millions, how many we cannot say. For its area was vast; and he himself had added Egypt and other countries. Already under the later Republic, the Roman world had covered almost the entire Mediterranean region, and then Augustus' great-uncle and adoptive father, the dictator Julius Caesar, had made it into an empire of continental Europe as well by conquering the whole of central and northern France, and extending the frontier as far as the Rhine.

A princess of the mid-first century.

20

It was at one of the Rhenish frontier fortresses that Nero's mother, Agrippina, had been born in AD 15. Her birthplace was a German town, a Roman cantonment later named after herself, Colonia Agrippinensis (Köln). When her son eventually came to the throne, she had lived through three memorable and terrible reigns, those of Tiberius (AD 14–37), Caligula (Gaius) (37–41), and Claudius (41–54). In spite of the aberrations of each successive ruler – which lose nothing in the telling by the ancient historians – the empire, as a whole, carried on effectively enough. But the lives of those near the emperors were hazardous. As a girl Agrippina herself had seen frightful things.

When she was fourteen her mother, from whom she inherited her name, was arrested by Augustus' successor Tiberius and exiled to an island, where she was beaten up by an officer and permanently blinded in one eye. Forcible feeding failed to prevent her from starving herself to death – though not before two of her sons, the young Agrippina's brothers, had likewise met with violent and horrible fates. One, denounced for homosexuality and relegated to another island, committed suicide after his executioner had shown him the noose he was to be strangled with, and the hooks for dragging his body to the Tiber. His brother, confined in a dungeon of the palace, was reduced to eating the stuffing of his mattress before he too was killed. These events must have left a mark on their sister.

The mother of Nero

In the year before her mother's arrest, at the age of thirteen, Agrippina had become engaged to Nero's father Cnaeus Domitius Ahenobarbus, a grand-nephew of Augustus. The name of this great family meant 'Bronze Beard', and an earlier generation had heard the remark that it was no wonder their beards were bronze since their faces were of iron and their hearts of lead. But they were often able and cunning, in a ferocious sort of way, and Cnaeus' father had been appointed the executor of Augustus' will – although he had once refused to let that emperor dissuade him from the practice, which even by the standards of the time seemed inhumane, of having every defeated fighter killed after a gladiatorial show.

Cnaeus himself was described by one of Tiberius' officers as a very distinguished young man,[3] but the unpleasant stories about him were persistent and circumstantial. He was more than unreliable financially, it was said

Agrippina's deranged brother, the emperor Caligula (Gaius) (AD 37–41).

– and he had been dismissed from the staff of an imperial personage because he had murdered a freedman for refusing to drink with him. Cnaeus Ahenobarbus also gouged a man's eye out in the Forum for saying something he did not fancy; and riding on the Appian Way in his chariot, he once deliberately ran over a boy and killed him. At the end of the reign of Tiberius (AD 37) he was running into trouble over charges of treason, adultery, and incest. But he survived because the old emperor then died and was succeeded by Caligula, the surviving brother of Agrippina. It was now, at Antium (Anzio), that Cnaeus' wife gave birth to the only child of the marriage, on 15 December AD 37.[4] This was Nero: though he was not called that yet but was born with the name Lucius Domitius Ahenobarbus. His father Cnaeus, when he heard the news of his birth, was later said to have remarked jokingly that the product of collaboration between Agrippina and himself was bound to turn out a disaster. Cnaeus died of dropsy three years later.

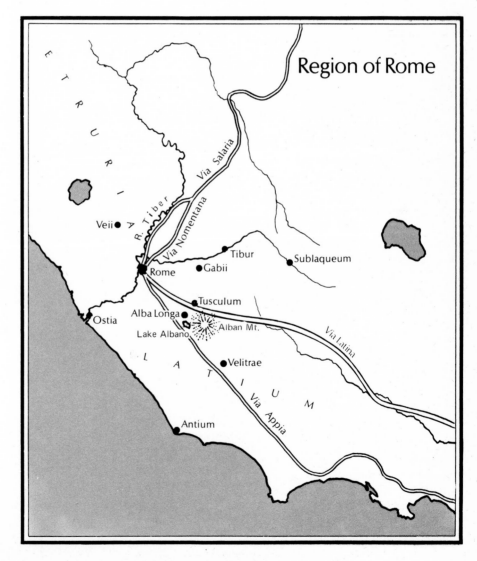

Meanwhile Agrippina and her two sisters enjoyed the perilous and probably sexual favours of their savagely unhinged imperial brother. He honoured all three of them by having their names associated with his own in vows and oaths; and they were depicted on his coins standing in a row, bearing the attributes of goddesses. But this precarious sunshine came to a sudden end in AD 39 when Agrippina was accused of joining with a lover in a plot against Caligula at Moguntiacum (Mainz). She was driven into exile, though not before she had been forced to bear the ashes of her executed paramour back to Rome, in hideous parody of a historic pilgrimage which her mother had piously undertaken with the ashes of the great Germanicus.

This happened a year before Nero's father died. He left his three-year-old son a third of his estate; but Caligula, who was co-heir, seized this share and added it to his own two-thirds. Stranded with no money, no father and a mother in exile, the infant Nero was taken into the house of his father's sister Domitia Lepida. There he lived for about sixteen months, in rather squalid conditions, looked after by a male ballet-dancer and a barber. When Caligula died in AD 41, and his uncle Claudius became emperor, Agrippina was recalled from exile and Nero got his inheritance back. His mother married again: her husband was a rich, obsequious, subtle, elegant orator called Crispus Passienus,[5] who conveniently and promptly died in about 44 — perhaps with suspicious promptitude, since his wealth passed into his widow's hands. However, life was very difficult for eminent women at this time owing to the jealousies of Claudius' dreadful young wife Messalina. But Agrippina somehow managed to survive, though it was later said that Messalina had tried to do away with Nero while he lay in his bed. If so, the attempt failed, and the boy was provided with a guardian of the highest rank – a man who had held the consulship, Asconius Labeo. He was also given two Greek tutors, Anicetus and Beryllus.[6] In AD 47, when he was nine, he made his first public appearance at a military exercise; and he was duly applauded as the descendant of a glorious line.

In 48 there was a great upheaval when Messalina was forced to commit suicide. Tacitus attributes this to a riotous party she gave with her lover Gaius Silius while the emperor was away, but in all probability she had been

above: Agrippina with her sisters on a brass coin of Caligula. She is personified as 'Security' (leaning on a column), Drusilla as 'Concordia' and Julia Livilla as 'Fortuna'. 'S C' (*Senatus Consulto*) indicates that this branch of the currency was approved by a decree of the Senate, operating under imperial control.

The suicide of Messalina

left: A sad child of about Nero's time.

right: A sculpture believed to represent Nero.

involved in a plot to place Silius on the throne. Claudius decided to marry again, and after various candidates had been considered his choice fell on Agrippina. She was the recommendation of the Greek finance minister Pallas, who urged the emperor to unite the two branches of the house of Augustus – since it would be perilous to let a woman who bore such a great name have the chance to marry into another family.

Claudius was profoundly susceptible to female influence, and the thirty-four-year-old Agrippina rapidly became more important than any imperial woman had ever been before. The position of emperor was theoretically personal and not hereditary or dynastic, and the constitution had no place for empresses. But Messalina had been jeered at as a woman who had virtually usurped such a position, and now Agrippina very nearly turned the sneer into reality. She was soon awarded the name 'Augusta'. All emperors called themselves 'Augustus', but even the original Augustus' venerated wife Livia had not been designated 'Augusta' until after her husband's death; and there was something strikingly novel about the gold and silver coins which now showed the name and portrait of Claudius and the name and portrait of Agrippina. No ruler's wife, in her lifetime, had ever been accorded such honours before. People remembered, long afterwards, how she looked presiding at a pageant, wearing a mantle of cloth of gold.[7]

This woman, with her appalling background, was avid for power and wealth, and the open display of both. Her coin portraits are not very revealing about her looks, though we may suspect that some rather formidable portrait-busts of the period display her features. What we are told is that pride and ambition were masked by a grave, cold and respectable manner. These were the concealments needed to achieve her aim, which was to win the throne for her son Nero. The trouble was that Claudius already had a boy of his own, Britannicus, born of his marriage with Messalina. He was about four years younger than Nero, but his lineage was more thoroughly

Claudius and Agrippina on a silver coin of Ephesus (Selçuk in Turkey). On the reverse is 'Diana of the Ephesians', whose supporters ejected St Paul.

Claudius, an idealized portrait on the gold coinage of the beginning of his reign (AD 41–2).

imperial – and he was the emperor's son. Agrippina, therefore, had to devote all her endeavours to readjusting the balance in favour of his step-brother.

For this she needed allies. She was helped, out of fear, by those who had brought down her predecessor Messalina. But her principal ally was Seneca, at this time about fifty-four years of age. Seneca was one of the most extraordinary men of his own or any other epoch. His parents were highly conservative members of a leading family of Italian expatriates settled in southern Spain, at Corduba (Cordova). His father was a distinguished rhetorician, and the young Seneca had rapidly become the most eminent literary figure of his time – public speaker, Stoic philosopher and essayist, tragic dramatist, writer of epigrams. John Aubrey once remarked: 'Dr Kettle was wont to say that "Seneca writes, as a boare does piss, scilicet, by jirkes".' But Seneca was immensely fashionable with the young, who adored his rhetorical fireworks and the abrupt, restless, pointed mannerisms that made his style the embodiment of the Latin Silver Age. Addicted in his youth to occultism, Seneca suffered from acute neuroses, due partly to ill-health so chronic that he often contemplated suicide. Under Caligula, who described his style as mere sand without lime, Seneca had become the leading speaker in the Senate, and it is a pity that none of his dazzling oratory has survived.

But his attentions to a sister of that emperor (a sister, that is to say, of Agrippina too) got him into trouble at the beginning of the next reign, when the young Messalina, who was jealous of the lady, had him condemned to death. In fact, however, he was exiled to Corsica. He hated the experience and the island, and wrote home grovelling flatteries of Messalina and Claudius' minister Polybius. But when Agrippina married the emperor, she organized Seneca's recall, secured his appointment to the high rank of praetor, and put him in charge of Nero's education and prospects. She

A typical portrait of an imperial personage of the age. Perhaps Messalina.

Cities in many parts of the empire issued their own token coinages. Here Hippo Diarrhytus (Bizerta, Tunisia) shows Claudius, apparently on the centenary of its foundation as a colony in AD 53–4.

reckoned that Seneca was a safe investment. He had every reason to be grateful; and if, as seemed the case, he was ambitious, his future lay in her hands.

Nero probably had more or less the normal education of an upper-class Roman. Seneca no doubt taught him personally, as well as supervising the whole programme. As regards Greek studies, the boy was given an eminent specialist tutor, Chaeremon, who had been head of the Museum at Alexandria. He was also professor of grammar in that city, and held the further office of Sacred Scribe, being an expert on Egyptian religious antiquities, about which he wrote esoteric works. Chaeremon was a follower of the Stoic school founded by Zeno (c.300 BC), who had done more than anyone else to give philosophy an ethical content, and Seneca himself had developed considerable Stoic leanings. But Nero was also provided with a second Greek tutor, Alexander of Aegae in Macedonia, who favoured the Peripatetic philosophy of Aristotle (d.322 BC), now revived as a school of metaphysics and logic. Rumour had it that Agrippina, more traditionally Roman in her approach, tried to correct Seneca's bias towards a philosophical curriculum for her son.

Very soon after her elevation, Agrippina took an immense step towards the realization of her ambitions. For she persuaded Claudius to allow his own daughter Octavia to become engaged to Nero. They did not marry for another four or five years, but the engagement was significant. Not only was she the daughter of the emperor, but, as her name indicated, she was the great-grand-daughter of Augustus' sister Octavia, by both lines of descent. At the time of the engagement she was only about nine years old. Augustus had allowed girls to be formally engaged at ten and married at twelve, but it was not unknown for these ages to be anticipated. Indeed Octavia had first been betrothed at the age of one. This first fiancé had been an aristocratic marriage connection of the imperial house, Lucius Silanus Torquatus, but Agrippina, even before her own wedding to Claudius, got him framed on a charge of incest, and on the day when she and Claudius married he cut his own throat.

In the following year AD 50, on 25 February, the young Nero was formally adopted as Claudius' son. The imperial minister Pallas, who had recommended Agrippina to Claudius, was behind the new step as well, for it was he who reminded the emperor that there was perfect precedent for the adoption of a stepson, since Augustus himself had adopted his stepson Tiberius. Tiberius had succeeded his stepfather on the throne, and the hint regarding Nero was unmistakable. And Nero, one of the classic surnames of the Claudian house, was what the boy was henceforward called: first, for a short time, Tiberius Claudius Nero, then Nero Claudius Caesar Drusus Germanicus. His name Lucius Domitius Ahenobarbus was dropped; and he and his mother took it amiss when the young Britannicus addressed him by the discarded name – either inadvertently, or as a deliberate, childish affront.

The position of the nine-year-old Britannicus was becoming difficult. He still received, outwardly, the honours due to the emperor's son. But his tutor was put to death. And since Nero was the older, he took official precedence over Britannicus. Nero's name is found before his stepbrother's on inscrip-

left: A boy of the time of Nero – possibly Nero himself.

29

tions; and the official coinage of Rome now portrayed and celebrated Nero, whereas Britannicus is nowhere to be seen. It is interesting to note how the coinage reacted elsewhere in the empire. In the provinces, where governors and cities gambled on their futures by the choice of which young prince to place upon their coins, most local issues prefer Nero, as does the mint master of a dependent king, the ruler of Pontus in Asia Minor. But right up to the end of Claudius' life the governor of Judaea continued to name the two of them together, in order to be on the safe side; towns in Asia Minor entitled to issue their own coinage did the same, and added portraits of them both.[8] On the Danube a provincial authority, probably the governor of Moesia (Bulgaria), issued a large brass coin (*sestertius*) with a Latin inscription in honour of Nero,[9] but apparently he, too, added another honouring Britannicus.[10]

These coinages mostly occurred after Nero's career had moved farther forward: as it rapidly did. He was formally declared an adult on 5 March, AD 51, even before he was fourteen, which was the earliest legal age. He was also permitted to march, carrying a shield, at the head of a parade of the Praetorian Guard. Gifts of money were distributed to the soldiers in his name, and various distinctions were conferred on him, including the rank of consul or proconsul outside Rome and membership of all the four great boards of priests.

He thanked the Senate for this spate of honours in his first public speech. Oratory was a traditional part of the education of young Roman nobles, and one in which Nero's tutor Seneca excelled – though he was accused of directing his pupil to the study of modern oratory (his own) instead of to historic, classical precedents. At all events, in 53 Nero obtained the opportunity to deliver a Latin speech, in support of an application by the people of Bononia (Bologna) which had been ravaged by fire; and he also spoke in Greek to back a similar plea from Apamea in Syria, damaged by an earthquake, and again to support tax exemptions requested by Rhodes and Ilium (Troy). It had always been found useful for rising youths to obtain supporters in the provinces by this means, and an oration in support of Ilium was particularly appropriate, since the house of Julius Caesar, into which Nero's ancestor Augustus had been adopted, traced its origins back to legendary Troy.

When Claudius went off to the Alban Mount to celebrate the annual Latin Festival, he left Nero officially in charge of Rome as its 'prefect' (AD 51). This involved hearing lawsuits, and the emperor left orders that only simple and insignificant cases should be brought before the boy. But his instructions were ignored, and leading speakers eagerly competed to appear before the prince.

These pleasant activities were by no means typical of the last years of Claudius' reign. The emperor, now in his sixties, was a curious mixture of administrative wisdom and personal absurdity, sensible liberalism and suspicious ferocity. Sodden and sensual, he was too much influenced by Agrippina, and by the Greek ministers who were collaborating with her. Agrippina was pathologically nervous, and struck malevolent blows all

The emperor Claudius

round to avert real and imaginary threats to the position of herself and of
Nero.

Treason trials, which had already reached considerable though still con-
trollable proportions under Augustus and Tiberius, were revived; and informers proliferated. Altogether during his reign Claudius put to death at
least thirty senators, and two or three hundred knights. Messalina had
inspired a good many of these executions, but a very substantial proportion
of them belonged to his last five years, while Agrippina was his wife and
almost co-ruler of the empire.

A good deal of play was made with the treasonable possibilities of astrology
and magic, which most of the population, including the majority of the
educated class, believed in. One victim, towards the end of the reign, was
Nero's paternal aunt Domitia Lepida (the mother of Messalina), who had
taken him into her house when he was three. A woman almost as formidable
as Agrippina, she was hated by the empress for her imperial blood. Further
resentment was caused by her influence on Nero, to whom her attitude was
more indulgent than his mother's. So Domitia Lepida was accused of magical
practices directed against Agrippina's life – an accusation which had disposed of several other rivals of the empress already. For good measure, it
was added that Lepida had allowed her Calabrian slave-gangs to imperil
public order: a good emotive charge in a society which was terrified of its
slaves and remembered their ancient revolts. She was tried before Claudius
as head of the family. One of the greatest Greek ministers, Narcissus (who, in
the competition regarding Claudius' remarriage, had backed one of
Agrippina's rivals), did his best for Lepida. Nevertheless, she was sentenced
to death – and Narcissus was forced into retirement. Under the influence of
his mother, the seventeen-year-old Nero gave public evidence against his
aunt.

31

The death of
Claudius

All the same, Agrippina felt that her position was precarious. When Tacitus says she was frightened by prodigies and omens – the birth of half-bestial children, and a pig with hawk's claws – he was probably right. More serious, however, was the fact that all her power had not quite availed to give her supreme control. The Senate actually had the nerve to expel from its ranks a sinister informer and prosecutor who was one of her most cherished agents. Worst of all, the emperor was quite unpredictable, and capable of suddenly saying and even doing the most worrying and frightening things. Agrippina decided that she dared not wait any longer for Nero's accession to the throne; something terrible might happen to either of them at any time. And so, according to Tacitus, she found a convicted poisoner Locusta, and suborned the imperial food-taster to serve up what the woman had prepared. 'Later', says the historian, 'the whole story became known. Contemporary writers stated that the poison was sprinkled on a particularly succulent mushroom. But because Claudius was torpid – or drunk – its effect was not at first apparent; and an evacuation of his bowels seemed to have saved him. Agrippina was horrified. But when the ultimate stakes are so alarmingly large, immediate disrepute is brushed aside. She had already secured the complicity of the emperor's doctor Xenophon; and now she called him in. The story is that, while pretending to help Claudius to vomit, he put a feather dipped in a quick poison down his throat. (Xenophon knew that major crimes, though hazardous to undertake, are profitable if you can bring them off.) The Senate was summoned. Consuls and priests offered prayers for the emperor's safety. But meanwhile his already lifeless body was being wrapped in blankets and poultices.'[11]

It looks as though the historian has artistically combined elements from at least two contradictory accounts. Suetonius, who blends an even more blatant assortment of different stories, does not mention the shocking suggestion that Stertinius Xenophon of Cos, Rome's leading doctor, was involved. According to some versions Nero had a hand. But, in any case, at this stage of his career it was Agrippina who still took the initiative in everything. It is true, however, that her responsibility for Claudius' end was not unanimously accepted at the time.[12] Could the emperor, perhaps, instead have died a natural death? But the opposite was very quickly believed, and the probability lies in that direction. The satirist Juvenal, then, is likely to have been right when, half a century later, he wrote of Agrippina's mushroom:

> The vegetable that settled the hash
> Of one old dotard, saw off his tremulous headpiece
> And beslobbered, drooling chops to some
> nether heaven.[13]

And so it was that on the day following this event, at the hour authorized by the astrologers, Nero made his appearance at the entrance of the palace and was saluted as emperor of Rome.

A woman of the imperial house often identified (though without complete certainty) as Agrippina. Found at Velleia near Parma, Italy.

33

2 Nero's Mother in Charge

Whether Nero was a party to the murder of Claudius or not, he later made a joke about it – remarking that mushrooms are the food of the gods. The point of the remark was that Claudius, after succumbing to one of these vegetables, had at once been officially deified as a god of the state. This strange institution of Roman official divinization dated back just under a hundred years to Julius Caesar, who after his death had been pronounced by his political heirs and the Senate to be a god, Divus Julius, and had a temple built in his honour. Neither he nor any of the Caesars who succeeded him were ever formally declared gods in their lifetime at Rome. Although there were state-sponsored cults of living emperors in the provinces, metropolitan Rome never officially accepted the Greek practice of hailing living rulers as divinities. But in the capital, as elsewhere, the concept of posthumous deification had come to stay.

Early emperors whose rule had gained favour received the honour. The first of them, Augustus, had been declared a god when he died; but his successors Tiberius and Caligula were not. Claudius, apart from killing too many of the upper class, had not been a bad ruler, but all the same it was clearly rather strange that he should now be deified. After all the decision regarding his deification mainly lay in the hands of his wife – who had apparently murdered him. By a further irony, it was she who now became the priestess of the Divine Claudius, and she, too, who gave orders for the construction of his temple on Rome's Caelian Hill.[1] An impressive series of coins was struck with the head of the new god, inscribed DIVVS CLAVDIVS AVGVSTVS; and on the day of the funeral Nero delivered a speech, elegantly composed for him by Seneca, in which he pronounced the late emperor's praises. When Nero began to talk of his stepfather's foresight and wisdom, reports Tacitus, nobody could help laughing[2] – rather unfairly, but they could hardly be blamed for signifying their disapproval since he had put a lot of their colleagues to death.

Tacitus also observed that the earliest days of a new reign are always an anxious time.[3] Everyone's utterances, and even the expressions on their faces, are keenly scrutinized. But one thing that seemed startlingly apparent was that Agrippina was the great power in the state. When his escort commander made the customary request for a password, Nero replied 'the Best of

35

Mothers'. Be that as it may, she had broken all records: not only was she the daughter of a great commander, but the sister of one emperor, the wife of another, and now the mother of yet a third.

Eastern coins hailed her as goddess and the parent of a god, and even the official metropolitan coinage of the Roman state – which was usually more conservative in its designs – now openly declared, for the first and last time ever, that a woman, the emperor's mother, was more important than the emperor himself. The people all over the empire were being told, in no uncertain terms, that the real ruler of the empire was Agrippina. For these gold and silver coins, which are proved by their inscriptions to belong to the period 4–31 December, AD 54, devote one side to the heads, facing one another, of Agrippina and Nero. One side shows Agrippina's names and titles, and the other shows Nero's. But Agrippina's are on the *obverse* of these pieces, beside the heads, and Nero's are in a less distinguished position on the reverse. Furthermore Agrippina's designations are couched in the nominative case normal to monarchs, whereas Nero's are in the dedicatory dative – the coins are only dedicated to him, whereas it is announced that they belong to Agrippina.[4]

It is not surprising, then, to learn that in this first period of the reign she was managing all the business of the empire. It was generally believed that she exercised her control over Nero by means of an incestuous relationship. This was a stock charge, but it was also a stock practice; and in this case the rumour was probably accurate, especially as Nero said as much himself – in addition to expressing particular fondness for a girl who looked like his mother.

right: Nero's wife Octavia on a coin of Alexandria, AD 56–7.

Overleaf

left: Agrippina and Nero appear together on this gold coin minted at Rome in December AD 54. Agrippina is given precedence over her son: the inscription round the portraits is in her honour. *right:* Agrippina and Nero, again together, on a coin of AD 55. But Nero now takes precedence, and the inscription refers to him.

The power behind the throne

left: Nero's uncle Caligula (Gaius).

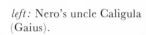

Agrippina's arrival at the summit of power did not cause her to relax her vigilance against every conceivable rival. Consequently, the list of casualties among aristocratic Romans lengthened. One of her first victims – without, it was said, the young emperor's knowledge or approval – was Marcus Silanus, brother of the man who had failed to survive his engagement to the girl Nero subsequently married, Octavia. Although innocuous enough to be known as the Golden Sheep, Silanus, like Nero, was a great-great-grandson of Augustus, and for this equality of relationship he paid the inevitable penalty. So, in the years to come as in those just past, did other leading members of his family. So, in fact, did everyone else who had the same perilous connections, or anything like them. By the time Nero had reigned for a dozen years, he had become the only surviving descendant of Augustus. Tacitus recounts the fates of all the others with detailed grimness and indignation. But the melancholy tale was a by-product of the imperial system. At this stage in imperial history, the regime never felt safe while there were other descendants of Augustus about – especially as Nero himself was not of unmixed imperial blood. That is why further Silani succumbed to violent deaths in 64 and 65,[5] and other men with imperial marriage connections, Faustus Sulla and Rubellius Plautus, were exiled in 58 and 60 and both murdered in 62. As far as we know, it was not even found necessary to level any specific charges against them. Whatever sections of the population found the reign of Nero enjoyable (and they were many), those members of the aristocracy who had any blood of the Caesars in their veins were not among their number. Indeed, none of them survived it.

Permissive Rome

Nero himself soon began to derive a great deal of enjoyment out of being emperor. In the first place, it gave him unlimited opportunity to indulge his highly developed and widely ranging sexual tastes. His own reported view on the subject is significant. 'I have heard some people say', reports Suetonius, 'that it was Nero's own unshaken conviction that no man was chaste or pure in any part of his body, but that most of them concealed their vices and cleverly drew a veil over them; and that therefore he pardoned all other faults in those who confessed to him their obscene practices.'[6]

This permissive approach was fashionable in smart Roman circles; it was the mode to look at everyone with a pretty disillusioned eye. Such an approach is extremely conspicuous in the uninhibited prose and verse of the contemporary novel the *Satyricon*, written by Nero's friend Petronius. It also comes out clearly in some admirable contemporary sculpture. At Pompeii, for example, Caecilius Jucundus is displayed as a wily and vulgar *faux bonhomme*, with wrinkles, warts, and flapping ears. In the same spirit the contemporary Greek poet Lucilius, who got agreeable subsidies from Nero, developed the new idea of giving his epigrams a final punch-line about people's personal peculiarities – the sort of thing later introduced into Latin by Martial.

A bronze head of Lucius Caecilius Jucundus, a rich banker of Pompeii (or possibly his father). Like Petronius in his contemporary novel, the *Satyricon*, the sculptor enjoys each coarse detail.

> Nicylla dyes her locks, 'tis said,
>   But 'tis a poor aspersion.
> She buys them black, they therefore need
>   No subsequent immersion.[7]

What Petronius did was to concentrate in a similar sort of way on people's sexual lives. Very much in the same spirit as Nero's own attitudes, he penetrated every respectable façade by demonstrating that anyone who did not admit he went in for sex and enjoyed it was talking nonsense.

> Find me any man who knows
> Nothing of love and naked pleasure.
> What stern moralist would oppose
> Two bodies warming a bed together?[8]

That, however, puts his attitude at its simplest: since in fact Petronius thought up an immense number of perverted variations of the activity. He is identifiable with a man called Titus Petronius Niger, who reached the consulship some eight years after Nero's accession and is recorded in an inscription discovered in 1946.[9] He became one of Nero's intimates, and the *Satyricon*, published soon after 60, sets the tone of Neronian society. It is a brilliant, many-sided work, but its dominant subject is multifariously lubricious sexuality. The book parodies traditional themes of the Wrath of Gods by purporting to write of the wrath of Priapus the fertility god, whom sculptors always portrayed with a vast erection. Petronius has been described by psychoanalytically-minded critics as the first writer who was a confirmed voyeur. When, in the end, he fell out of favour and was forced to commit suicide, he sent Nero a detailed account of all the peculiar sexual activities which he, the emperor, had engaged in, giving the names of everyone involved.

It must have been strange reading, because from all accounts Nero's tastes in this direction were inexhaustible. It is true that charges about sexual irregularities were an even commoner feature of gossip than they are now, and that they particularly centred round the imperial court, which was a fascinating mystery to the outside world. Moreover, such scandal was particularly likely to gather round a youthful emperor; especially as it very soon became clear that he took no interest in his wife Octavia, who was only fourteen when he came to the throne. Nevertheless, the stories about Nero's sexual behaviour were so persistent that there must have been something in

The sex-life of Nero

42

them. His activities were also astonishingly varied. He was alleged to go to bed not with his wife but with his mother, and with boys younger than himself, and with elder men; and not merely slaves either, which would have been somewhat less disreputable, but free-born citizens. He was also said to have gone through a mock marriage ceremony with a male Greek variously described as one of his ministers, Doryphorus, or a certain Pythagoras, perhaps his cupbearer of that name. Tacitus glumly remarks on the trans-sexual aspects of the affair. 'In the presence of witnesses, Nero put on the bridal veil! Dowry, marriage bed, wedding torches, all were there. Indeed everything was public which, even at a natural union, is veiled by night.'[10] Suetonius adds that on this wedding night he imitated the screams and moans of a virgin being deflowered.

Suetonius, while collecting a great deal of material that is valuable, throws in an immense amount of filth as well. But even this has its psychological importance: partly (on the assumption that some of it is true) for our estimate of Nero, and certainly for our assessment of the sort of talk that emanated from his court. So it is worth adding that, according to the biographer, the emperor approached these nuptials in the right spirit. For he came to them straight from a game he had invented. This involved his dressing up in skins, getting into a cage, and then being released from it in order to charge at men and women, who were standing bound to stakes, and subject them to oral outrages.

Nero's liaison with Acte

We can understand that, with this sort of thing going on, it may have come as a relief to his principal advisers, Seneca and the Guard commander Burrus, when Nero started an affair with a young girl. They must also have been glad she was not of aristocratic family, with all the complications which that would have involved. For his mistress was a freedwoman called Acte, who had originally been bought as a slave in Asia Minor and then taken to Rome, perhaps as a member of Octavia's domestic establishment.[11] Nero became extremely fond of Acte. There were rumours that a royal Greek ancestry was being invented for her so that they could marry, though such a step must generally have been regarded as out of the question. No identifiable portraits of Acte have survived, and we do not know what she looked like. However, it is clear that she was not the pathetic waif of romantic literature, for inscriptions have revealed that she was given villas at Puteoli (Pozzuoli) and Velitrae (Velletri), and potteries in Sardinia; while her household included two chamberlains, a messenger, a baker, a eunuch and a Greek singer.

Nero was helped to pursue his liaison with Acte by his smart young friends. One was Annaeus Serenus, who was Commander of the Watch, or chief of the fire brigade and the police. Serenus, a relation of Seneca – who dedicated some high-minded treatises to him – pretended to be Acte's lover himself, in order to conceal from the world what was really happening. And an even more intimate crony of the emperor, Otho, some five years his senior, accommodatingly acted as go-between. Otho exercised great influence on the young Nero. 'Affable, pliant and corrupt', says Ronald Syme, 'he was a choice luxury product of the Neronian court.' When, later, he became emperor for a few months (69), he issued coins with neat portraits showing a

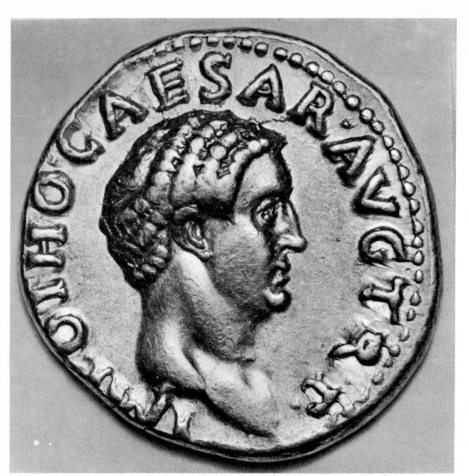

good head of hair: but we are told that it was a wig. Short, knock-kneed and flatfooted, Otho was vain and devoted to his mirror; and it was his custom to soften his beard by rubbing his face with bread soaked in water. He also used to have his body hair plucked, which was regarded as a homosexual custom and seemed to raise questions regarding the nature of his relationship with Nero.

Otho was in wild reaction against an over-disciplinary upbringing, and his main effect on the youthful ruler was to show him that, if you are going to be extravagant, you must do it in the grand manner. 'When one day', says the biographer Plutarch, 'Nero put on some expensive scent and favoured Otho with a sprinkle of it, he, entertaining the emperor the next day, ordered that gold and silver pipes should suddenly shower the same perfume freely throughout the whole room like water.'[12] Otho also introduced the innovation (imitated by the clownish Trimalchio in Petronius' novel) of having his feet and those of his guests drenched in scent at the dinner-table.[13] Although a profitable connection with Augustus' wife Livia had helped to make his family extremely rich, at one period Otho's debts amounted to two hundred million sesterces – perhaps the equivalent of between half a million and a million pounds (see Appendix 3 for the impossibility of finding a more exact equivalent).

So Otho helped Nero to meet Acte secretly. Agrippina, on the other hand, was profoundly opposed to his association with the girl. She took the Roman view that an affair with an insignificant Greek slut must not in any circumstances be allowed to become so serious. Besides, it directly interfered with her own ascendancy. And indeed, already in AD 55 soon after Nero's accession, the official coinage shows clearly that her position in the state was sharply deteriorating. For at some time during that year a new gold and silver coinage was issued with significantly different designs from its predecessor. The heads of Nero and Agrippina still appeared. Now, however. they no longer faced one another but faced in the same direction, with the head in front partially eclipsing the one behind; and the head in front is Nero's. Furthermore, his name and titles have now been altered from the dedicatory dative to the monarchic, possessive, nominative; and his and Agrippina's designations have changed places, so that his are now on the more important obverse side of the coin. These changes are neither fortuitous nor meaningless. They were meant; and they were noticed.

Agrippina's violent temperament found this sort of situation difficult to endure. She veered sharply from excessive severity towards Nero to extravagant complaisance, finally even offering her own bedroom and bed for his lovemaking with Acte. Nero's friends were unimpressed, and suspicious. And it no doubt reached the ears of those concerned that the dowager empress was sneering at Burrus, commander of the Praetorian Guard, for being a cripple, because he had a maimed hand, and that she had been heard describing Seneca as 'the deportee with the professorial voice!'.

These principal advisers of Nero had already, at the outset, had occasion to feel nervous about her methods. They cannot have thought it a good thing that the reign should be inaugurated by a political murder, the killing of

Livia, the wife of Augustus, personified as IMPERIAL JUSTICE. Otho's Etruscan grandfather became a Senator through her influence.

45

Marcus Silanus. Nor had they liked Agrippina standing behind a curtain, as she did, to listen to meetings of the Senate. On another occasion, when Nero was receiving an Armenian delegation, she entered the room and was clearly on the point of mounting the emperor's dais and taking her seat there beside him. Under Claudius she had attended imperial hearings, but had sat on a separate dais. Her intention to join Nero on his own dais caused dismay. Seneca quickly whispered to him to get up and go and meet her. When the emperor rose and moved forward, the conference stood adjourned; and the scandal was averted.

But more disturbing still was the fact that Agrippina, whose attention such snubs obviously did not escape, suddenly started taking an interest in Nero's pathetic, rejected – and according to some accounts attractive – thirteen-year-old stepbrother Britannicus, whose prestige had been enhanced by his father's deification and whose claim to the imperial crown might be regarded as better than the emperor's own. Nero easily got into a panic; and he did so now. Tacitus describes an incident which upset him still further.

The fate of Britannicus

During the amusements of the Saturnalia (December, 54), the young men had thrown dice for who should be 'king' of the revels, and Nero had won. To the others he gave various orders causing no embarrassment.

But he commanded Britannicus to get up and come into the middle and sing a song. Nero hoped for laughter at the boy's expense, since Britannicus was not accustomed even to sober parties, much less to drunken ones. But Britannicus composedly sang a poem implying his displacement from his father's home and throne. This aroused sympathy – and in the frank atmosphere of a party at night, it was unconcealed. Nero noticed the feeling against himself, and hated Britannicus all the more.[14]

According to Tacitus, this helped to drive the emperor to his first murder. The historian remarked earlier that the poisoner employed by Agrippina to kill Claudius, a certain Locusta, 'had a long career of imperial service ahead of her'; and now, some time early in 55, he reports that Nero himself enlisted her professional aid. The first efforts to poison Britannicus however proved unsuccessful, and an attempt on his life by his tutors likewise failed. But then Locusta and a guards officer got together and concocted a new mixture which might be suitable for use at dinner. Britannicus was placed with some of his contemporaries at a table separate from Nero's.

A young contemporary of Nero and Britannicus.

He was handed a harmless drink. His taster had tasted it; but Britannicus found it too hot, and refused it. Then cold water containing the poison was added. Speechless, his whole body convulsed, he instantly ceased to breathe.

His companions were horrified. Some, uncomprehending, fled. Others, understanding better, remained rooted in their places, staring at Nero. He still lay back unconcernedly – and he remarked that this often happened to epileptics; that Britannicus had been one since infancy; soon his sight and consciousness would return. Agrippina tried to control her features. But their evident consternation and terror showed that she knew nothing. . . . After a short silence the banquet continued.

Britannicus was cremated the same night. Indeed, preparations for his inexpensive funeral had already been made. As his remains were placed in the imperial mausoleum, there was a violent storm.[15]

Britannicus, at Hippo Diarrhytus (Bizerta). The local coinages were assiduous in honouring imperial princes, especially potential heirs. Hippo guessed wrong.

Is this gruesome story true? Evidently there was foul play of some sort. Britannicus' collapse did not look natural, whatever Nero might say; and the haste with which the body was cremated seemed to point to murder. Moreover, an eye-witness informant survived: the subsequent emperor Titus, a friend of Britannicus who was actually reclining beside him at the same table. According to one account, preserved by Suetonius, Titus even shared the fatal dose, and was ill for a long time afterwards.[16] Anyway he could presumably give historians some idea of what had happened.

But obviously neither he nor anyone else was able to know for certain whether Nero was the assassin. Nearly every writer declared he was.[17] But was he? It is true that both Tiberius and Caligula began their reigns by eliminating their nearest rivals in the imperial house, and that Nero might be expected to do the same. But it does seem extraordinary that the new emperor, possessing all the resources in the world necessary to murder a boy living in his own palace, should choose such a public occasion for the purpose. Or was this a kind of double bluff on Nero's part, based on the assumption that the public character of the scene would make people less likely to believe that he could have been responsible for anything so conspicuous? This may, perhaps, seem rather far-fetched. If, on the other hand, the murderers were people without intimate access to the palace, the selection of such an occasion was more probable. The murder of Thomas à Becket is a reminder that, if the autocrat is irritated or frightened by someone, it is quite likely that one of his henchmen will kill that person, in order to forge an additional link with his master. It has happened again in modern times.

One of the ambiguities is the role of Seneca and Burrus. They could have argued that the coexistence of the two stepbrothers created an impossible situation, and that the security of the state made it necessary for one of them to go: otherwise there might be civil strife, and millions of people would suffer. But we shall never know for certain who the murderer was.

However, one thing is clear enough. Agrippina, who appeared threatening before, had now received a mortal threat herself. But she was too tough a personality to let it get her down, and if Britannicus was no longer available as a target for her sympathy she decided instead to show sympathy with his sister, Nero's estranged wife Octavia. It seemed very much as though

right: A boy identified as Britannicus – but it can only be a guess.

Agrippina was looking round for support, with a view to future action. There were also rumours that she was trying to raise funds. And so steps were taken by Nero and his advisers. She was deprived of her military escort, including a party of German guards who had recently reinforced it. Then she was moved out of the palace into a mansion of her own. 'When Nero visited her there, he would bring an escort of staff-officers, hurriedly embrace her, and leave.'[18] She was encouraged to spend time in her mansion on the Pincian hill, or in her villas at Tusculum or Antium. After 55, her head and name never appeared on the Roman coinage again. She continued to arouse Nero's suspicions, but her active role was ended. The possibility that there might be a ruling empress at Rome had vanished, never to return.

Even if she murdered Claudius, as seems so probable, his deification was her idea, and her role as the cult's priestess had been part of her political position. And so, from now on, the coins and inscriptions pay much less attention to the memory of Claudius. It was rumoured that Nero was negligent about building the new god's temple (though this is doubtful, since a good deal of the masonry still remains today). And Nero's request to the Senate that a statue should be erected to the memory of his own, real, father was another move away from the Claudian connection. It is true that he was still married, officially, to Claudius' daughter Octavia. But to all intents and purposes the marriage was at an end, if it had ever really started; and from now on the estrangement between him and his wife was complete.

Vindictive people gathered round in the hope of putting an end to Agrippina altogether. They included one of Nero's aunts, Domitia, who had shared an earlier husband with Agrippina and was the sister of Domitia Lepida, whom Nero's mother had framed. Another of the vultures, not surprisingly, included a lady of the Silanus family. She was the sister of men whom Agrippina had hounded to their deaths; furthermore, her lover had cooled because Agrippina, supposedly her friend, had told the man that his intended bride was a nymphomaniac and an old one at that. One of Domitia's freedmen – the male ballet-dancer Domitius Paris, who was intimate with Nero – reported to him one evening that his mother was plotting against his life. Nero, as might have been predicted, was stricken with terror. But the report was probably not true: or not true yet. Accordingly Burrus – who did not forget his former association with Agrippina, and needed to be careful because his own position was being threatened at this time – urged legal correctness, and warned the emperor it would be unwise to condemn her unheard. She was therefore allowed to vindicate herself, which she did with tactful gusto; and, with the exception of Paris who was close enough to Nero to get away with it, her latest batch of accusers were liquidated.

3 Nero and his Helpers

Meanwhile Nero, eager to have a break from government affairs, derived pleasure from going to the theatre. He also liked to watch – and applaud – the fights between street-gangs which formed factions favouring this or that male ballet-dancer. But he had to give up this amusement when public order was so gravely disturbed that it became necessary to order the dancers to leave Italy. Nero also formed an embarrassing taste for going out brawling and pub-crawling at night – a custom which rapidly caused crowds of criminals to spring up and engage in similar disorders. The deliberate squalor of the emperor's nocturnal rambles was one of the many features in his life which are close to Petronius' *Satyricon*. For there, too, great emphasis is laid on just the same sort of disreputable wanderings, in modern drop-out spirit; indeed the novel is a sort of low-life parody of the *Odyssey* itself, or of the travellers' tales which figured so largely in Greek romantic novels.

And so Nero prowled the city by night, in disguises and false wigs, beating up passers-by and taking liberties with women and boys.[1] On one such occasion a passing senator called Montanus, who is probably identifiable with a poet of the same name, received a blow from the emperor and hit him back. But he committed the mistake of apologizing, which made Nero think that Montanus had known whom he was hitting. So the senator was forced to commit suicide – and in future when the emperor went on his nightly outings he was accompanied by guardsmen and gladiators, ready to beat up any victims who looked like offering resistance.

The influence of the Greeks

When Petronius' anti-heroes go debauching in the streets, the streets are those of south Italian towns. Often these are Greek. So are the crooks and vulgarians he writes about. This was traditional stuff: centuries ago the comic dramatist Plautus had already brought countless farcical Greeks on the stage, so as to illustrate lax behaviour without attributing it to Romans. The Romans, or those who were educated, claimed to venerate Greek culture, but the angry contempt they felt for contemporary products of Hellas was to be summed up, half a century later, in the satires of Juvenal, who deplored the slick, subservient Greeks of a Greek-struck Rome.

However, it was all very well making fun of Greek toadies. What seemed a great deal more exasperating was the fact that certain Greeks and easterners

Seneca, Nero's tutor and advisor until he fell into disfavour. Seneca is back to back with Socrates in this double portrait.

were gaining a large measure of control over whole ranges of important Roman affairs. The hold was not as large as it might have been, because many rich Greeks remained content with their own local lives. Nevertheless, it was considerable. Petronius tells us at length how Trimalchio had speculated in trade until he became a multi-millionaire. And it is this wealthy, successful type of Greek or Greek-speaking oriental who really infuriated Juvenal.

> When such men as these wear the purple, when some creature,
> Blown into Rome along with the figs and damsons,
> Precedes me at dinner-parties . . .
> > Things have reached a pretty pass.[2]

In the time of Claudius and Nero, Greeks had still not penetrated very extensively into the official ranks of Roman public life; we know of only one possible Greek senator of the time, and twelve knights. However, Nero sent out Greeks or Hellenized easterners as governors of the enormously rich province of Egypt – which was controlled by a personal agent of the emperor[3] – and a number of other such men were concentrated in key positions at the imperial court itself. Although once they had been slaves, they were now the emperor's Secretaries of State or Ministers — in the sense not of cabinet members, but of important departmental heads. So these men, although totally alien in birth and largely alien in upbringing from the traditional ruling aristocracy of Rome, were nearly the most important men in the empire, second only to the emperor's policy-controlling council of his topmost Roman advisers and friends. Apart from them, no other senator was as

Claudius.

A mosaic from Pompeii showing a scene from a comic play, by Dioscurides of Samos (though whether he designed the mosaic or the painting it was copied from is uncertain).

influential as these hard-working Greek and eastern administrators; and they had their own important chains of contacts all over the Roman world, particularly in commercial, industrial and shipping circles.

Augustus had collected some clever Greeks together to help him with his work, and so did his successors. But it was only under the much more bureaucratic regime of Claudius that the emperor, ageing and increasingly un-self-reliant but too unfamiliar with senatorial society to call upon its aid, had allowed these ministers to attain their enormous power. As a literary device, Tacitus symbolically brings together the three most mighty of them all, supposing that they came to a meeting with the emperor Claudius at the moment when he had allowed Messalina to be disposed of and was wondering whom to marry next.

One of the three men who met to advise Claudius was Narcissus, who dealt with all business relating to governors, commanders and imperial agents (procurators) in the provinces. He was called the Minister of Letters (*ab epistulis*) because these governors and the rest were the only people entitled to write the emperor a letter. Through his handling of this correspondence, the minister, though officially not responsible for major decisions, had a considerable say in matters of strategy and defence. This was, in Narcissus' day, the top post, and his personal fortune of four hundred million sesterces (for possible modern equivalents, see Appendix 3) was the largest sum known to have belonged to any individual, other than rulers, throughout the whole of antiquity. However, it was not to be expected that he would survive

Claudius' marriage with Agrippina for long, because he had tried to get him to marry one of her rivals. Narcissus did, in fact, manage to last until about the time of Claudius' death: but in retirement, and latterly in prison. Tacitus and Dio Cassius record that he just survived Claudius. Tacitus says Agrippina murdered him at the beginning of the new reign, Seneca that he went down to hell by a short cut and was there to receive Claudius when he arrived.[4] Nero, who was sorry to lose Narcissus, apparently divided up his job into two parts, relating to Latin and Greek correspondence. We hear of the head of his Greek department, Beryllus, formerly his tutor – and apparrently bribable. But we also learn that he had to go to Nero for approval of a decision. The ministers were not totally independent; and, in particular, these divided Secretaryships of Letters were no longer as important as some of the other jobs.

Claudius on a silver coin. This artist, in the province of Asia (W. Asia Minor), has adopted a more realistic approach than was usual at the time.

The other secretary who became great under Claudius was the *a rationibus* or Minister of Finance or Accounts, in whose hands he concentrated, not financial policy or the collection of taxes, but the management of the empire's accountancy and the disposition of its revenues; and this duty remained in the hands of a single official throughout the reign of Nero. At the meeting about Claudius' remarriage the minister of the day, Pallas, had backed the winner, because it was he who urged the claims of Nero's mother. The degree to which he was feared and flattered became clear when the Senate, through the agency of one of its highest patricians, showered honours upon his head, including a bogus declaration that he was of royal Arcadian stock. On this occasion Pallas accepted the insignia of a praetor (the senatorial rank second only to consul), but declined a gift of fifteen million sesterces,[5] as he could well afford to, since he already possessed vast estates on the Esquiline Hill. But when Agrippina lost her power in 55, Pallas was forced into retirement. He was still a sufficiently impressive figure to be able to extract agreement that his accounts should be regarded as balanced; and, as he swept out of the palace, a host of dependents surrounded him. Yet he soon suffered the lot of fallen potentates, for he was charged with plotting against Nero's life – in company with some of his own freedmen. But the accusation could not be true, he convincingly protested, because he never deigned to utter a single word to the members of his household: he just nodded to them, he said, or waved his hand, or if necessary jotted down a message.

Probably Pallas was succeeded by a certain Phaon – who remained quietly in office until Nero's death. It is characteristic of Roman and Greek historians that, until the moment when he will briefly play a part in a melodramatic scene, they tell us nothing whatever about Phaon or his work. The quiet operation of the vast financial machine was not news like the death of a blue-blooded senator.

The third Secretary of State who was present at the matrimonial conference was Callistus. He was the Minister of Notes, *a libellis*, in charge of Rome's relations with cities and communities all over the empire: *libelli* being the name of the communications, less distinguished than letters, which their leaders were entitled to send to the emperor. And this minister had a second department, which controlled the appointments and promotions of a great number of personnel. Callistus, successor of Polybius whom Seneca had flattered while in exile, was a jovial character, and he too was very rich indeed: Seneca remarked that he once saw the man who had been his slave-master standing and waiting at his former slave's front door.[6] But Callistus had not wanted Agrippina to become Claudius' wife, because he had a candidate of his own; and since his candidate was struck down by Agrippina it is unlikely that he himself survived into the new reign. His successor under Nero was Doryphorus, whom Nero went to bed with and donated gifts of huge estates and farms – on one occasion presenting him with ten million sesterces to annoy his mother. Within the Ministry one of those in charge of dealing with communications and appeals from Greek communities was Stertinius Xenophon of Cos, the doctor who was believed to have put a poisoned feather down Claudius' throat.

There were other important officials too. One, for example, the secretary *a cognitionibus*, prepared all documents for judicial cases brought before the emperor; he may sometimes have combined these duties with the Minister of Notes. Another was the *a studiis*, whose functions are uncertain. The duties of all of them fluctuated widely from time to time, depending greatly on the personal influence of whoever held this or that post at a given moment. Indeed when the historians do happen to mention these men, they never seem to be engaged in their normal departmental duties at all, but appear exclusively in connection with spicy political dramas and intrigues – which in fact only occupied a small part of their time. One of Nero's ministers, whose duties we do not know, was a certain Claudius of Smyrna, who married a rich and beautiful wife, rose from slavery to be a knight – second only to a senator in rank – and outlived his employer by a quarter of a century, leaving an enormous fortune and earning elegies from the two most famous poets of the day, Statius and Martial.

Nero was conscious of the immense jealousies aroused by these great imperial freedmen, and evidently intended at first not to let them have too much power. But the only way to avoid this (since senators would not or could not do these jobs) was by working all day himself, and that he was not prepared to do. So the Greek functionaries soon reasserted themselves, although more behind the scenes than under Claudius. Two years after Nero's accession the Senate launched a malignant counter-attack against the excessive licence of freedmen; and what some at least of the senators had in mind was a desire to insult the influential ministers. But the emperor, faced with a difference of opinion, gave a judiciously non-committal ruling.

Nero's advisers This difference of opinion arose within his council. That body, because of its personal character, resembled an American President's cabinet rather than a British Prime Minister's. But it was more fluid and usually more informal than any modern cabinet. It consisted of twenty or thirty Roman senators who were the emperor's friends and acted as his principal advisers. They met, most frequently – or some of them did – for consultations on judicial and semi-judicial matters, with particular reference to the range of legal cases which the emperor had accepted as his personal responsibility. More rarely, but still quite often, they were convened to discuss and advise on matters of general policy. At the outset of his reign Nero assured the

Senate that he proposed to rely on such advice – an assurance which they favoured, since the council was composed of their own members, and provided a counterblast to the autocracy of emperors and the influence of freedmen alike. And indeed, during his first years as emperor, this imperial council played a larger part than ever before or after.[7]

The most important advisers were Burrus, commander of the Praetorian Guard, and Seneca; and the ancient historians sometimes imply, perhaps with some oversimplification, that important decisions were taken on their advice alone. It is said that they encouraged Nero in debauchery so that they would have a free hand to run the government themselves. Whether this is true we cannot say; but it is possible that, out of a desire to keep decisions in their own experienced hands, they tried on occasion to divert him from interventions that would have been naive or undesirable.

The birthplaces of the two men show how two highly civilized areas, southern France and southern Spain, had risen to a virtual equality with Italy. Burrus came from Vasio (Vaison) – his origins attracted Claudius, who had been born in Gaul himself – and Seneca's home-town was Corduba (Cordova), which belonged to an area that was highly productive of Roman senators. The historians' accounts are too inadequate to give a clear idea of

what the specific influences or policies of Burrus and Seneca were. But it is at least clear that both of them did a lot to advance the careers of provincial senators like themselves – for example a certain Pompeius Paulinus, who originated from Burrus' province and was the brother of Seneca's wife.

The commander of the Praetorian Guard had by now gained a share in branches of judicial work that had previously been undertaken solely by the emperor himself.[8] The occupant of the post, Burrus, is presented by Tacitus as the typical sound soldier, but this is cliché character-casting which seems to bear little relation to his career. In fact he had served as a personal and financial agent of emperors and of Agrippina[9] – whose downfall in 55, as has been seen, he was not prepared to accelerate. In the same year he went through a bad period when Seneca narrowly rescued him from being superseded by the son of Nero's nurse.

Whether Seneca was the real master of the world during these years we cannot say, since the historians do not tell us what support he could mobilize. With the exception, therefore, of a few people such as Pompeius Paulinus, we do not know who the men were upon whom he could rely, or how important their influence was. It is only by chance, for example, that we learn a little about his relative Annaeus Serenus, who became Commander of the Watch and helped Nero with his affair with Acte, but died young from eating poisonous fungi. (The analogy with Claudius' end looks sinister, but every year the Italian newspapers are full of stories of people who make the same mistake.) Tacitus, attracted by the Platonic situation of Seneca as the Philosopher behind the young ruler's throne, gives us a too stylized version of his power. There were other powerful men about as well, though we know little or nothing of what they did. But the historians were probably right in supposing that Seneca was more important than anyone else except the emperor. To show the world his position, he secured for himself a consulship, the senior annually elected office (56),[10] and obtained one also for his brother, Junius Gallio, known as the man who once interviewed St Paul.

above: Nero at the age of eighteen.

Seneca's philosophical essay *On Clemency* was written towards the end of 55, a year after Nero's accession. And it is to Nero himself that it is dedicated, on the grounds that once the emperor, when he was signing a death-warrant, had cried out 'I wish I had never learnt to write!'[11] The story is very probably true: although fear could make him kill, Nero hated the brutality of death. And so Seneca's watchword was Clemency. His study on the subject earned the admiration of Calvin and Corneille, and was a source of Portia's speech on mercy in Shakespeare's *Merchant of Venice* – 'it becomes the throned monarch better than his crown'.

The immediate purpose of *On Clemency* was to serve as a prospectus and compendium of how Seneca thought Nero ought to rule. 'Happiness is vouchsafing safety to many, calling back to life from the brink of death, deserving a Civic Crown for clemency. No decoration is fairer or worthier a prince's eminence than this crown awarded *for saving the lives of fellow citizens* – not trophies torn from the vanquished, not chariots blooded with barbarian gore, not spoils in war.'[12]

Nero on an imperial coin issued at Alexandria in Egypt, AD 56–7. His name and titles appear in Greek.

Seneca was powerful enough to get this message translated into the government's official publicity. For it is obviously no coincidence that, between the end of 55 and the year 60, the standard gold and silver coins of the state, the *aureus* and *denarius*, show this oaken wreath, the Civic Crown, as their exclusive and unvarying reverse design. A contemporary poet, Calpurnius Siculus, also had much to say about clemency in his flatteries of the emperor,[13] and Nero himself too, in numerous speeches, pledged himself to display the quality. No doubt he spoke under the influence of Seneca – though not necessarily under his exclusive influence, since such ideas were in the air.

But Seneca's essays went further still. For he set himself the task of out-lining the whole doctrine, a commonplace among the more enlightened rulers of later Greece, that monarchy is an 'admired slavery' devoted to service and morality. And yet there also persists through his work the abundant realization that autocracy is in charge at Rome – and has come to stay. Clemency itself is the virtue not of a Republic but of an autocracy;[14] Tacitus uses the word for some of his most ironical sneers and, because of its despotic ring, very few emperors – none for two reigns before or after Nero, and not even Nero himself – include it among the array of imperial virtues paraded on their coins. Yet it was an appropriate enough quality for the ruler of an empire so vast that Seneca and his philosophical masters could equate it with the human brotherhood which their Stoic school, source of the *lingua franca* of Graeco-Roman ethical thought, proclaimed as its ideal.

Nero was sufficiently influenced by this attitude to hate the idea of men fighting against each other as much as he hated judicial executions and gladiatorial slaughters. With such sentiments going round, the poets hailed him as provider of eternal peace.

> Joy, joy to all, to every race
> From where the southern lowlands lie
> To where the north wind takes the sky.[15]

Seneca's youthful acquaintance with philosophy and its practitioners had affected him with the violent excitement of a religious initiation. At first he had been interested in doctrines of a more mystic sort, and even after he had passed on to Stoicism he retained a strongly ascetic approach. He asked, on these grounds, to be excused the dubious pleasures of attending Nero's dinner parties and bestowing upon him the ceremonial morning kiss.

A contemporary compatriot, Columella of Gades (Cadiz), who wrote on agricultural affairs, described Seneca as a man of extraordinary talent (which he was) and extraordinarily high principles (of which more will be said in the next chapter). Another contemporary, the elder Pliny, remarked that he was 'by no means an admirer of frivolities'.[16] Both, however, are referring not so much to his philosophical achievements as to his business acumen – the management of his vast estates. For all his asceticism, he was gigantically wealthy, and it was held against him that four years in Nero's favour brought him 300 million sesterces from the emperor. As an example of his grandeur (strangely blending with personal austerity), we are told he possessed five hundred identical tables of citrus wood with ivory legs. It ran in the family. His father-in-law always travelled with twelve thousand pounds of silver plate, and his brother Annaeus Mela, who avoided an official career, amassed a large fortune as director of Nero's imperial domains. To his other brother Gallio, Seneca wrote – perhaps in 58 when he was at the height of his power – frankly defending the philosopher's right to be as rich as he could manage. And he was certainly famous for his generosity.[17]

The government of Nero's empire under these auspices was, on the whole, painstaking, correct and beneficial. The emperor had served notice that he would respect the position of the Senate. The poets proclaimed the same fact, and a public reminder of the point was continuously offered on all Roman coinage from the end of 55 to 60–1. For the inscription on these coins, EX s*(enatus)* c*(onsulto)*, indicates that they were issued by a decree of the Senate, a reference which had not appeared on imperial gold and silver coins before and which, although it had little or no meaning in terms of power – and indeed it was probably the emperor who moved the senatorial decree – meant a lot in terms of prestige. The government of the empire, in general, was a fairly static and passive affair, mostly set in motion by pressures from below, but in Nero's first years it was thoughtful and enlightened. There were improvements of treasury administration, measures in support of public order, provisions against forgery, and instructions that provincial governors and their officials must not hold gladiatorial or wild beast shows – for which, in the past, large sums of money had been harshly raised from local popula-

Nero aged twenty-three.

tions by governors who hoped to win supporters to screen their own irregularities.

Moreover, in Nero's first seven years, Rome witnessed twelve accusations of Roman officials by provincials – mainly in wealthy Asia Minor – and six of the defendants, including three imperial agents, were convicted. At the beginning of his reign Nero had promised the Senate good judicial administration, and he took a lot of trouble about this. In the law-court over which he personally presided, he preferred to defer his judgement on a case until the following day, and then gave it in writing; and he ruled that, instead of a case being presented as a whole, first by one side and then by the other, every relevant charge should be debated separately. On withdrawing to study a problem of law, he never consulted openly with his judicial advisers or assessors, but made each of them write out their opinions, which were then incorporated in a single memorandum; Nero mulled it over in private, and came to his own conclusion, appending to the document, or getting his minister to append, the imperial verdict.[18]

Tax reforms

In 58, for the first time as far as we know, Nero showed an embarrassing sign of administrative independence. This was when he suggested to his council that indirect taxation all over the empire should be totally abolished. What prompted him to intervene in this field was the continuing flow of complaints about the private tax-gatherers *(publicani)*, to whom, as in the bad old days of the Republic, the collection of many taxes was still farmed out. It is uncertain whether he thought of the idea himself, or whether others thought of it for him; if so, they are unlikely to have been Seneca and Burrus. At any rate he now proposed to eliminate the whole evil, root and branch. Modern suggestions that his proposal was really more limited and prosaic are unlikely, since this was just the type of popular, sweeping gesture that appealed to him.

But it had the manifest disadvantage that, if it were put into effect, a great deal more money would have to be raised from direct taxation instead. The principal indirect tax was the customs or import duty levied at various points throughout the empire and on its frontiers. Presumably Nero, or those who encouraged him to promote the scheme, calculated that the abolition of this duty would stimulate trade to such an extent that the revenue from direct taxes would greatly increase. But these calculations were quite as uncertain as a British Chancellor's annual budgetary calculations today. The idea involved vast, unpredictable risks, and Nero's advisers, with much praise of his noble generosity – the quality traditionally vaunted by Roman aristocrats – ventured to dissuade him.

Behind the incident may be seen an early clash between Nero's impulsive liberalism and the more cautious feelings that prevailed among most leading Romans. However, good came out of the conflict, because the opportunity was taken to ensure that some of the worst abuses of tax-collecting were abolished.

The grain supply

At the same time merchant ships were exempted from property tax. This was one of a number of measures taken to facilitate the transport of grain to

Rome from overseas. That was a major preoccupation of all emperors, and although in fact they usually fell from power, in the end, for other reasons, they had some justification for feeling that their thrones largely depended on their success in this field. In spite of the protests of many moralists and Italian agriculturalists, Rome was only saved from starvation by these ships which imported the grain of north Africa and Sicily. It was a partially parasite capital which needed seven million bushels of this grain every year,[19] a quarter of it coming from Egypt. The city also contained many poor and destitute people who were only kept alive by state-organized distributions of grain below market price, or completely free of charge. These subsidies had been in force for two centuries, and the number of registered recipients was probably, in Nero's reign, about 200,000 – as much as one-fifth of the total urban population.

The great Alexandrian grain ships took eighteen days to reach Italy; or sometimes they got there in half that time. Seneca describes how at Puteoli (Pozzuoli) in the Bay of Naples – the main port of Rome, which Ostia was only beginning to replace – the whole population used to turn out on the breakwaters to meet the vanguard of the approaching fleet.[20] People were

The remains of what was once an impressive building at Ostia, which started to become an important harbour-town under Claudius and Nero.

very sensitive and anxious about this grain supply, and complained with great readiness if they thought that anything had gone wrong with the arrangements. Petronius vividly describes the sort of grumbling that went on in Puteoli itself, or a town not far off.[21] At Rome, whose inhabitants so largely depended on these supplies, people were even more excitable, suspicious, and nervous. They were at the mercy of any and every rumour about empty granaries, shipwrecks, alleged displacements of grain cargoes by luxury imports, and speculators trying to corner the market. The imperial government felt obliged to spend an immense amount of time counteracting such worries and improving supplies of grain. And no ruler was more attentive to this problem than Nero.

One of his subsequent coins shows a sketch of the port of Ostia – reminding everyone that Nero had completed, or was using, the new harbour begun by his predecessor, much closer to Rome than Puteoli. The port was protected from the open sea by two moles six and eight hundred metres in length, as well as by a sunken, concrete-filled ship a hundred metres long. Nero's coinage also reported that, in addition to the usual grain distributions, he twice gave their recipients additional presents, the first of these special hand-outs taking place in 57 and the second at some uncertain date thereafter. The practice was traditional, but the sums distributed by Nero, 400 sesterces a head, were larger than any since the early days of Augustus. The coins also showed Romans their fine new Macellum Augusti, or market for meat, fish and vegetables, which he opened for them in 56 or 57 and later rebuilt after it had been burnt down.

By such measures he achieved his aim, the creation of a close, emotional bond of gratitude and affection between himself and the large, potentially disorderly, population of the capital. For they could be a perilous threat to the regime; but they could also be its mainstay. At a later date Nero abandoned a foreign trip because the people of Rome felt so anxious about how they would fare if their benefactor went away. Graciously cancelling his plans, he took the opportunity, as Tacitus reports, to rub in what a kindly ruler he was.

His patriotism came before everything, Nero asserted; he had seen the people's sad faces and heard their private lamentations about the extensive travels he planned – even his brief absences they found unendurable, being accustomed (he

A painting of ships from the Temple of Isis at Pompeii.

The recently excavated
Great School of
Gladiators at Rome,
probably newly built at
the time of Nero's
accession.

added) to derive comfort in life's misfortunes from the sight of their emperor. Just as in private relationships nearest are dearest, he said, so to him the inhabitants of Rome came first; he must obey their appeal to stay![22]

The people liked such protestations. . . . Their principal interest was the grain supply, and they feared it would run short if Nero was not with them.

Bread and circuses

And, Tacitus adds, they also loved the amusements the emperor provided for them. For this was the second element in the 'bread and circuses', *panem et circenses* – the classic recipe by which the Caesars kept the favour of the metropolitan population. Nero was as attentive to the 'circuses' as to the

63

bread. Under Augustus, Games had been held in Rome on sixty-six days every year. Nero on his accession increased the total by several days, causing something like a strike among the firms that provided charioteers. In 57 he built an imposing new wooden amphitheatre for gladiator and wild-beast shows; it was the forerunner of the stone Colosseum, but located elsewhere, in the Field of Mars.

But Nero, true to his dislike for violent death unless he felt himself threatened, significantly ruled that no gladiator should be killed in these bloody contests – not even the condemned criminals whose execution by this means was traditional. His policy was to reduce the gladiator fights to harmless fencing matches, in which representatives of all social classes (and, later, of both sexes) were encouraged to take part. What he was trying to do was exactly in line with the opinions of Seneca, who wrote harrowingly on the horrors of these duels and deaths. Indeed it was Seneca who delivered the first known unambiguous attack on the whole institution of gladiators, so repugnant to his Stoic concept of the human brotherhood.[23]

But it was impossible for the emperor to go so far as abolishing gladiators, and he did not even try – presumably with Seneca's pained but practical concurrence. On the contrary, despite the security problems displayed by riots in the amphitheatre at Pompeii and an attempted break-out by gladiators at Praeneste (Palestrina), Nero felt it necessary to lavish money on these displays. At one of them the arena was flooded so that a naval battle, Athenians versus Persians, could be staged. Another time the gladiators' weapons and equipment were studded with amber. And so were their coffins: which showed that the veto on fights to the death had been too much in advance of the times, and could not be maintained.

Nero also spent enormous sums on wild-beast fights. Seneca objected to these, at least in theory, telling stories of desperate suicides by the combatants. Seneca's contemporary Petronius was another who found this sort of carnage horrid.

> Rome rampant
> On a victim world.
> New shapes of slaughter everywhere,
> Peace a pool of blood.
> With gold the hunter's snares are set:
> Driving through Africa, on and on: the hunters at Hammon,
> And the beaters threshing the thickets where the flailing
>   tiger screams.
> Hunters, hawkers of death. And the market for murder
>   at Rome:
> Fangs in demand. At sea, sheer hunger prowls the ships;
> On silken feet the sullen tiger pads his gilded stage,
> Crouches at Rome, and leaps! And the man, gored and dying,
> While the crowd goes wild.[24]

Though he became a close friend of Petronius, the emperor was not in a position to hold such views; or at least he could not put them into effect. Instead, he exercised his ingenuity to provide amusing and startling spec-

right: Nero in his nineteenth year, portrayed on a coin of Antioch.

overleaf: A relief of an animal-fight in the arena. Nero organized immense displays of this kind, and was himself reported to have taken on a lion, perhaps doped.

62660

tacles. On the day when the arena was flooded, fishes and other sea animals
were launched upon the waters, and polar bears were set to kill seals. When
the amphitheatre was dry, spectators were able to watch the slaughter of
many a rare beast, including maned, bearded and 'bristly' oxen (the last
probably gnu), and 'horned boars' which may have been warthog from the
sources of the Nile. There were also hippopotamuses .to be seen and
slaughtered.[25] Later, an elephant carrying a Roman knight was reported to
have appeared balancing in the air on some sort of a track made of ropes,
though it is difficult to see exactly what happened. Bull-fights, the precursors
of modern Spanish contests, were also to be seen; and the cavalry of the
Praetorian Guard took on four hundred boars and three hundred lions.

Machinery, evidently of considerable sophistication, was installed to
enable the ground to yawn open: whereupon was disclosed a magic wood of
glittering bushes and scented fountains, infested with exotic wild animals.
The poet Calpurnius Siculus witnessed this misplaced *tour de force*, and
described it in verse scarcely more stimulating than this translation.

How oft I, inly terrified,
Witnessed, as side withdrew from side,
The arena's level scene dispart,
And grisly monsters upward start
From bursting rifts of deep sunk ground.
How often from that gulf profound
Gold-branching arbutes sprang to view,
With fountain spray of saffron hue.[26]

69

The poet was justified in feeling a certain amount of alarm, for careful steps had to be taken to protect spectators from the beasts. There was probably a wooden barricade, surmounted by strong nets hanging from elephant tusks fixed to the awning's masts, and in front of the seats were arranged horizontal cylinders (at least one of them of ivory) which rotated so that no animal could climb over them into the crowd.

Corbulo, the greatest general of Nero's time.

Rome often seemed infinitely more important than the rest of the empire together – and the amount of space devoted to its affairs by the aristocratically-minded ancient historians suggests that this was often what they thought too. But still the capital was not everything; and the government had to devote continuous, unobtrusive attention to the vast imperial territories, and above all to the immensely long frontiers.

The only frontier which presented serious problems was the eastern one, for Parthia, a feudal state in Iraq and Iran, was the one substantial foreign power with which Rome had to contend, anywhere in the world. The relations between the two governments were perpetually bedevilled by the mountainous kingdom of Armenia, which extended north of Mesopotamia as far as the Caucasus. Both Rome and Parthia always coveted that country, and neither was ever able to reduce it to subordination for long; though the Romans at least, and presumably the Parthians too, often boasted publicly that it had been conquered. Above all, neither of the two empires could allow it to be absorbed by the other. Each felt the territory was a dagger pointed at its own heart.

Campaigns raged in this area during a large part of Nero's reign. Like his Parthian counterpart Vologases I (51–78), he never took the field himself. Nevertheless, the important decisions he had to reach must be considered in any estimate of his character and achievement. When it became clear, as it did immediately, that there was a power vacuum in Armenia, and that the Parthians aspired to fill it, Nero at once appointed to the area one of the leading generals of the day, Corbulo. His mother, who had been married six times, gave him a host of valuable connections; and his own deeds, like his physical features, were remembered by later generations partly because he wrote his memoirs, but chiefly because his daughter married the future prince and emperor Domitian. Corbulo had won his prestige not by a career of great victories, for there were few to be gained, but by the strict discipline which often gave the generals of this epoch their reputations. He was a plain-spoken man (he once called a colleague a plucked ostrich), and it was not long before he got involved in a quarrel with the governor of Syria. But meanwhile Parthia, in domestic difficulties, backed down, and Nero soothed the generals' quarrel by a tactful announcement honouring them both for this success.

The first important development occurred in about 58, when Corbulo tried to arrange a meeting with the man who had taken over the kingship of Armenia, Tiridates. He was the Parthian nominee for its throne, being the half-brother of Vologases himself; but Corbulo had advised him to petition Nero, in which case he might be allowed to remain king with the approval of Rome as well as Parthia. This was an interesting policy, since, if adopted, it would mean an end to the dreary succession of fighting which had alternately placed Roman and Parthian puppets on the Armenian throne for brief and precarious periods. A Parthian nominee was to rule Armenia in peace because he was also going to obtain the favour of Rome. Nero and his council – for the policy which Corbulo was trying to execute was no doubt not his own but theirs – evidently reckoned that a show of submission by Tiridates was enough to persuade the Roman public it had obtained the victory which emperors, for the sake of their reputations and skins, were always obliged to claim they had won.

The formulation of this pacific yet face-saving policy was one of the major achievements of Nero's government. It made the poets talk even more loudly of the new era of peace. But the policy did not prove successful immediately. Corbulo failed to get his meeting with Tiridates, and instead fought two campaigns against him and his Parthian backers. The fighting seemed to go reasonably well. But fighting in Armenia rarely turned out to have the successful result which it had at first seemed to promise; and nothing, for the present, was settled.

On this silver coin, the Fortune or spirit of the great Greek city of Seleucia on the Tigris is presenting a wreath or diadem to a seated king of Parthia.

4 The Death of Agrippina

The emperor was not as attentive to these far-off happenings as he might have been, because he had other things on his mind. In 59 he decided that his mother had become intolerable, and that she must be killed. His reasons for this monstrous decision are not, at first sight, apparent. She had evidently ceased to play an active part in the government nearly four years earlier. And he did not often have to meet her. Tacitus is by no means at his best when he tries to explain the situation. According to him, Nero was scared because his mistress Acte convinced him of the dreadful consequences his incest with Agrippina might have on the army's loyalty. But, even if these relations with his mother were more than just salacious gossip, they surely belonged to a period some years earlier, when Nero had still been fond of her. So the historian's indication that this was still a live issue in 59 is an anachronism.

On the other hand his second explanation of Nero's assassination of Agrippina – suggesting that the atrocity was prompted by the emperor's future wife Poppaea – is an anachronism from a later date. Poppaea is supposed to have told him, with many womanly upbraidings, that it was only Agrippina who stood in the way of his divorcing Octavia and getting married to her. In fact, three more years went by after 59 before Nero took these steps. Poppaea's early relations with Nero were so conjectural that no less than five conflicting accounts of them have come down to us, two contradictory versions appearing in Tacitus alone. It looks probable that he and other historians antedated her influence over Nero in order to provide a tidy, somewhat novelettish course of events to explain the murder of Agrippina. But, in fact, the emperor is most unlikely, first, to have plucked up his courage to the supreme horror of matricide in order to facilitate his divorce and remarriage, and then, subsequently, to have failed to divorce and remarry for another three years.

Suetonius is probably much nearer the truth in suggesting that Nero became frightened by the violent and threatening remarks that he was told Agrippina was making. As we have seen, he was always easily roused to fears for his own safety; and when he killed that was nearly always why. Furthermore, apart from the doubtful case of Britannicus, there was a typical pattern about most of the killings and suicides for which Nero may be regarded as

73

responsible. First, there came a considerable period of estrangement, when the future victim was far away from Nero, sometimes in exile, always under surveillance. Death only came some years later when informers or other interested parties had reported, not always accurately, what the disgraced person was saying or had said. As one of these typical sequences of events unfolded, the timid Nero was always able to work himself up into a genuine frenzy of anxious conviction that his life was at stake. It is easy to believe that this is what happened in the case of Agrippina. He, on his side, must in any case have been desperately eager to emancipate himself from her psychological ascendancy. And she, by all accounts, was not careful with her tongue, and would have been likely to express herself quite freely in her own home about aspects of her son's life which she disliked – and they were many, including, for example, his love of Greeks and all they stood for, and his passion for having a good time in his own way. It is also not impossible that Agrippina *was* thinking of striking Nero down; or at least that she was listening to people who had such thoughts in mind. At any rate that is what he came to believe. And he could all too easily be reminded of the perils that

Probably Agrippina, with long sceptre and sacrificial bowl.

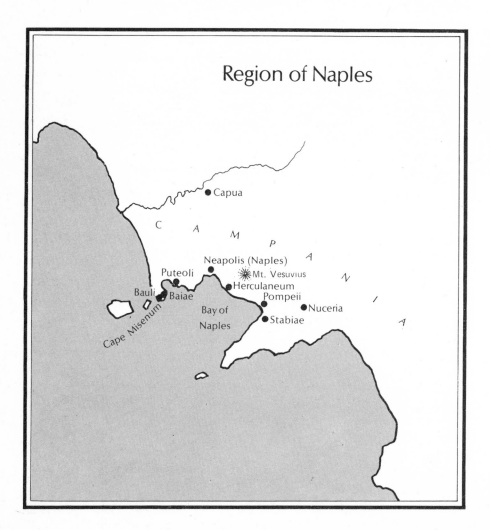

Region of Naples

74

would ensue if his mother contemplated marriage with some imperially descended or related personage. No island exile could be safe enough for such a lethal woman, even if she was his mother. Her survival, he felt, would mean a risk of civil war, endangering the subjects whom it was his duty to protect.

And so a proposal by his former tutor Anicetus, who was now commander of the fleet at Misenum beside the Bay of Naples, gained Nero's attention. Anicetus suggested that she should be eliminated by means of a collapsible ship; and the emperor agreed. He was accustomed to attend the annual festival of the goddess of Minerva at the fashionable, noisy resort of Baiae, not far from Misenum, and he invited his mother to join him there. They dined together at Bauli, on the bay between Misenum and Baiae, in a mansion which probably belonged to Agrippina. It was a very cheerful and friendly party; according to one account the host was the emperor's friend Otho, who had helped to arrange Nero's affair with Acte. Then Nero left for Baiae by land, and Agrippina departed for the same destination by sea.

It was a quiet, starlit night and the sea was calm. The ship began to go on its way. Agrippina was attended by two of her friends. One of them, Crepereius Gallus, stood near the tiller. The other, Acerronia, leant over the feet of her resting mistress, happily talking about Nero's remorseful behaviour and his mother's reestablished influence. Then came the signal. Under the pressure of heavy lead weights, the roof fell in. Crepereius was crushed, and died instantly. Agrippina and Acerronia were saved by the raised sides of their couch, which happened to be strong enough to resist the pressure. Moreover, the ship held together.

In the general confusion, those in the conspiracy were hampered by the many who were not. But then some of the oarsmen had the idea of throwing their weight on one side to capsize the ship. However, they took too long to concert this improvised plan, and meanwhile others brought weight to bear in the opposite direction. This provided the opportunity to make a gentler descent into the water. Acerronia ill-advisedly started crying out, 'I am Agrippina! Help, help the emperor's mother!' She was struck dead by blows from poles and oars, and whatever ship's gear happened to be available.

Agrippina herself kept quiet and avoided recognition. Though she was hurt – she had a wound in the shoulder – she swam until she came to some sailing-boats. They brought her to the Lucrine lake, from which she was taken back to the villa at Bauli.[1]

Nero was not the first despot to lure his mother out onto a boat to assassinate her. This had already been done in Heraclea Pontica (Eregli in Turkey) in c. 300 BC when queen Amastris was killed at sea by her two sons.[2] But that does not mean that the story of the attempt on Agrippina's life is fictitious; though the partial precedent may signify that Anicetus, as befitted a former professor, had been reading history. However, the idea of the collapsible ship was taken from a more recent event. It was derived from a vessel used in Nero's aquatic Games, whose hull opened automatically to let animals out into the water.

Agrippina understood very well what had happened. She sent a freedman, Agerinus, to tell Nero that by divine mercy and his lucky star she had survived a serious accident; but that he must not trouble to visit her at present, since she needed to rest. But when the messenger entered Nero's presence, the emperor dropped a sword on to the ground and declared the man had been caught red-handed in an attempt on his life. Agerinus was placed under guard.

Meanwhile news of Agrippina's mishap had become known, and huge crowds started gathering on the shore. They were dispersed by troops. Agrippina's servants now melted away from her house; and Nero made a second and successful attempt. He did not trust his praetorian guardsmen to do the deed, but dispatched Anicetus and two naval officers. They arrived at the villa, and struck their fatal blows. The body was cremated on a dining room couch the same night.

Nero, it was reported, remained in a state of terror until senior praetorians came to offer him their congratulations on his narrow escape; and deputations from the neighbouring towns soon did the same. This made him feel better, and he bestirred himself to leave for Neapolis (Naples). From there he wrote the Senate a letter, reporting that Agrippina's freedman had been caught in the act of trying to murder him, and that she, conscious of her guilt as instigator of the outrage, 'had paid the penalty'. The letter then reiterated every charge that could possibly be brought against his mother, from the reign of Claudius onwards. It included the outburst: 'I can hardly believe that I am safe from her now. Nor do I derive any pleasure from the fact.'[3]

The murder of Agrippina

The murder took place at some date between 19 and 23 March, AD 59. On 28 March, as we learn from an inscription, the members of the Arval Priesthood – an élite body including some of the most politically knowledgeable noblemen in the state – held one of their periodical religious meetings at Rome. They were accustomed to offer sacrifices for members of the imperial family. But this time they did not offer one. It was still too difficult to know who ought to be sacrificed for, and how to express it. Then on 5 April they met again and duly offered a sacrifice. By now there was a senatorial decree to guide them, and they gave thanks for the safety of the emperor.

But Nero still did not come back to the capital. He postponed his return until September. It was an awkward interval; and unpleasant graffiti were to be seen along the streets.

> Alcmaeon, Orestes and Nero are brothers.
> Why? Because all of them murdered their mothers.[4]

And yet, on the whole, Nero was extremely well received when he finally returned to Rome. The murder had no immediate effect on his standing. It was possible for senators and others to avert the eye from speculations about what may actually have happened on the Bay of Naples, and to reflect that the coexistence of Nero and Agrippina had been creating an intolerable situation, perilous for the state and for its leading men, who could easily have become fatally engulfed in the venomous hatred between imperial mother and son. It was a relief that this situation had come to an end. And now, from one province and another, loyal addresses duly poured in.[5] Nero promptly restored men whom Agrippina had driven into exile; and it was probably with conviction that her birthday was declared a day of ill omen.

Politically speaking, this was not such a serious crisis as the melodramatic accounts of the historians so unforgettably suggest. It could have been rather awkward, it is true. But the problem had been surmounted without too much difficulty.

It was generally believed that Nero's dispatch to the Senate, announcing his mother's hostile act and subsequent death, had been composed by Seneca. And Tacitus adds that, when the senior praetorian officers went and congratulated Nero immediately after the event, they did so on the prompting of Burrus. He and Seneca are unlikely to have been privy to the murder, but Tacitus suggests how, afterwards, they probably made the best of a bad job. Evidently they still felt it essential for the security of the state, and of themselves, to do everything possible to help Nero. It was largely through their diplomacy, therefore, that he was given such a good reception when he returned to the capital.

How Burrus really felt can only be guessed. Tacitus remarks, with a good deal of plausibility, that he was nervous about how the army might react to the downfall of the woman who was daughter of the beloved Germanicus; and Nero himself had not felt able to entrust her assassination to the guardsmen. As for Seneca, his attitude can to some extent be reconstructed from his writings. These, the philosophical essays and tragic dramas alike, repeatedly dwell on the difficult problem of harmonizing personal standards and political activity. This is very different from the rich young 'satirical' poet Persius who was also writing at this time. For he, although his astringent approach was poles apart from Nero's court, never says or hints a critical word about the political situation. In the works of Seneca, on the other hand, there is a great deal of talk about the evilness of tyrants,[6] of whom the last emperor but one, Caligula (37–41), was taken as the stock type.[7]

> Excessive power seeks power beyond its power . . .
> A violent power no ruler wields for long,
> A moderate lasts and lives.[8]

Seneca also has praise for the Stoical, saintly sort of person who opposes a tyrant: the historical figure of Cato, who a hundred years previously had fought against Julius Caesar, is transfigured (as by earlier writers) into a sage of this kind. Seneca is evidently conscious of the precedent of Plato (who refused to compromise with the tyrant Dionysius of Syracuse) and is quoted by Tacitus as claiming, later on, that Nero had often had more reason to complain of his freedom of speech than of his servility. Seneca is acutely aware that there can come a point of no return. 'I will keep my promise to go out to dinner if it is merely cold, but not if there is a snowstorm.' The tyrant may become so tyrannical that the best thing his advisers can do is to remove him from the scene. 'If all hope of his sanity be for ever gone, my kindness which I return to him shall be therewith a kindness to the world. Departure from this life is his best remedy, and it is best for him to pass away who will never come to himself again.'[9]

These words may have been written soon after Nero's accession; more probably they belong to c. 63. At all events, the appalling act of matricide in

59 not only abruptly ended any surviving dreams of the philosophically orientated prince, but, one might have thought, must have made Seneca give up all hope of his former protégé, and feel as Hamlet felt.

> O heart! Lose not thy nature; let not ever
> The soul of Nero enter this firm bosom;
> Let me be cruel, not unnatural!

The act was certainly horrifying. And yet, for practical reasons of state, Seneca evidently decided that the breaking-point had not yet been reached. The national interests seemed to require the conclusion that the emperor had still not brought matters to the point of no return.

This is a perpetual dilemma for collaborators. Might they not, they can always wonder, be of more service to their countrymen, as well as to themselves, might they not be able to avert even worse evils, if they stay at their posts? Their retirement might make it more likely for the state to disintegrate into violence. And that, evidently, is what Seneca decided in 59. His own personal safety had recently been threatened by a malignant prosecutor. And he was all too well aware that theory and practice did not and could not always coincide.[10] An implicit admission to that effect appears in his later work *On Anger*, in which he quoted an aged courtier's remark that he had survived by receiving injuries and being grateful for them.[11]

An unknown Roman of the fifties or sixties AD.

In other words, even if the collaborator could do some good by remaining at his post, it had to be realistically accepted that his possibilities in this direction were severely limited. In another epoch Thomas Warton wrote,

> Could Boileau to reform a nation hope?
> A Sodom can't be mended by a Pope!

The prospects of reforming Nero were equally discouraging. As Seneca himself rather pointedly observes, speaking about despots in general, 'if the tyrant desires stage-artists and harlots, and such gifts as may soften his fierceness, I will gladly let him have them'.[12]

But if Seneca, in spite of such gloomy reservations, believed that this undignified role was worth while, so did the historian Tacitus. Unlike many later critics, he implies a favourable verdict on Seneca's efforts. In the appallingly difficult conditions of these perilous imperial regimes he felt that Seneca's attitude was the right one. Tacitus' own father-in-law Agricola, whom he admired, had played an even more unprotesting role under the even more tyrannical Domitian (81–96) – and it therefore seemed to the historian that Seneca's dogged, unobtrusive persistence, without many illusions or even hopes, had been equally praiseworthy. 'Let us keep back', wrote Seneca to his friend Lucilius Junior of Pompeii, 'as far as we can, from slippery places. Even on dry ground we do not stand too steadily.' And in his last letter of all he added that the most successful men are also the most miserable.

And so Seneca had now shown how very far he was prepared to go along with Nero. Moreover, it may have been at about the same time that he displayed a new degree of willingness to amuse the youthful and cynical court. This point was marked by his publication of a savage piece of mockery, in mixed prose and verse, about the death of Claudius. It was apparently known as the 'Pumpkinification' (*Apocolocyntosis*) of that emperor, a mocking parody of Deification (*Apotheosis*).[13] The work has been generally attributed to *c.* 54–55, immediately after Nero's accession; but this date is probably wrong, since although Agrippina was apparently the murderer of Claudius she had also been made the priestess of the cult of the new god. So it would scarcely have been practical for a man in Seneca's position to have made fun of the deified emperor so offensively when she was at the height of her power; or even, one may surmise, while she was living at all. A feature of this literary effort, which casts a strange light on its author's versatility, is that Augustus is made into one of Claudius' fiercest accusers. This is a far cry from the days of 54–5 when official coinage had shown Divus Augustus and Divus Claudius riding together in a ceremonial elephant-drawn chariot. We learn independently that Nero himself considered the deification of Claudius a joke,[14] and it was perhaps now, when the patroness of that event was out of the way, that the mockery became open.

5 An Emperor who Sings, Acts and Races

For Nero, Agrippina's disappearance chiefly meant that he was now able, without feeling inhibited or irritated by her disapproval, to plunge into the activities which she despised and he enjoyed more than anything else in the world: singing, acting, and chariot racing.

At the beginning of his reign he had moved in the society of male ballet-dancers or *pantomimi*. These performers, whose profession and art dated back to the time of Augustus, were handsome athletic young men who danced and mimed in gorgeous gold-embroidered tunics, purple cloaks, flowing silk robes and beautiful, tight-lipped masks. For each successive role, they changed both costume and mask, even in the course of a single piece. They were silent as they danced; 'their gestures', declared Seneca, 'flowed as fast as words', with every position of the hands and fingers possessing its own significance. A prince of Pontus in Asia Minor asked Nero to present him with a dancer he had seen in Rome, because the man's expressive gestures would enable interpreters to be dispensed with at the Pontic court.[1] Huge orchestras and massed choirs provided a thrilling accompaniment for these performances; the poet Lucan, Seneca's nephew, profitably wrote fourteen librettos for such choirs.

The ballets, and a variant called Pyrrhic dances, were ambitious. But things could go wrong. On one occasion, when there was an elaborate staging of the myth of Daedalus and Icarus flying through the sky, Icarus fell to the ground, right beside Nero's couch, and spattered the emperor with his blood. And the modern fashion for authentic sexual activity on the stage was anticipated by a ballet showing the love-making of the Minotaur with Pasiphae. In the myth, Pasiphae had disguised herself as a cow for the purpose; and now, on the stage, it seemed to the spectators that a dancer disguised as a bull was actually engaged in intercourse with a girl who was inside the hind-quarters of a hollow wooden heifer. (Realism was fashionable; at a performance of a comic play called *Fire* the scenery was really set alight, and the actors were allowed to carry away the burning furniture.)

The partisans of the leading dancers were as impassioned and hysterical as those of a modern pop-singer, but with the difference that they included senators and knights. The beautiful dancer Mysticus possessed an unusual

A scene from a tragedy.

83

left: Behind the scenes at the theatre: preparations for a performance. A mosaic from Pompeii.

distinction, because not just one knight but two died in the very act of making love to him.[2] Teachers and scholars of this art of the ballet sprang up everywhere, and at many a private theatre performances were staged in which husbands and wives competed to partner the gorgeous young men in their dances.[3] One lady of the period, Aelia Catella, was still ballet-dancing in her eighties.

The excitement and rivalry aroused by the public appearances and performances of the stars could rapidly degenerate into violent brawling between factions and gangs. This amused Nero, but became so serious that in 56 his government was obliged to clamp down. His previous experimental withdrawal of the guards battalion, which was normally on duty at these shows, had to be reversed, and for a few years the dancers were expelled from Italy.

Such repressive measures, however, did not descend on Nero's particular friend Paris, the ballet-dancer who had helped to poison his mind against Agrippina – a woman likely to have been far from sympathetic to the type of exotic entertainments he provided. Next Paris secured a court verdict against his own former slave-mistress, Nero's aunt Domitia, suing her successfully for the sum with which he had purchased his enfranchisement.[4]

Paris was such an outstanding dancer that his interpretation of Mars

right: The Flight of Icarus in a painting from Pompeii.

overleaf: A relief of dancing Bacchants – the kind of role that Nero liked acting.

above: Allegedly the sage Apollonius of Tyana: but most philosophers were given these grim expressions. Apollonius was in danger of his life under Nero.

making love to Venus, in which he took both parts in succession, persuaded even an ascetic holy man, Apollonius of Tyana in Asia Minor, that there really was something to be said for this sort of thing. Paris used to join Nero's table after dinner to amuse him, but he was also the emperor's dancing master. This, however, ultimately caused his downfall (in 67); because the emperor, who had entertained the ambition to dance the part of Virgil's Turnus, felt sour because he never became a successful pupil.

Nero very soon decided that he really preferred another art instead. This was tragic drama – in the sense in which that was understood in his day. The performance of the old Greek and Latin tragedies had been totally changed. Originally they were dialogue interspersed with lyrics; now there were only scraps of dialogue, and the lyrics were everything. The great performers of the day sang these lyrics as solos, acting and gesturing as they sang. At the same time they accompanied their own songs on the lyre, which was held in greater honour even than the pipes because it was harder to play. The strings, it was said, 'were made to resound like the human voice'.

Nero devoted a great deal of energy to becoming a successful singer and lyre-player and tragic actor. His voice, though not very strong, was a deep, cavernous, muffled bass. He trained it with the utmost conscientiousness. Music had formed part of his childhood curriculum, and he early developed a taste for it. Soon after his accession, he summoned Terpnus, the greatest lyre-player of the day, to sing to him after dinner for several nights in succession until very late. Then, little by little, he began to study and practise himself, and meticulously undertook all the usual exercises for strengthening and developing the voice. He would lie on his back with a slab of lead on his chest, and used enemas and emetics to keep down his weight.[5] He also followed a careful diet. He avoided apples, which experts considered harmful to the vocal chords. Dried figs were regarded as good for a singer, but fresh figs bad. He also refrained from eating bread on fixed days every month. All vegetables of the onion family were believed to be good for singers, and on certain days Nero ate nothing but chives preserved in oil – a recipe which, in consequence, was recommended thereafter by the medical profession. It is good to know after this (and after Suetonius' report that he suffered from body odour as well) that the emperor scented not only his bath-water, but his hands and the soles of his feet.

A throaty bass voice like his, we are told, was thought to be best adapted to conveying emotional or pitiful or dramatic situations;[6] and those were the parts he welcomed. In Greek drama it was the kind of part you could find most easily in Euripides, whom Nero consequently favoured. But in his time tastes had become far more melodramatic and bizarre. In the rhetorical tragic dramas of Seneca, which were written not so much for public performance as for private recitation, some passages are so macabre that they can scarcely be read without producing a feeling of nausea.[7] And there are equally morbid stretches in the *Pharsalia* (Civil War) which his relative Lucan wrote about the strife between Pompey and Caesar.

That was the right spirit for Nero. He liked to sing and act tragic, desperate, shocking roles – like Nauplius unjustly sacrificed by the Greeks in the

An amber statuette of an actor, from Nola in Campania, not far from Nero's favourite city, Naples.

Trojan War, Attis castrated, and even the incestuous Oedipus blinded, as
well as Orestes, who committed matricide: parts, one would have thought,
which Nero might have regarded it as tactful to avoid. He also enjoyed acting
as a beggar, a runaway slave, and lunatic. At one imperial performance a
young member of his bodyguard, who was standing in the wings without
evidently paying very much attention to the performance, suddenly looked
at the stage, and saw the emperor wearing rags and chains; Nero was acting
the part of Hercules gone mad. Whereupon the soldier (although he could
have noted that the chains were made of gold) committed the unfortunate
gaffe of rushing forward and releasing him.

Nero was also perfectly prepared to sing and act women's parts – for
example Niobe, turning to stone because her children were massacred.
Another of his favourite roles was Canace, whose incestuous bastard by
her brother was thrown to the hounds. This gave rise to a joke: 'What is the
emperor doing? He is having a baby.'

Even if he was a failure as a ballet-dancer, Nero flung himself with enthusiasm into the dramatic aspects of these parts. 'You danced the whole programme according to the book', declared the admiring Greek poet Lucilius.
The same poet also mocked at performers who acted three of Nero's favourite
parts badly – which was a delicate way of saying that the emperor had done
them better.

He liked to sing and act in masks representing the features of whatever
woman happened to be arousing his interest at the time. His fellow-lyre-
players enjoyed agreeable patronage. Even Terpnus, no doubt, found it

A scene from a tragedy is
depicted in this painting
from Herculaneum:
Orestes, with Pylades,
gazes at his mother
Clytaemnestra and her
lover Aegisthus. Strangely,
Nero liked acting the part
of his fellow-matricide
Orestes.

worth his while to have to play and sing to the emperor until a late hour of the night. His colleague Menecrates, whose songs were mangled by Trimalchio in Petronius' novel, was presented by the emperor with an estate and a palace. Other huge properties went to Spiculus, who not only played the lyre but fought as a gladiator as well.

Most of these singers and musicians were Alexandrians. But their songs were hummed in the streets of the capital, and Roman ladies knew them all. Trimalchio's dinners were like the theatre, with music being played incessantly. What all this Neronian music sounded like is not quite clear. It was predominantly melodic, without any counterpoint or harmony as we understand it, and lacking our highest and deepest notes. It would probably come as a shock to modern westerners – it might sound like some sort of a mixture between Gregorian chant and the musical traditions of the Arabs, Indians or Chinese. And as for the accompaniments to dramatic displays, ancient writers were quite convinced that, like the rest of these performances, they had an erotic, depraving effect. They excited listeners so much that their hands began to stray: 'Their soft and effeminate notes provoke immodest touches and lascivious tickling.'[8]

Nero as poet So this singing and lyre-playing and tragic acting became, and remained, the greatest interest in Nero's life. It also involved the composition of poetry, because the songs lyre-players sang were very often composed by themselves. Menecrates, for example, was famous for this. And so Nero, too, wrote some of his own songs – with preference for orgiastic subjects, such as *Attis* and *Bacchants*. His songs, like those of other musical idols of the day, were sung everywhere. Apollonius of Tyana, whose reluctant conversion to the ballet was mentioned, nearly got into trouble when he passed a musician singing Nero's songs in the street, because he was seen not to be applauding with sufficient vigour.[9]

But Nero's poetic ambitions went far beyond short songs. A scholar named Annaeus Cornutus from Lepcis Magna in north Africa – a relative or freedman of Seneca – fared worse than Apollonius when he, too, was not complimentary enough. The emperor declared he was contemplating the composition of an epic on Roman history, and he wanted Cornutus' opinion on the length which was appropriate for such a poem. Attendant courtiers rapidly interposed that four hundred books would not be too long for such a masterpiece, but Cornutus said he did not agree; he considered that would be *much* too long – indeed useless. He was not asked to court again. Indeed, he left Italy. And Nero did not persevere with his Roman epic.

But he did write a poem on the Trojan War, a theme which, although exceedingly well-worn, was once again very fashionable at this time – partly because the imperial family traced its lineage back to mythical Trojan origins. It is a pity Nero's composition is lost, because it must have revealed a lot about his character and attitude. For its Trojan hero was not Homer's brave and virtuous Hector, but Paris who was traditionally a weakling: in Nero's version however, this misunderstood type, without revealing his identity, fought a series of wrestling bouts in which he defeated all comers, including tough, manly Hector himself.[10] Half a century later the satirist

Juvenal made savage fun of Nero's poem. That other mythical figure Orestes, he says, may have been a matricide, but at least he did not write a *Trojan War*.

> *He* never sang on the stage
> Or composed a Trojan epic – and what, in that bloody regime,
> Cried out for vengeance more when the military took over?
> Such were the acts of this prince of the blood, and such
> His accomplishments – how he adored inflicting that ghastly voice
> On audiences abroad, and winning Greek parsley wreaths!
> So deck his ancestral statues with concert-tour souvenirs . . .[11]

As literary criticism, too much need not be made of this. There is no reason to suppose that Nero's voice was bad; if it had been hopeless, he is unlikely to have decided it was his fortune. The same applies to his poetry. Apart from half a line about thunder, and the epithet 'amber-coloured' with which he described Poppaea's hair, only four of his lines have survived. One, about doves' feathers ruffled by the wind, was quoted with approval by Seneca; it runs smoothly and delicately with a long, sensuous Greek epithet.[12] The other three lines attributed to the imperial hand are about the source of the River Tigris, and they somewhat recall similar geographical digressions in the *Pharsalia* of the young Lucan.[13] There is little wrong with Nero's lines, as examples of the fashionable silver Latin of the period. But they do not form a substantial enough corpus to say whether Nero was a good poet, or, if so, how good. His verse, like his singing, no doubt followed the currently fashionable taste for the picturesque, colourful, sonorous, sensational and pathetic – a taste with a whiff of the quaint and archaic. Another poet of a very different type, Persius, was a pupil of Cornutus whose unfortunate comment to Nero has been mentioned. Persius' belief in poetry 'tasting of bitter nails' got him within hailing distance of perilous controversy when he criticized this fashionable type of verse.

> 'They filled their fierce horns
> With Mimallonean bellowings.' Or, 'The Bassarid,
> About to rip the head from the gambolling calf', or
> Again, 'The Maenad, ready to rein in the lynx
> With braids of ivy, redoubles the Dionysian
> Cry, and reverberant Echo returns it'. Do you think
> Stuff like that would get written if our generation
> Hadn't been born without balls? Maenads! Attis! Watery
> Saliva slopping around on the lips with the rest
> Of the spit![14]

A commentary written in the margin of a manuscript says the lines branded in this passage as effeminate Hellenisms had been composed by Nero himself. But Persius was writing while the emperor was still alive, and the completely escapist character of the rest of his work makes it most unlikely that he could have been so rash.

Without going so far as a contemporary pastoral poet who ranked Nero's poetry above Virgil's, the epigrammatist Martial later described him as a

This painting from Pompeii shows the sacrifice of Iphigenia – the sort of high drama that Nero enjoyed acting and singing in.

fellow-poet who was *doctus* – a writer, that is to say, who knows his job, who understands the forms and rules of his art.[15] Our major sources for this period, dating from a later one, are strangely contradictory about Nero's poetic achievements and methods. Tacitus allows him very little credit; in his way he is as rude as his contemporary Juvenal:

A contemporary head of Nero in his twenty-second year.

> Nero aspired to poetic taste. He gathered round himself at dinner men who possessed some versifying ability but were not yet known. As they sat on, they strung together verses they had brought with them, or extemporized – and filled out Nero's own suggestions, such as they were. This method is apparent from Nero's poems themselves, which lack vigour, inspiration and homogeneity.[16]

But this idea that Nero's poems were merely a sort of post-prandial combined operation is flatly contradicted by Suetonius:

> Nero turned his hand to poetry, and would dash off verses without any effort. It is often claimed that he published other people's work as his own; but notebooks and loose pages have come into my possession, which contain some of Nero's best-known poems in his own handwriting, and have clearly been neither copied nor dictated. Many erasures and cancellations, as well as words substituted over the lines, prove that he was thinking things out for himself.[17]

Suetonius is curiously emphatic here, and almost seems to be deliberately correcting his impressive contemporary Tacitus; which is a thing he very rarely attempts to do. And surely the version of Suetonius is the one that must be preferred, partly because of the circumstantial nature of his evidence and partly because the bias of Tacitus is extremely clear. Coming as he did from one of the Roman cities in southern France or northern Italy, he strongly reflects their strait-laced, provincial attitude about the arts, more ancient Roman than the Romans. Nero offended profoundly against this conservatism, not only by all his singing and acting and dancing, but by his versifying as well. The only form of literature which had long been socially correct for the Roman upper classes was oratory. Tacitus sourly notes that Nero was the first ruler to need to have his speeches written by someone else: an emperor who could write his own speeches would have been respectable. But poetry was much less so; and when Tacitus writes of his own contemporary Domitian, whom he hated obsessively, his bogus connoisseurship of poetry, among other forms of literature, is one of the things he chooses to sneer at. Public figures were supposed to have better things to do; and so Juvenal mocks amateur poets. Whereas Nero could hardly even be described as an amateur! He not only went in for this sort of thing, but was really keen about it: this was indeed something to be sneered at. Augustus, as usual, had shown his sense of public relations and aristocratic opinion when he mentioned, with a feeble joke, that he himself had begun a poetic tragedy – the *Ajax* – but he had not bothered to finish it.[18]

After the death of Agrippina, Seneca and Burrus and the rest of the imperial council found it quite impossible to keep Nero off the stage. So they concentrated, instead, on what did seem capable of achievement; namely that his spectators should be hand-picked and his shows held

right: Two paintings from
Herculaneum, near
Naples. *Above:* a
prize-winning comic
actor; *below:* a concert.

privately in a theatre of his own in the Vatican Gardens across the Tiber. It was decided that an appropriate arrangement for the emperor's stage début – or the most appropriate one that could be devised in Nero's present frame of mind – was to hold displays that were to be called 'Youth Games'. It was hardly practicable to exclude a Greek element altogether, but attention could be diverted from this by explaining that the Games contained a strong Roman flavour as well. For they were to be a religious affair devoted to the well-being of the emperor and held under the auspices of the fine old Roman deity Youth (Juventas), whose cult possessed virile, martial associations because Juventas was the goddess of the *juvenes*, the young men of military age. Furthermore, the occasion was the first shaving of Nero's beard, which was an ancient family festival of the Romans. The occasion could therefore be excused, up to a point, by its intimate, domestic, traditional character. And so, to the accompaniment of a holocaust of sacrificed bullocks, he deposited his shavings in a pearl-studded golden box and dedicated them in the Temple of Jupiter on the Capitol. The novelist Petronius seems to have been skating on slightly thin ice when, soon afterwards, he makes his ludicrous Trimalchio put his own shavings, too, in a golden box, deposited in a private chapel.

A feature of the subsequent entertainments was that not only Nero but a number of noblemen and noblewomen also took part and entered the competitions. (This was one of the occasions when the octogenarian Aelia Catella performed.) The emperor's advisers probably calculated that this would make his own participation seem less conspicuous and disreputable. But it only added to the gloom with which conservatives viewed the entire proceedings. Their attitude is wholeheartedly reproduced by Tacitus:

There were many volunteers for the Youth Games. Birth, age, official career, did not prevent people from acting – in Greek or Latin style (pantomime or ballet) – and from accompanying their performances with effeminate gestures and songs. Eminent women, too, rehearsed indecent parts. In the wood which Augustus had planted round his Naval Lake, places of assignation and taverns were built, and every stimulus to vice was displayed for sale. Moreover, there were distributions of money. Respectable people were compelled to spend it; disreputable people did so gladly. Promiscuity and degradation throve. Roman morals had long been impure, but never was there so favourable an environment for debauchery as among this filthy crowd. Even in good surroundings people find it hard to behave well. Here every form of immorality competed for attention, and no chastity, modesty or vestige of decency could survive.[19]

It is indeed probable that the atmosphere of the occasion was lax: though not necessarily quite as corrupt as Tacitus leads us to suppose, because what he really objected to, in spite of the private character of the occasion, was the first stage appearance of the emperor. 'The climax was Nero's stage début. Meticulously tuning his lyre, he struck practice notes to those beside him. A battalion attended with its officers. So did Burrus, grieving – but applauding all the same.'[20]

Seneca, it appears, was there too, and the successive items of the imperial repertoire and programme, *Attis* and *Bacchants* and so on, were announced to

right: A Bacchanalian dance, in a wall-painting from the Villa Doria Pamphili, Rome.

overleaf: A music lesson. Nero took lessons from Terpnus, the leading lyre-player of the day.

the audience by Gallio, Seneca's brother. Seneca and Burrus were indeed trying to make the best of things. But royal performances have always been mocked at by traditionalists, ever since Saul's daughter Michal sneered at David for leaping and dancing before the Lord.[21] And, in this case, Tacitus had a chorus of contemporary disapproval to base his hostile version on: both the Jewish historian Josephus and the source used by the biographer and essayist Plutarch are among those who claimed to have noted, at the time, the disastrous political results of Nero's histrionic efforts.[22] The trouble was that he was the first ruler in all recorded history, and indeed almost the only one of any real importance, to consider himself *primarily* as a singer and stage performer.

He was aware of potential criticisms, and tried to meet them in the sort of terms reactionaries would understand. 'Singing', he declared, 'is sacred to Apollo: that glorious and provident god is represented in a musician's dress in Greek cities – and in Roman temples as well.'[23] All the same, it seemed inadvisable to his counsellors to run the risk that the applause might be less enthusiastic than was required. So the matter was seen to. 'For this was the occasion when the corps of knights known as the Augustiani was formed. These powerful young men, impudent by nature or ambition, maintained a din of applause day and night, showering divine epithets on Nero's beauty and voice. They were grand and respected as if they had done great things.'[24] This fan-club, based on the gangs of youths that had surrounded the monarchs of the Greek empires, was later swelled by other sections. These included a bevy of wavy-haired, scented, beringed young boys, acolytes who acted as mute chorus on the stage; and a troupe of Alexandrian seamen whom Nero sent for because he had been captivated by the rhythmical applause of certain Egyptian sailors at one of his performances. Finally the whole claque was more than five thousand strong, and by now it had perfected special techniques of expressing appreciation: the 'bees' making a loud buzz or hum, the 'hollow tiles' clapping with hollow hands, and the 'flat tiles' keeping their hands flat while they clapped. Whenever Nero sang, each section leader received a sum of 400,000 sesterces.

All this protected the emperor adequately from any unfortunate audience reactions. Nevertheless, as a performer, he always remained completely incapable of escaping from the anxieties of his own temperament. Occasions were found to repeat the Juvenalia quite soon and often, but the same nervousness which caused Nero to deal out death readily when in a state of alarm continued to reach the most fantastic heights whenever he performed in a contest.

This trepidation and anxiety, his competitive behaviour towards his opponents, and his awe of the judges, can hardly be credited. 'As if his rivals were of quite the same station as himself, he used to show respect to them and try to gain their favour, while he slandered them behind their backs, sometimes assailed them with abuse when he met them, and even bribed those who were especially proficient. Before beginning, he would address the judges in the most deferential terms. . . .'[25]

Surely it must have been clear to himself and everyone else that he was going to receive extravagantly favourable treatment every time he appeared

A chariot-race at Pompeii.

on the stage. Besides, this was what he liked doing more than anything else in the world – what he lived for. And yet the prospect of a competition filled him with utter panic every time.

When taking part, he observed the rules most scrupulously, never daring to clear his throat and even wiping the sweat from his brow with his arm. Once indeed, during the performance of a tragedy, when he had dropped his sceptre but quickly recovered it, he was terribly afraid that he might be excluded from the competition because of his slip, and his confidence was restored only when his accompanist swore that it had passed unnoticed amid the delight and applause of the people.[26]

Nero's interests in the entertainment world were however by no means limited to the theatre. He was also passionately fond of horses, and had been ever since his childhood. As a boy he was forbidden even to mention the word 'Circus', in the interests of high-mindedness, and when he first came to the throne he used to play every day with ivory chariots on a board. After his accession to the throne, he was obliged, in his official capacity, to suppress rioting by charioteers; but he himself intervened when an official, obstructed by charioteers' owners objecting to the amount of work demanded of their men, tried to replace their horses by dogs. Nero awarded pensions to veteran racehorses – dressing them up in human clothes – and entered enthusiastically into the strife between racing factions, which caused frequent disorders but absorbed passions that might otherwise have found more perilous out-

The substructures of the Circus Maximus, where Nero avidly followed the racing. He rebuilt the Circus after the fire of AD 64.

lets elsewhere. The factions were distinguished by colours – Greens, Blues, Reds and Whites – and Nero keenly backed the Greens. He wore green in the Circus Maximus, where the major races took place, and had the track strewn with green copper dust.

His advisers must have realized that he would sooner or later want to compete in horse-races himself. And after Agrippina was out of the way, this moment could be delayed no longer. Nero was quite as prepared to justify this activity as he was ready to defend singing. 'Chariot-racing', he declared, 'was an accomplishment of ancient kings and leaders: it was honoured by poets, and closely associated with divine worship.' So Seneca and Burrus, apparently even before the Youth Games, started making the best of this situation as well. Their method was the same as for his acting. That is to say, they encouraged him to have a *private* racecourse: the Circus begun by Caligula in the Vatican valley across the Tiber was completed (its obelisk now stands in the Piazza San Pietro), and there he could drive his horses remote from the public eye. 'But soon', says Tacitus, 'the public were admitted – and even invited. And they approved vociferously. For such is a crowd: avid for entertainment, and delighted if the emperor shares their tastes. However, this scandalous publicity did not satiate Nero, as his advisers had expected. Indeed, it led him on.'[27] He had definitely embarked on the slippery slope – a strange one for an emperor – of exchanging amateur for professional status.

The Neronian Games   However, personal performances were not all that he was interested in; he also wanted to raise the artistic standards of the Roman population. He was prepared to postpone his own public appearances on the stage, provided that he could first achieve the introduction to the capital of the civilized, Greek kind of public Games, instead of the more savage Roman types of entertainment. And so in AD 60, the year after his Youth Games, he founded a festival to be held at Rome after the Greek style, the Neronian Games.

Its competitions were divided into three sections: music, poetry, eloquence; athletics and gymnastics; and chariot-racing. The new institution was modelled, in a general sort of way, on the classic Greek festivals, and it resembled the Pythian contests of Delphi more than the Olympic Games, since there were no musical contests at the latter.

The Neronian Games took place on 13 October, the anniversary of the emperor's accession. The government paid for the new festival, which was given precedence over other Games by the fact that its president was not a praetor, as was generally the case, but a more senior official who had served as consul. He was chosen for this privilege by lot. The festival was Romanized to the extent that it was to take place every five years – the quinquennial interval that played a part in traditional Roman civic and religious institutions, instead of the four years that separated the festivals of Greece.[28] On coins it was therefore described as the Five-Yearly Contest (*certamen quinquennale*).

It was also possible to point to Augustan precedents for this Greek type of festival – and these were always useful. One such inspiration was provided by Games founded in honour of Augustus at Neapolis (Naples), the city of which Nero was particularly fond. These Neapolitan Games were held every four years in the Greek fashion, as befitted a city which, although partly Italianized, cherished its Greek origin. At first the events it comprised had been athletic and equestrian – in the last year of his life Augustus had attended them in person – but then, perhaps in AD 18, musical competitions had been added; and it was from here that Greek contests of various types had spread to other parts of Italy. Augustus had also celebrated his victory over Antony off Actium (in north-west Greece) by reconstituting an ancient athletic festival there; this Actia equalled the major Games of Greece in importance, and he had a new stadium built to house its contests. What is more, the same emperor had inaugurated Actian Games at Rome (though they may not have survived his death), encouraging men and boys of the upper class to take part in them. Again a stadium (of wood) was constructed for the purpose – the first mention of such a building in the western Roman world; and the conventional Greek programme was probably followed.

A later conception of Nero, in bronze.

So Tacitus overdramatizes when he implies, in his *Annals*, that Nero's introduction of this Greek type of festival to the capital was a sensational novelty. However, he plays fair when he describes the first Neronian Games: his account of the occasion is a good deal more relaxed than his description of the Youth Games – because on this new occasion there was at least not the disgrace of the emperor personally taking part. The *Annals* represent, it is true, the conservative viewpoint,[29] reflecting a distrust for Greek Games which even appears in the writings of some of Nero's friends, such as Seneca and Lucan;[30] the whole business will just turn the young men into shirkers, gymnasts and perverts. But then Tacitus goes on to give the other side quite fairly as well. Dancing and chariot-racing were ancient institutions; payment for them by the government would spare the purses of state officials, besides giving the public less excuse to pester them for additional Greek shows; there was even something to be said for a permanent theatre, which would put a stop to the expense of building so many temporary ones. And prizes for oratory and poetry ought to encourage talent. 'These nights – not many, out of a period of five years – are for gaiety, not immorality. Besides, in such a blaze of lights, surreptitious immorality is impossible.'[31]

In any case, it had to be admitted that these first Neronian Games passed off without scandal. For one thing the ballet-dancers, whose presence so often caused rioting in the past, were banned. They had by now been allowed back into Italy from their places of exile, but they were not permitted to perform in the Games because these were treated as a sacred occasion like their Greek prototypes. As for the emperor, although he did not take part himself, it was considered advisable that he should win a prize all the same. So he was declared the winner for oratory.

Tacitus leaves the Neronian Games with a characteristically acid remark: 'Greek clothes, which had been greatly worn during the festival, subsequently went out of fashion.'[32] This must have disappointed the emperor who, regardless of Seneca's disapproval of brightly-coloured male clothing, predictably favoured Greek costume. Nero himself often appeared in public in a brilliantly-coloured variety of Greek robe, which combined the simplicity

A passion for things Greek

of the tunic in its upper part with the flowing fullness of a toga below. It was worn with a scarf round the neck, and without belt or shoes. Certain Romans were accustomed to wear such a garment on the relaxed annual holiday of the Saturnalia, but otherwise it was generally reserved for women. However, that is how Nero liked to dress. He also violated the conventional decencies by appearing in public in a sort of flower-patterned mini-tunic, a short, unbelted garment with a muslin collar.

It was this same passion for things Greek which had prompted him to include an athletic and gymnastic section in his Games. This was very alien to most Romans, who despised athletes as over-trained and over-specialized lumps. The emperor, on the other hand, viewed them with marked favour, amateurs and professionals alike, and spent a lot of time watching them perform. It must have been difficult for readers not to think of him when Seneca wrote disapprovingly of people who never failed to note the form of each and every athlete as soon as he appeared on the Roman scene.[33]

And so, for his festival, Nero built a new gymnasium in the Field of Mars, the most splendid in all Rome (it was struck by lightning two years later, but rebuilt in 66). Nearby were magnificent new Baths, again the finest of their kind. 'What is worse than Nero?', declared Martial, 'what is better than Nero's Baths?'[34] Like the gymnasium, the Baths offer nothing for the visitor to see today; but their impressive ground-plan can be reconstructed, and a great many pieces of different kinds of expensive marble have been found on the site. From an architectural point of view, this was a pioneer building, already incorporating the soaring halls and cross-vaults which are known to us from baths and halls of the decades immediately following Nero's death.

Less tactful, no doubt, than Seneca, the rough, outspoken Cynic philosopher Demetrius stamped into the new buildings and denounced public Baths as an unnecessary expense, and bathing in general as enervating and degenerate.[35] He was later banished from Italy (and even the easy-going emperor Vespasian later found it preferable that so frank a man should reside elsewhere). While Demetrius was visiting the gymnasium, he saw Nero himself engaged in his exercises, naked except for a loincloth and singing lustily as he went through his routine. This had become a little complicated, since Nero had ambitions not only as a vocalist but as an athlete; and it had not been possible to limit his interest in athletics, any more than his passion for acting and singing, to the role of a mere spectator. He was a very keen wrestler, and it was widely believed that he might compete in this capacity at the next Olympic Games.

He also had to think about his training as a charioteer. At this period, charioteers were accustomed to apply boar's dung both externally and internally, as a remedy against injury; and Nero drank the ash of it in water.

All these measures, inconsistently combined with an uninhibited sex life and a continual round of parties, would have cast a strain on any constitution, and Nero's physique cannot have been particularly impressive. But his health was excellent all the same. Only three possible illnesses can be noted in the fourteen years of his reign, and only one of them is beyond a doubt.

He did not suffer from any lack of medical advice. For one thing, the new

Nero's medical advisers

Baths encouraged the hydrotherapy that now came back into fashion at Rome. Its successive leading practitioners originated from Massilia (Marseille): the wealthy astrologer Crinas, and then his critic Charmis who prescribed cold baths even in winter and was always dipping aged ex-consuls in icy water.

When Nero came to the throne, the head of the profession was the immensely rich Stertinius Xenophon, who was the first to call himself 'chief doctor', as well as 'doctor of the emperor'. The problems of courtiers are illuminated by a monument in his honour at his home-town Cos; its inscription called him 'Lover of Claudius', but later on this was erased in favour of 'Lover of Nero', and subsequently that term, too, was rubbed out in its turn.[36] If, as was suspected, Xenophon had helped to kill Claudius, that may explain why, under Nero, he was found no longer serving as a doctor at court but working in one of the emperor's ministries, receiving Greek delegations. Nero might not be too keen on receiving medical treatment from a man who knew how to assassinate emperors.

At any rate, Nero employed two other doctors. Both happened to be called Andromachus. One of them, a Cretan, invented an antidote to the bites of poisonous animals, which he himself, contrary to modern etiquette, praised in a long poem. Nero also received a letter from another doctor, Thessalus of Tralles in Asia Minor, who founded a popular new medical school, the Methodici. Although Thessalus could not compete with the smart doctors from Massilia, he confidently attacked all his predecessors, and even if, as he claimed, he himself had learnt all he knew in six months, his monument on the Appian Way described him as *Iatronices,* the champion doctor. But his famous compatriot Galen of Pergamum, who wrote on medical matters in the following century, described him as ignorant and arrogant.[37]

Galen was also shocked by another Neronian practitioner from the same country, Xenocrates of Aphrodisias. The treatments he was accustomed to prescribe included the eating of human brains, flesh, liver and blood, as well as secretions from hippopotami and elephants – a series of remedies which must surely have appealed to the lovers of all those ghoulish descriptions in Seneca's and Lucan's poetry.

6 Hard Realities of an Emperor's Life

Nero's growing preoccupation with the dramatic and athletic arts was rudely interrupted by a scandal. One of the most important state officials was the Prefect of the City, a sort of security chief, who was responsible for the maintenance of order in the capital and enjoyed powers of summary jurisdiction. In AD 61 the holder of this office, Lucius Pedanius Secundus, was murdered by one of his slaves. 'Either', says Tacitus, 'Pedanius had refused to free the man although he had previously agreed to a price, or the slave, infatuated with another male member of the household, found his master competing with him, and regarded this situation as intolerable.'[1] The traditional consequences of such a murder by a slave were grim. Ancient custom required that not only he, but every other slave residing under the same roof, should be executed: and Pedanius owned four hundred – including, of course, many women and children.

The situation that had now arisen was particularly embarrassing because Nero and some of his most enlightened advisers would have liked to depart from the tradition. As we have already seen, the emperor himself, however murderous when he saw himself threatened, hated authorizing executions, and his reluctance to do so had inspired Seneca to write his treatise *On Clemency*. For Seneca, too, was appalled by the brutality of Roman executions – and particularly by the various ways in which slaves were put to death;[2] for example he deplores the horrible burnings of slaves alive, in 'the shirt which is woven and smeared with the food of flames'.[3] He repeatedly stressed that slaves are part of the human brotherhood in which he, as a follower of the Stoics, believed; and in one magnificent, historic letter to Lucilius Junior he elaborated the point.

I'm glad to hear, from these people who've been visiting you, that you live on friendly terms with your slaves. It is just what one expects of an enlightened, cultivated person like yourself. 'They're slaves', people say. No. They're human beings. 'They're slaves.' But they share the same roof as ourselves. 'They're slaves.' No, they're friends, humble friends. 'They're slaves.' Strictly speaking, they're our fellow-slaves, if you reflect that fortune has as much power over us as over them.[4]

A Roman soldier from the Column of Nero at Moguntiacum (Mainz).

The rest of the letter, like other writings of Seneca, goes on at length to deduce the conclusion that slaves have to be decently treated.[5]

109

Petronius even attributes the same view to the vulgarian Trimalchio. 'My dear people, slaves are human beings too. They drink the same milk as anybody else, even though luck's been against them!'[6] This was evidently how a lot of people were talking. It is very likely that Nero's feelings on this subject were the same as those of his friends Seneca and Petronius. The ministers he saw every day had all at one time been slaves, and might be expected to encourage his sympathy with the servile condition. And so we read in the pages of the lawyers that Nero, at some time during his reign, ordered the city prefect of the day to pay attention to slaves who complained about unjust treatment from their masters[7] – rather ironically, in view of what had happened now.

For obviously, in a society like Rome's, the liberals were not going to have things all their own way. Indeed in 57 the Senate, far from relaxing its vigilance, had actually added to the punitive rules. For henceforward, if a man was murdered by one of his slaves, not only were all the others to be executed but the same sentence was to be extended to any who had been liberated in the dead man's will, if they were in his house at the time. This, of course, was in case any slave should be tempted to hasten his own testamentary liberation by violent means.

The murder of Pedanius Secundus may have caused Seneca particular embarrassment, because the dead man, like himself, came from Spain; his home-town had been Barcino (Barcelona). Pedanius may therefore have been a friend, and a valued political supporter. And the situation nearly got out of control: for the population of Rome took a hand. Except when they were agitating about the grain-supply or indulging in gang warfare on behalf of this or that ballet-dancer or Circus faction, the ordinary inhabitants of the city rarely intervened in governmental affairs. But now they did. They disliked the aristocracy – which was no longer in a position to act as their munificent patrons – and were therefore unsympathetic with its traditions. And the fate impending for the innocent slaves seemed archaic, brutal nonsense.

Furious rioting began. The Senate-house was besieged, and a debate took place in crisis conditions. According to Tacitus, the spokesman for the conservative cause was a certain Gaius Cassius Longinus, an extremely eminent lawyer and consul – one of the first professional jurists to be entrusted by an emperor with a consulship and important commands. Curiously enough, and Tacitus no doubt relished the paradox, he was known for the broadmindedness of his legal reforms. But he came from a stern Republican family, and he himself, while governor of Syria, had enforced unusually strict military discipline. The details of his alleged speech need not be studied too literally, since Tacitus is echoing the late Republican historian Sallust, whom he admired. Yet it was easy enough to see what Cassius' arguments must be: that Roman society, with its large submerged slave population held down by force, would collapse altogether if crimes such as this were not ruthlessly punished.

Nowadays our huge households are international. They include every alien religion or none at all. The only way to keep this scum down is by intimidation.

DE BRITANN(is). This coin of Roman Britain depicts Claudius' arch at Rome commemorating his conquest of Britain. He also erected another similar arch at the port of embarkation in Gaul.

Innocent people will die, you say. Yes! And when in a defeated army every tenth man is flogged to death, the brave have to draw lots with the others. Exemplary punishment always contains an element of injustice. For individual wrongs are outweighed by the advantage of the community.[8]

Those of the other senators who had a sneaking sympathy for the slaves did not dare to speak up, and the vote went in favour of the mass execution. 'However', continues the historian, 'great crowds ready with stones and torches prevented the order from being carried out. Nero rebuked the population by edict, and lined with troops the whole route along which those condemned were taken for execution.'[9] This was a sad and disillusioning role for a government influenced by Seneca, humane spokesman for the rights of slaves. And it was sad, also, for a young emperor with some liberal ideas. It was one of a number of incidents which successively alienated Nero from the harsh realities of Roman life.

Slaves had to be suppressed at home; and recalcitrant subjects had to be suppressed abroad. This, too, was not a task which Nero enjoyed, since, amid the applause of his poets, he preferred peace. In the east, he had made an initial attempt to put his wishes into effect, but recently circumstances had defeated him. Now it became equally impossible to avoid repressive hostilities in Britain.

Julius Caesar's two invasions of the island more than a hundred years previously had been among the least successful of his enterprises, achieving nothing better than extended reconnaissances. The chain of semi-dependent states which the Romans liked creating outside their frontiers had not proved attainable in England, where the native tribes, encouraged by the Channel barrier, remained obstinately independent. Finally under Claudius, during the years AD 43–8, the south-eastern part of the island had been conquered, and a diagonal frontier established roughly along the rivers Severn and Trent, from Seaton in Devon via Aquae Sulis (Bath) and Ratae (Leicester) to beyond Lindum (Lincoln). At least three dependent kingdoms had been established, two within the new boundary – the Regni in western Sussex and the Iceni in East Anglia – and one outside it, the Brigantes in Yorkshire. The British leader against the Romans in the south-east, Caratacus, had been defeated, and fled first to central Wales and then to Queen Cartimandua of the Brigantes. She handed him over to Claudius (AD 51), who, surprisingly, spared his life.

And so the activities of a peacetime province began. The Romans quickly began to exploit British metals. Silver was extracted from Mendip lead deposits as early as 49, and coins of Nero have been found in slag-heaps of Wealden iron. But Britain was still very much a frontier area. In this respect it resembled Armenia, at the opposite extremity of the empire. There Nero's first plan had been to give formal independence, under supervision, to a native prince Tiridates. He must have been tempted to do the same in Britain, for there was a very suitable—a much more suitable—local candidate available. This was Cogidubnus, who ruled the Regni inside the Roman province and bore the exceptionally honorific title of 'King and Imperial

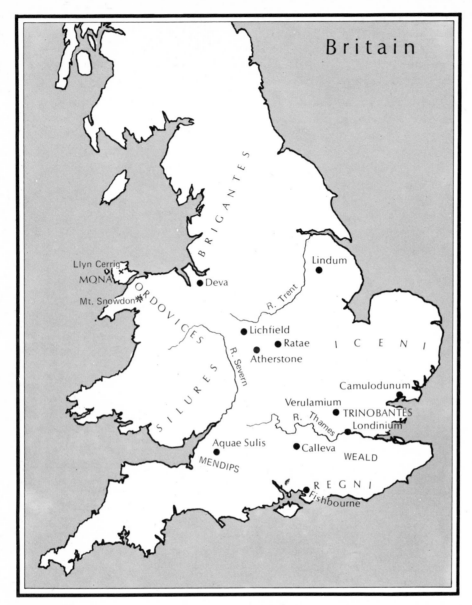

Britain

Llyn Cerrig
MONA
Mt. Snowdon
BRIGANTES
ORDOVICES
SILURES
R. Trent
R. Severn
Deva
Lindum
Lichfield
Ratae
Atherstone
I C E N I
Camulodunum
Verulamium
TRINOBANTES
R. Thames
Londinium
Aquae Sulis
Calleva
WEALD
MENDIPS
R E G N I
Fishbourne

Legate'.[10] At his capital Noviomagus (Chichester), an inscription of 58–60, now lost, paid punctilious reverence to Nero, and at Fishbourne, on the Sussex coast, he was already completing the colonnaded residence and government offices which were later expanded into the vast palace excavated in recent years.

However, the situations in Armenia and Britain were different in a vital respect. Beyond the former country there was a major independent power, the kingdom of the Parthians, and the acceptance of Tiridates had largely been intended to achieve good relations with them. Beyond the British border, on the other hand, there was no such major power. Moreover, the boundary itself was makeshift and unsatisfactory, and it was tempting to deal with the disturbed areas beyond it by annexing Wales and later perhaps

Yorkshire too. Nero's peace-loving tendencies could be overborne by the likelihood that conquests and glory were easily available: a prospect which attracted all emperors, and those of their advisers who had an eye on publicity at home.

In 58, therefore, a new governor of Britain was appointed with instructions to pursue an aggressive policy of annexation. His name was Quintus Veranius. A Greek writer, Onasander, paid Veranius the honour of dedicating to him a scholarly essay on generalship, for he was regarded as one of the most distinguished commanders of the day. But the entire plan had to be postponed, because very soon after taking up his duties Veranius died. All he had done was to conduct certain minor raids into Wales. But his will was found to contain the boast that, if he had lived two years longer, he would have 'reduced the whole province' – by which he possibly meant the entire island. Tacitus, who quotes the assertion, might have been expected to approve of it, since he shared the old Roman pride in military aggressions and annexations. Instead, however, he offers a sneer. But that is because Veranius' will also contained gross flattery of the emperor. And, in any case, the historian was not prepared to imagine Nero as a conquering supreme commander on the traditional Roman model.

Veranius' successor Gaius Suetonius Paulinus immediately resumed the forward movement. He devoted two seasons to the reduction of north Wales,

A flagon, a platter with a few pieces of bone, a coin, a blue glass bead, the remains of a mirror and a heap of cremated bones – all dating from the time of Claudius or Nero and found at Norwich.

left: An enamelled bronze terret (a ring for driving-reins) from a hoard of seven horse trappings found at Saham Toney, Norfolk, probably of *c.* AD 50–70.

including Snowdonia, and pushed ahead as far as the Irish Sea. Quite soon, however, it became clear that all this activity would remain ineffective if Mona (Anglesey) were not reduced. This island – Mon Mam Cymru, the legendary mother of Wales – was full of grainfields and pastures which gave the mainland much wealth. But above all it was the headquarters of the Druids, fanatical priests who were central figures in the resistance movement. A hoard of objects that has been found at Llyn Cerrig Bach consists of offerings or tithes they had collected or been given. The hoard includes war-material, some of it from as far afield as south-west Britain and Yorkshire. Prisoners' chains were found among the booty; and war-trumpets which had been brought all the way from northern Ireland. Though Mona was already thickly populated, it gave sanctuary to many foes of Rome from Wales and elsewhere, and provided a supply base to others who were still in the hills.

Claudius had proscribed the Druids; Nero must stamp them out. And by taking such action, the Romans could add, they would not only be demolishing a hostile native cult of vast ramifications (far more extensive than any ancient author hints), but they would also be eliminating the practitioners of uncivilized, savage rites. These included the butchery of human victims for sacrifice and augury, in which the Druids 'drenched their altars in the blood of prisoners and consulted their gods by means of human entrails'. The new governor Paulinus, in an earlier command in north Africa – against the tribesmen of the Atlas – had gained his reputation by striking at the plainlands that supplied the hill-peoples. Now, he proposed to do the same again by occupying Mona; and from his base at Deva (Chester), he moved to the attack.

The Roman legionaries got across the strait, but only with difficulty. The crossing itself was painful, and their morale was vulnerable to the magic spells which were the speciality of the Druids.

Flat-bottomed boats were built to contend with the shifting shallows, and these took the infantry across. Then came the cavalry; some utilized fords, but in deeper water the men swam beside their horses. The enemy lined the shore in a dense armed mass. Among them were black-robed women with dishevelled hair like Furies,

Two Roman legionaries of Nero's time, depicted by northern sculptors. From the column of Nero erected by the tradesmen of the Roman camp at Moguntiacum.

brandishing torches. Close by stood Druids, raising their hands to heaven and screaming curses.

The weirdness of the spectacle awed the Roman soldiers into paralysis. They stood still – and presented themselves as a target. But then they urged each other (and were urged by the general) not to fear a horde of fanatical women. Onward pressed their standards and they bore down their opponents, enveloping them in the flames of their own torches.

Suetonius garrisoned the conquered island; and the groves devoted to Mona's barbarous superstitions he demolished.[11]

The Druids died or fled, but their cause was by no means finished. During the Civil Wars in the empire after Nero's death, they reappeared to make trouble in Gaul – announcing that the burning down of the Roman Capitol, which had just occurred, was a sign of the anger of the gods, and meant that the centre of world dominion had shifted to north of the Alps.[12]

Nevertheless, as far as it went, the operation entrusted by Nero to Paulinus had been successful; though the success was very far from permanent, since only seventeen years later Tacitus' father-in-law Agricola had to seize Mona all over again. He was also obliged to crush the Ordovices, the nearest tribe on the Welsh mainland, which Paulinus had evidently not succeeded in reducing.

The reason why Nero's governor did not achieve more was because, while he was mopping up resistance on Mona, a dangerous rebellion had broken out in East Anglia. The rebels were the Iceni. This tribe, which lived in the flat country of Norfolk, Suffolk and Cambridgeshire, had been ruled long and successfully, under Roman supervision, by its king Prasutagus. Now he was dead (59), and he had made the emperor co-heir with his two daughters. As a client king he could not legally bequeath the succession. But evidently he had hoped that with Nero's support his daughters would be able to succeed, jointly, to the tribal throne. The Romans decided otherwise. Perhaps they had always intended to absorb this client territory when its ruler died. In any case, they were nervous about its reliability, because the Iceni had resented inclusion within Claudius' Roman frontier. Now their nervousness was much increased by the presence of the deceased monarch's formidable widow Boudicca (Boadicea). Although, according to the historian Dio Cassius (see Appendix 2), she was 'more intelligent than women usually are', Boudicca had not been made one of his principal heirs, so that even if the kingdom had continued it would not have become hers. For Prasutagus, in making his will, no doubt realized that Rome, which had experienced trouble bolstering up queen Cartimandua of the Brigantes, in Yorkshire, did not want to have to deal with another dowager as well.

As it was, however, the Romans had now decided that the royal family of the Iceni should cease ruling altogether. It cannot have been an enjoyable task to break any of this news to Boudicca. 'In stature she was very tall, in appearance most terrifying, in the glance of her eye most fierce, and her voice was harsh: a great mass of the blondest hair fell to her hips; around her neck was a large golden necklace; and she wore a tunic of divers colours over which a thick mantle was fastened with a brooch.'[13] Even if this descrip-

Silver coins of the Iceni, from the Honingham (Norfolk) hoard of 341 pieces, probably concealed c. AD 60. The coins date from the first half of the first century AD.

tion bears certain conventional marks of the Noble Savage, the local agents of the emperor were evidently alarmed by this ferocious woman, who referred to the emperor as 'Miss Domitia Nero' and felt comfortably unhampered by his governor, who was far off in Wales. And their alarm induced the imperial officials to behave very high-handedly.

Roman provinces normally contained both a governor and an imperial agent or procurator (largely concerned with financial matters), and they sometimes operated at cross purposes. In addition to the latter, and to some extent under him, the emperor had various other local representatives, mainly former slaves, looking after particular imperial estates and properties and interests. In 53, Claudius had taken the dangerous step of giving the decisions of his principal agents in each province equal validity to his own; and Nero's administration inherited this decision and suffered from its effects. Although government, generally, was good, we hear of iniquitous behaviour by his agents who got above themselves – for example in Spain and Egypt. In the latter province, in which such officials had a stranglehold, an edict by a governor issued immediately after Nero's death reveals that there had been a good deal of petty crookedness.

In Britain, where things were now going particularly wrong, Seneca did not help matters, for, according to one account, he had lent the Britons ten million sesterces, and insisted on repayment with the appropriate interest added; and although this can scarcely be regarded as unreasonable (even for a moralizing philosopher), it seems to have been one of the contributory causes of British discontent. However, the unrest was caused not so much by Seneca's loan as by Roman taxation. For semi-civilized tribes of this kind did not like paying regular taxes: they far preferred erratic and irregular exactions, however severe.

Unfortunately, however, they had these as well, over and above the normal levying of taxes. For the Roman agents now proceeded to confiscate lands which Claudius had left in the hands of the Icenian notables. According to the official version of the principal imperial agent, Catus Decianus, he was only requesting the repayment of loans made by Claudius; but it came to much the same thing. His intention, no doubt, was to leave the British so impoverished that they would not be in a position to rebel. The Romans had reason to know that the immediate result of annexation was often a revolt, and they may have reckoned that the seizure of the major estates would make this impossible. But, if so, they miscalculated, because a savage revolt was precisely what followed.

As soon as the Iceni rose, their neighbours the Trinobantes, who lived in Essex, joined them, apparently accepting Boudicca as the leader of the whole movement. The Trinobantes, again, had particular grounds for complaint. When south-east England came under the control of Claudius, their territory had from the first been treated as conquered soil. On the site of their old native capital at Camulodunum (Colchester), Claudius had founded a new capital for the whole province, populating it with a 'colony' or settlement of Roman ex-soldiers. These took sizeable lands away from the dispossessed native nobles, and generally failed to win the confidence of the local people, who felt they had no protection against any further grabs the

A Roman glass cup from Camulodunum (Colchester), of the first century AD.

settlers might feel inclined to make. There was also a garrison, which did not behave any better. Furthermore, Claudius' new foundation included a large and sumptuous temple dedicated to his own divinity, as was customary at provincial capitals. Standing on the site of the later Colchester Castle, it was the centre of a cult which proved costly to the British. They were invited to elect, each year, a native high priest and priestess of the divine ruling emperor. The incumbents were involved in heavy expenses – which they duly recouped from their own unfortunate peoples. And the tribes which had to pay for the upkeep of the temple and priesthoods were painfully few, probably only numbering ten altogether.

The system had worked in Gaul, where it provided an effective nucleus of loyalty to Rome. But the Britons, with no such tradition of common meetings behind them, were by no means ready for such a sharp transition from independent to provincial status. It was only in certain areas, notably parts of Hertfordshire, that native huts were beginning to be replaced by houses of Roman type, and warrior-chiefs by land-owners. Romanization had not gone as far as the Romans thought. They miscalculated again when they gave Camulodunum amenities but not defences: it possessed a Senate-house and a theatre but no fortifications.

The result was that the Roman population of Britain, and Nero's government at Rome, suffered a fearful disaster. Camulodunum was overrun in two days, and its small garrison, which had barricaded itself in the temple, succumbed in the general massacre. A relief force failed to get through, and the unpopular imperial representative Catus Decianus fled to Gaul. Then the river port of Londinium (London), of which we hear for the first time, likewise fell to the rebels; and so did Verulamium (St Albans). Paulinus, who was now back in the south-east, had been obliged to make the terrible decision to let these towns go. The number of Romans or Romanized Britons slaughtered by the British was estimated at seventy thousand or more.

Nevertheless, Boudicca's prospects were limited, because she had received no aid from beyond the frontier in Yorkshire, where Cartimandua, having been helped by the Romans against her own dissident population, was not prepared to oppose their regime. And so, perhaps somewhere near Atherstone in Warwickshire, Paulinus defeated the rebels in a decisive battle. Both Tacitus and Dio Cassius describe the engagement as a rhetorical set-piece. But although the two accounts are equally circumstantial, they are wholly incompatible with one another. After the battle, too, there are discrepancies. According to Tacitus, Boudicca poisoned herself. In Dio Cassius' version, she fell ill and died. At all events, the independence movement was finished.

Nero now had to decide whether to adopt a policy of repression or conciliation. Paulinus favoured the former approach, while the new imperial agent, Classicianus, who disliked him and was married to a noble Gaulish girl (his tomb is in the British Museum), favoured leniency. The emperor sent a powerful Greek freedman and minister, Polyclitus, to investigate the situation. After he and his enormous escort had come and gone, it became clear that he had reported in favour of a conciliatory approach. Consequently,

The gravestone of Marcus Favonius Facilis, centurion of the Twentieth Legion. It was found at Colchester, where it was carved during the first years of the Roman occupation.

Peaceful Romanization

after a decent interval, Paulinus was replaced. Tacitus blames his successor for failing to revive the aggressive policy, but it would not have been timely – especially as Nero needed some of the legions for the east. Tacitus also refrains from giving the next governor after that any credit for his discreet policy of peaceful Romanization. But this is because the historian wants to reserve all possible praise for the subsequent governorship of his own father-in-law Agricola.

The British towns were rebuilt, and the imperial cult revived; but it was moved to the more convenient centre of London, which soon became the capital for the first time. Warlike figures appeared on the Roman coinage, so that chauvinists would have nothing to complain about. But a policy of peace was adopted.

Meanwhile Armenia, on the frontier at the other end of the Roman world, had likewise experienced a period of war. The pacific policy which Nero had tried to put into effect – by recognizing Tiridates, the protégé of Parthia and half-brother of its king, as Rome's nominee as well – had not proved practicable. Corbulo, the distinguished Roman general on the spot, had sought to arrange a meeting with him, but failed; and so warlike operations recommenced. This meant that, for the time being at least, Nero was obliged to change his policy. It was impossible to go on trying to sponsor a prince who was up in arms against Rome. Consequently, the imperial government decided to revert to the bad, impracticable old policy of installing instead of him a pro-Roman, anti-Parthian puppet (*c.* AD 60). This collaborator Tigranes V, who did not even belong to the native royal family but came from Cappadocia in Asia Minor, was duly installed in Armenia with the backing of Roman troops. At the same time strips of his territory were handed over to several neighbouring monarchs, in the hope that they would then refrain from opposing or molesting him; though this can scarcely have done anything to endear the alien Tigranes to the Armenians.

Such arrangements were doomed to failure. One wonders whether Nero himself, or one of his advisers who had favoured the earlier, peaceful, face-saving approach, was not, at this point, rather cynically giving way to conservative pressure and adopting the traditional, anti-Parthian type of policy – but in conditions which ensured it could not succeed. At any rate Tigranes, whether egged on by Romans or not, almost at once made an unprovoked large-scale attack on the neighbouring country of Adiabene (Assyria) – which was a Parthian dependency. The result, naturally, was that the Parthian king Vologases I openly took the field against Tigranes; and the Armenian question had now become a major Partho-Roman issue. Vologases ceremonially crowned Tiridates as king of Armenia, ordered him to expel the foreign usurper, and mobilized his own forces for large-scale supporting operations.

At this point the government of Nero decided, apparently on Corbulo's recommendation, to divide the eastern command (AD 61). Behind the southern reaches of the Asian frontier – the section remotest from Armenia – lay the populous Roman garrison province of Syria, whose very great wealth

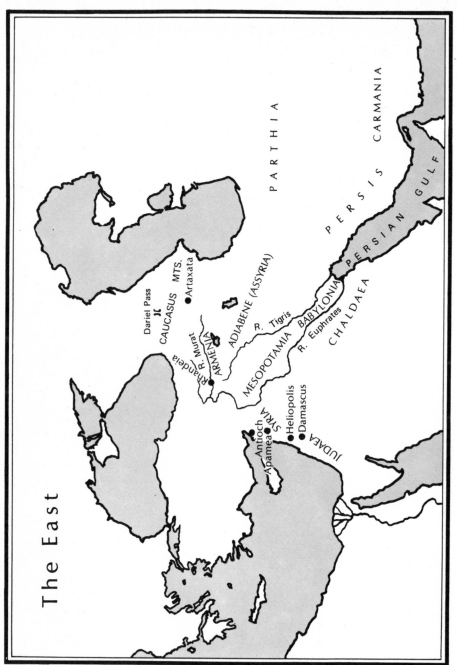

The East

Dariel Pass
CAUCASUS MTS.
● Artaxata
Rhandeia
R. Murat
ARMENIA
ADIABENE (ASSYRIA)
R. Tigris
MESOPOTAMIA
BABYLONIA
R. Euphrates
CHALDAEA
PARTHIA
PERSIS
CARMANIA
PERSIAN GULF
Antioch ●
Apamea ●
SYRIA
● Heliopolis
● Damascus
JUDAEA

right: The Parthian rebel
Vardanes II (*c.* AD 54–7),
on a coin of Seleucia on
the Tigris. Internal
agitators of this kind
made King Vologases I of
Parthia reluctant to fight
against Rome.

overleaf: The art of the
borderland between the
Roman and Parthian
empires is well represented
in this relief from the
court of the Temple of
Bel, Palmyra. The three
gods wear cuirasses of
Graeco-Roman form over
oriental tunics and
trousers.

right: The remains of Nero's temple of Jupiter (Zeus) at Heliopolis (Baalbek in the Lebanon).

left: A Parthian monarch: probably Vonones II, king of Media (AD 51–2) and father of Vologases I.

at this time is still symbolized by the gigantic Neronian temple of Jupiter at Heliopolis (Baalbek). Whenever war broke out with the Parthians, Syria immediately became vulnerable; and so it was now decided that Corbulo should move his headquarters into that province in order to strengthen its defences, while a new general was to be sent out to deal with Armenia. Before leaving the north, however, Corbulo went to the help of Tigranes. The king of Parthia, who was under no illusions about the ultimately superior power of Rome, quickly offered negotiations for a far-reaching settlement. But his deputation to Nero, making proposals on these lines, achieved no progress. Meanwhile Corbulo left for Syria, and his successor, Paetus, arrived on the Armenian front in his place.

It now became clear that Nero's government had embarked on a new policy – no longer the establishment of a puppet on the Armenian throne, but direct annexation by Rome. In Britain, too, arguments in favour of further annexations had recently prevailed, and there the policy had only been reversed because the British rose in a rebellion, recently terminated. The same expansionist programme was now to be tried in Armenia. It was a bad idea; neither the local people nor the Parthians would put up with it, and the country was vast and mountainous, with savage, ill-defined and almost infinitely extended frontiers. But the scheme for a joint Partho-Roman appointment had failed, and the government had also evidently come to the conclusion that the imposition of the Roman nominee, Tigranes, was not going to work either, at least not without continuous and massive interventions; and so the unfortunate, imprudent man was quietly dropped.

However, the annexation policy ran speedily into trouble. For Paetus allowed himself to be surrounded by the Parthians in Rhandeia (a fortress somewhere north of the River Murat), where he was forced to capitulate. Apparently he was also compelled to agree to humiliating conditions, including the evacuation of Armenia pending discussions between Vologases and Nero. But of this we cannot be too sure, because our information comes ultimately from the memoirs of Corbulo, who hated Paetus and, though he had come back from Syria to help him, had not unduly hurried. Even Tacitus, though admiring Corbulo, admits that what he wrote had not always been fair.[14] Anyway, Paetus, as soon as the Parthians let him go, left the scene of his disaster, at a panic-stricken rate of forty miles in one day, abandoning his wounded as he went.

Since noblemen whose only fault was a connection with the imperial family were accustomed to receive merciless treatment from Nero, one might have expected that a commander like Paetus, who had grossly humiliated Rome, its emperor and its Eagles, was in for trouble. But not at all. When the defeated general got back home, expecting the worst, Nero told him he was pardoned. And he added with mild malice that he was imparting this news immediately, because prolonged suspense would damage the health of someone whose nerves were evidently so frail. So Paetus survived to hold a further eastern command in a subsequent reign.

In Armenia, as in Britain, the imperialists on Nero's council had failed to achieve their object. Back, then, to the beginning, and the peaceful policy of officially approving, as Rome's candidate, the man whom the Parthians also favoured, Tiridates. Probably this is what Nero, and those of his friends who felt the same way, had really wanted all the time; and his lenient reception of Paetus seems to confirm the suspicion. At any rate that is how things turned out. After a special meeting of the emperor's council, Corbulo, now transferred to the Armenian front once again, was encouraged to make warlike moves into Mesopotamia, so that, although he never fought a major battle, victory could duly be reported to the Roman Senate and public. Then he tried again to arrange a meeting with Tiridates (63); and this time it took place. Ceremonious courtesies of every kind were exchanged, and it seems to have been agreed that the Romans would evacuate Mesopotamia provided that the Parthians moved out of Armenia. Tiridates publicly took off his diadem and laid it at the feet of a statue of Nero. The diadem was to be restored to him by the emperor himself in Rome, to which it was planned that Tiridates should in due course pay a visit.

Nero's settlement had been hard to get, but when it was finally attained it was excellent. Tacitus and other historians cannot be expected to approve of it, because they were heirs to the aristocratic, expansionist tradition. But Nero's was a diplomatic solution which brought peace to the region for no less than fifty years, until Trajan reverted to the tougher policy and invaded Armenia and Mesopotamia again. Such a prolonged peace in these territories was quite unprecedented. The only ruler who had attempted a diplomatic settlement before, Augustus, was obliged to conceal the peaceful nature of his aims from Roman conservative opinion by issuing coins inscribed 'Armenia captured', 'Armenia captured again'. But Augustus' policy had not lasted, because his Armenian nominee was only reluctantly accepted by Parthia and in any case died soon after; whereas Nero's peace successfully endured. Much of the credit must go to him personally, because it was he, young though he was, who presided over the councils whose general directives, in his name, even strong-minded commanders like Corbulo were obliged to obey.

It was only a pity the success could not be more spectacular, because the sort of triumphs Nero liked best were those which permitted resplendent displays of pomp. But this, as we shall see, he was later to achieve on an unprecedented scale, when Tiridates, almost three years after the settlement of 63, made his appearance at Rome.

Nero's bronze coinage at his great eastern military base, Antioch.

7 Expansion and Exploration

Although Armenia was not annexed, the historians who disliked Nero were wrong to depreciate him for not adding to the empire, as virile emperors should: because elsewhere there did occur annexations during his reign. They were probably four in number, two relatively insignificant and two rather more important. On the borders of Italy itself the Cottian Alps, based on Segusio (Susa) and commanding the Mont Genèvre pass, were transferred from the rule of a dependent dynasty to direct Roman government. On the Syrian border, too, the magnificent city of Damascus, which had been controlled by an Arabian client monarch for over twenty years, appears from its coinage to have been re-annexed by Rome in 62–3, in order to strengthen the frontier defences.

In addition, at the top end of the eastern boundary, we again learn from coins that an important strip of territory in Asia Minor was added to the empire in 64, under the name of Lesser Armenia. This had been the dependent kingdom of Pontus; its monarch was now withdrawn and allowed to transfer himself to another fief he possessed at the south-eastern end of the peninsula. This Pontic kingdom, adjoined on the west by the long-established Roman province of Pontus and Bithynia, contained the formerly autonomous city of Trapezus (Trabzon, Trebizond), which now became an important frontier post.

Trapezus was strategically situated on the Black Sea, and throughout the period leading up to this annexation we have some dim, fragmentary pieces of evidence, mostly in the form of inscriptions and coins, which suggest that it was the policy of Nero and his advisers, over a considerable period, to make the Black Sea into a safe Roman lake like the Mediterranean. This, up to now, the Black Sea had not been.

There was the constantly shifting Partho-Armenian frontier situation on its Asian shores; and the European Black Sea coast was likewise by no means secure. Roman rule extended up as far as the Danube, and far beyond it the Cimmerian Bosphorus (Crimea) was ruled by a dependent monarch – the fortunate possessor of enormous wealth in grain – whose policing of the area also permitted a huge, lucrative traffic of slaves to Rome. But along the coast between Danube and Crimea, there were only pockets of Graeco-Roman civilization. The coins of one such place, Tyras (Belgorod) on the Dniester,

The fascinating contemporary art of the Euphrates, beyond Rome's Syrian frontier. The wall-painting is from the Temple of the Palmyrene Gods, Dura-Europos (Salahiya). The chief ministrant has a Greek name, Conon, but wears the tall white conical hat of a Persian magus or later dervish.

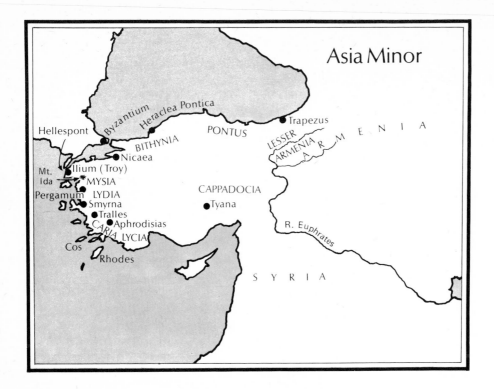

Asia Minor

are dated according to an era starting in AD 57, which suggests that this was the year in which Nero brought the city under imperial control. But in *c.* 60 there were threatening movements of tribes on the lower Danube, and Nero's governor Titus Plautius Silvanus Aelianus (a relation of Claudius' first wife) restored order in what is now Rumania. Transferring a hundred thousand Transdanubians south of the river – kings, women, children and all – he annexed a strip of Wallachia, and entered into a system of alliances with Moldavian chiefs and Greek coastal cities.

He also intervened in the Crimea, and subsequently claimed, as an inscription reveals, that he was the first to send large quantities of grain from this area to Rome.[1] The removal of the local monarch's head from the Crimean coinage in 62-3 – when Nero's head and name appear without any reference to the king – suggests that the Crimea itself was reduced to more direct dependence on the Romans, thus comprising the fourth of Nero's annexations. But, if so, the arrangement did not outlast his death. Before then there had been fresh tribal trouble in and around the Dobrogea (Dobruja).[2] So Nero's policy in the area remained uncompleted. However, it had evidently aimed at establishing the same measure of trading security in these distant regions as already existed in all the imperial territories further west and south.

Nero and his helpers, from motives ranging from scientific curiosity to acquisitiveness, were fascinated by remote countries, and eager that they should be explored. *The quest for amber*

For example, the emperor was keen to get amber. His immediate aim, it

In this portrait of Nero his hair is brushed up in front like a charioteer's. (Cf. p. 205.)

appears, was to make a fine display at gladiatorial Games. But there was more to it than that. Trading in amber from Jutland and the Baltic went back to the second millennium BC, but although amber routes were well established the commerce still remained in native hands. It would be a good thing to change this as far as possible, so that interested parties, including the emperor, could get hold of this lucrative luxury product at a cheaper price. But even beyond the uttermost stretches of the Roman empire, there were a full four hundred perilous miles to traverse before reaching the Baltic coast. At some time during Nero's reign, a Roman knight, the agent of the emperor's manager of gladiators Julianus, made the journey: crossing the Danube frontier at Carnuntum (Petronell), he penetrated northwards into what are now Czechoslovakia and Poland. He got to the Baltic, and eventually brought back so much amber that the emperor, at one of his shows, was able to plaster safety-nets, weapons and even coffins with the material.[3] But the longer-term results were more considerable, and Rome's northern trade profited.

Otherwise Nero's activities on and beyond the German frontier were not very significant. He employed German bodyguards,[4] refused to allow one of his governors on the Rhine to cut a Moselle-Saône canal because it might

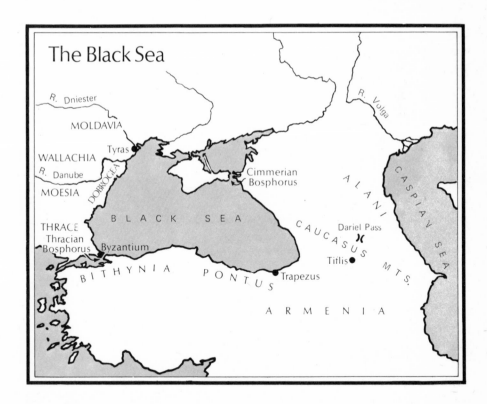

disturb the Gauls, and refused also to allow the Frisians to squat on a coastal strip of imperial territory between the Rhine and the Zuyder Zee. However the visit of the two Frisian delegates to Rome provided a laugh, because at the theatre, out of national pride, they had the effrontery to elbow their way forward and sit among the Roman senators.[5]

It was quite an achievement, in a single reign, to have explorers from Rome visiting not only the Baltic but central Africa as well. But that is what happened under Nero. The African expedition, which may have started out from Rome in 61, consisted of a small party of praetorian guardsmen including perhaps two officers.[6] After sailing to Egypt, they crossed the southern frontier of the empire near the First Cataract, this side of the present

From the Baltic to central Africa

Egyptian-Sudanese border. Then they proceeded south into the Sudan. They passed the Nile's junction with the Atbara and reached Meroe (Bakarawiga), capital of Napata – an independent state, with which Rome maintained a connection.

Here the Napatans provided them with a military escort, and they moved southwards once again. Finally they came to immense marshes, where they saw plants so 'entangled with waters' that they were impenetrable, except perhaps for a one-man canoe. This description clearly indicates the Sudd, the marshy area of floating islands of vegetation on the White Nile south of Malakal, in the Upper Nile province of the Sudan – a region not rediscovered until 1839–40.

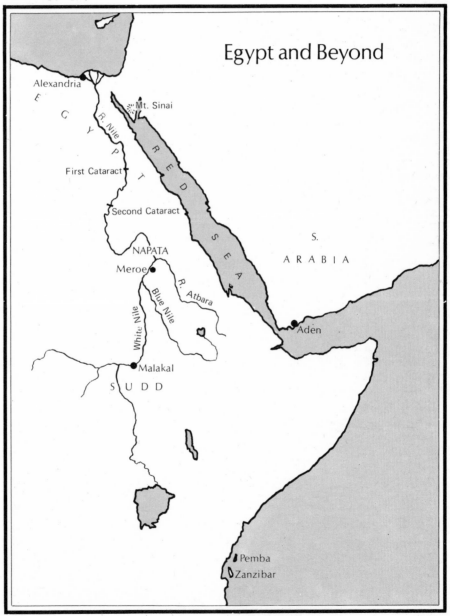

Egypt and Beyond

Nero's explorers had penetrated a thousand miles beyond the imperial frontier, as the crow flies – in reality, of course, their journey had been a very great deal longer. When they finally got home again, they were interviewed by Seneca, who listened to their stories of parakeets, rhinoceroses, elephants, dog-faced baboons – and, for good measure, dog-headed men as well. They also showed him – or more probably handed over – some ebony wood they had brought back. But they were obliged to report that the kingdom of Napata was poor and thinly populated and its capital Meroe crumbling. So if Nero and the government had hoped to use that state as a stepping-stone for political expansion, they did not pursue the matter any further.

However, the reasons why the emperor and Seneca had sponsored this remarkable expedition remain uncertain. Was it trade, or 'the flag', or scientific spirit? Perhaps a bit of all three. Trade and the flag, it is true, were by no means as closely linked as they became eighteen centuries later; and the imperial encouragement of commercial ventures was mostly indirect, consisting of the maintenance of unprecedented peace, secure roads, and safe seaways on which a single ship could carry six hundred people. Yet emperors were naturally in favour of business activity, which meant not only prosperity but tranquillity – or, to put it in another way, satisfactory political apathy.

Nero's ministers, too, had reasons for taking the same line, since they were Greeks and orientals acquainted with all the eastern merchants who controlled the empire's trade. Moreover, this was a time when sensational fortunes were being won by freedmen of eastern birth, the sort of people whom Petronius brings before us in his story of the self-made millionaire Trimalchio.

The Graeco-Syrian philosopher and polymath Posidonius (died *c.* 50 BC), who, less optimistically than Seneca, supposed that India was 7,700 miles from Spain.

Nobody gets enough, never. I wanted to go into business. Not to make a long story of it, I built five ships, I loaded them with wine – it was absolute gold at the time – and I sent them to Rome. You'd have thought I ordered it – every single ship was wrecked. That's fact, not fable! In one single day Neptune swallowed up thirty million. Do you think I gave up? This loss honestly wasn't more than a flea-bite to me – it was as if nothing had happened. I built more boats, bigger and better and luckier. . . . In one voyage I carved out a round ten million. . . . I invested in slaves, and I bought up the horse trade. Whatever I touched grew like a honeycomb. Once I had more than the whole country, then down tools! I retired from business and began advancing loans through freedmen.[7]

Rough seas could not, then, be controlled. But the lawlessness of human beings could be; and the provision of safe trading conditions was one of the motives which made the imperial government devote tireless attention to the maintenance of security throughout the empire. To have peace inside the frontiers you had to have good relations with the peoples just outside them: best of all (as earlier emperors had failed to achieve in Britain) you could maintain a continuous belt of little states that were ostensibly independent but really depended on Roman subsidies. The expedition into central Africa was linked with that sort of consideration. Napata, if it had not proved so weak, would have been precisely the kind of buffer-state which the Romans liked to maintain as a *cordon sanitaire*. Perhaps the Roman visitors gave it what encouragement they could against its neighbour on the other side: Axum in Ethiopia. But east of both kingdoms lay the Red Sea, in which Romans and their Levantine shippers were extremely interested because of the Indian trade, which was now based on a much improved knowledge of how the monsoons operated. It may even be, though this is still uncertain, that men from inside the empire had occupied some point in south-western Arabia not far from Aden, possibly Syagros (Cape Fartak). And travellers from imperial territory had reached even further south by Nero's reign – as far as a place called Menuthias, which was Zanzibar or Pemba.

Scientific exploration Nero was readily infected with enthusiasm for projects of exploration; it was he, later on, who tried to sound the depths of the supposedly bottomless Lake Alcyon near Lerna in Greece. This attitude owed much to Seneca, who was passionately interested in exploring from a scientific point of view. When he was young, he had lived in Egypt and had written a monograph about the country; and he compiled a study of India as well. Now he was preparing material for an eight-book work called *Natural Questions,* of which the greater part survives. Its subject is physical science in many aspects – the curiosities of fire, air and water, and the nature of winds, earthquakes and comets. No wonder Seneca wanted to interview the men who came back from central Africa: for he had hoped they would discover the source of the Nile.

This sort of activity was the geographical counterpart of his philosophical conviction that the earth was a single brotherhood, unified by Rome.

> In the broad world the ancient ways
> No longer can our steps confine:
> The Indian by Araxes strays,
> The Persian drinks the Rhine.[8]

The *Natural Questions* give the same thought more detailed expression, and it must have been exhilarating for Nero to hear Seneca offering himself or his council prognostications in this truly enlightened, scientific style:

The people of the coming generation will know much that we do not know; much is reserved for ages which will have forgotten our names: the world is a tiny thing, except that it contains questions enough for all the world. . . . Great discoveries come slowly, especially when the work goes slow.[9]

And Seneca, speaking as a Spaniard – a younger compatriot of the great geographer Pomponius Mela, who came from Tingentera near Gibraltar – wrote down some extraordinary examples of what he had in mind. For one thing he was convinced that Spain would soon be joined to the Indies by an oceanic link. He prophesied the discovery of a new transatlantic land which would displace semi-legendary Thule (Iceland or Norway) as the end of all things. A Graeco-Syrian scholar of the previous century, Posidonius, had expressed the view that Spain and India were about 7,700 miles apart. But Seneca, with an optimism unfulfilled until the age of aeroplanes, believed that before long these lands would be reached from one another 'in a very few days'.[10]

8 New Advisers and a New Wife

In AD 62 a number of people died who had played important parts in Nero's life. Four of these deaths had little effect on him, for the men had lost all influence long before. Two of them were former ministers: Pallas, who had reached a mighty position under Claudius; and Doryphorus, who had reputedly been Nero's lover in his earlier days. There is no real reason to believe the inevitable rumours that he accelerated the ends of either of these men.

It was a different matter, however, with the other two, Rubellius Plautus and Faustus Sulla. Rubellius could boast a descent from Augustus which was almost comparable to Nero's own, and Sulla was a descendant of the great dictator of that name and of Pompey, and had married Claudius' daughter. Like the two ministers who died in the same year, they had passed from the Roman scene some years previously. For Rubellius and Sulla were living in banishment. But, as we have seen, no private citizen related to the imperial house could be allowed to continue in existence for long; and men in exile generally did not have many years to live, because it was so easy to report their alleged remarks to the suspicious Nero. The decision to kill them, says Tacitus (who exploits these tragedies to the full) was due to another death which removed a check on such ferocious tendencies and in general exercised an important and far-reaching effect on governmental policy. For Burrus, too, had died. It was suggested that imperial poison had been at work, but he probably succumbed to a natural cause – an abscess or cancer of the neck or throat.

Nero decided to replace him, as commander of the Praetorian Guard, not by one officer but by two, an arrangement which had been preferred in earlier days by Augustus. The amount of administrative, judicial and advisory work the post involved, going far beyond purely military duties and including membership of the imperial council, justified the duplication – which also helped to avert the peril that a guard commander might gain too much power. But the division did tend to mean that one of the colleagues would become closer to the emperor than the other. And so it was now. One of the two new commanders was Faenius Rufus, who was liked by the guardsmen; and he enjoyed general popularity as well, because he had previously been in charge of the Roman grain supply and had managed the job without

Poppaea, on the imperial coinage of Alexandria (AD 64–5).

personal profit. But he did not have a very effective personality; and he was rapidly eclipsed by the other joint commander, Gaius Ofonius Tigellinus.

Tigellinus' career had been unusual. He was the son of a Sicilian from Agrigentum who had found it healthier to leave the island. The boy was brought up in the households of Agrippina and her sister, and was banished by Caligula on suspicion of adultery not with one of these imperial ladies but both. After living, for a time, as a fisherman in Greece, he appeared in south Italy. There he made good, becoming a landowner and breeder of race-horses for the Circus;[1] and it was in this capacity that he attracted the favour of Nero, who made him Commander of the Watch. Now, in 62, he was associated with Faenius Rufus in the command of the Praetorian Guard.

Tacitus gives Tigellinus an appalling character, accusing him of lechery, treachery, cruelty, greed and cynical bargaining with human lives.[2] Was he, therefore, only appointed to these senior posts because he was horsy like Nero, and because they enjoyed the same sort of parties? That would not, in general, be characteristic of the senior appointments of the reign, which showed a much greater degree of responsibility. On the other hand, we certainly know nothing good about Tigellinus. But Tacitus' reasons for hating him leave us with a suspicion that the new commander must have been a more capable, though possibly not a nicer, man than we are told. For one thing, the historian was a snob who strongly disapproved of people of humble origins becoming important; he specifically charges Tigellinus not only with 'vicious childhood and dissolute maturity', but with low birth. Secondly, Tacitus saw in him a reincarnation and repetition of the bogey-man Sejanus whose tenure of the same post under Tiberius had, in his view, made that reign the decisive epoch of Rome's degeneration. And Tigellinus was the enemy and supplanter of Seneca, whose side Tacitus could be expected to take.

Indeed, the appointment of Tigellinus, coming on top of the death of Burrus, was what made Seneca decide to retire. The waves of criticism against him, always considerable, now seemed likely to become stronger than he could cope with; he had got into too isolated a position to be able to continue a useful career as the emperor's adviser. His vast wealth was an obvious target, and more serious still was the fact that the emperor did not want to see much of him any more.

For one thing, his various philosophical utterances could be, and no doubt were, interpreted as reflections on the emperor's tastes – for example, on his love of charioteering and singing and athletics and wearing eccentric clothes. And no doubt there were always people ready to report that what he had written or said amounted to a criticism of Nero. When Seneca went to him to announce his retirement, adding a tactful offer to hand over his vast proper-ties, Tacitus reconstructs a brilliant exchange of insincere compliments between the two men. Nero is quoted as urging him not to withdraw. But Seneca was not to be persuaded. 'He expressed his gratitude: all conversa-tions with autocrats end like that. But he abandoned the customs of his former ascendancy. Terminating his large receptions, he dismissed his entourage and rarely visited Rome. Ill-health or philosophical studies kept him at home, he said.'[3]

A woman of Nero's time, believed by some to be Poppaea.

From now on, Seneca's writings swelled in volume. The new works included a treatise *On Leisure*, and the *Natural Questions*, and the elegant moral *Epistles* to Lucilius Junior. Once there were more of these than the one hundred and twenty-four that now survive; though Lucilius asked for not so much advice and more books.

The removal of Seneca and Burrus caused Nero to become less cautious, and helped him to summon up the courage to divorce Octavia. The marriage had been a complete failure; she did not appeal to him at all. And there seemed no prospect of Octavia having his child – either because she failed to become pregnant, or because her husband could not bring himself to do his part. But Roman rulers, as their coinage often shows, greatly relied on having children and heirs to protect their own positions against would-be supplanters.

above: A Roman woman of the time.

Besides, Nero had pensioned off Acte and fallen in love with another woman, Poppaea. As was pointed out earlier, the ancient tradition dating her great influence back to 59 is probably a fabrication. For it was not until 62 that the emperor made the change. It was a formidable and possibly perilous step, involving the degradation of a young wife of imperial ancestry, whose father had been Nero's own predecessor. Seneca and Burrus cannot have favoured the divorce,[4] but now they were gone. And in the very year of their departure Poppaea became pregnant. Now, at last, Nero had a chance of getting an heir, together with a wife whom he found infinitely more attractive than Octavia. So he summoned up the courage to take the plunge.

The frame-up of the presumably guiltless Octavia seems to have been inexpressibly sordid. In order to reconcile the Senate, the public and the army to the rejection of a woman of such tremendous birth it was necessary to smear her reputation thoroughly. A member of her household was therefore suborned to report that his mistress was having an adulterous affair with an Alexandrian slave who played the pipes. Her servants were examined and tortured, but many of them remained immovably loyal. Tigellinus himself presided over the investigations, but while he was interrogating one of the maids, Pythias, she spat in his face and cried: 'the private parts of my mistress are cleaner than your mouth!'

above: Octavia? or Poppaea?

Nevertheless, enough confessions were extorted to enable the divorce to go through. As her place of retirement, Octavia was given the mansion of Burrus – with the rather ominous addition of some estates that had belonged to Rubellius Plautus before his liquidation. Soon, however, she was sent further away to Campania, where she was kept under military guard.

But Nero had not reckoned with the volatile Roman population. In the previous year it had rioted in support of condemned slaves, and now crowds demonstrated vigorously in favour of this pathetic imperial girl who was still only just out of her teens. A rumour that Nero was going to take her back produced equally vociferous demonstrations of joy, which were promptly suppressed by the army. Poppaea was understandably upset. The allegations about Octavia's misconduct with the Alexandrian had clearly failed to gain acceptance, and some further charge had to be found. So Nero now mobilized his old tutor, the fleet commander Anicetus, to declare that he

right: Octavia, sister of Augustus and great-grandmother of Nero's wife Octavia.

overleaf: A racing chariot coming up to the turn in the Circus Maximus. The turning point is marked by three conical pillars. First century AD.

AE
EVSA

T.337.

himself had committed adultery with Octavia. Tied to Nero by complicity in Agrippina's death, the man had no alternative; and the emperor's council was summoned to hear a confession from him which actually exceeded the instructions he had received. Then it was thought best to remove him from the scene. He was told to retire to Sardinia, where he lived in comfort and died a natural death.

Nero issued an edict reporting that Octavia's choice of a lover showed her intention of tampering with the loyalty of the fleet. He added that she had become pregnant by Anicetus and had procured an abortion – an ill-considered charge, considering that he had previously accused her of sterility. She was moved from Campania, and confined on the island of Pandateria (Pantellaria). But there always remained the danger that some ambitious nobleman would rescue her and make her his wife. And so, only a few days after her arrival at Pandateria, she was put to death. Twenty or thirty years later a rhetorical tragedy, the *Octavia* – the only Roman historical play still surviving – was written to give dramatic and lyrical form to the whole story. Seneca appears on the stage to protest against the emperor's barbarity. The *Octavia* is a bizarre work, but perceptive in its presentation of three deeply frightened people – Octavia, Poppaea and Nero himself.

But now Poppaea was triumphant, for only twelve days after his divorce, Nero married her.

> Ah, you were beautiful on that high couch
> In the palace hall! Your loveliness astonished
> The Senate, when you burnt the holy incense,
> Sprinkling the altar with the sacred wine,
> Wearing the delicate marriage-veil of saffron.[5]

One of Nero's old friends who is unlikely to have been present at the wedding was Otho. Otho himself loved Poppaea and was her lover; and they may even have been married. However, not content with once having helped Nero over his affair with Acte, he was also responsible for introducing him to Poppaea. The ancient historians were fond of weaving legends round this triangular relationship. But what probably happened is fairly simple: Nero wanted her for himself, and consequently posted Otho to the remote governorship of Lusitania (Portugal) – where he acquitted himself quite well.[6] When his relations with Nero had become tense, it seems to have been Seneca who got him the job, thus probably saving him from destruction.

> Why is it Otho lives an exile's life?
> Because he dared to sleep with his own wife.[7]

Poppaea was hailed as Augusta, as Agrippina (but never Octavia) had been. Octavia's head had appeared on the coinage of Alexandria and eastern cities but never in the capital; now Poppaea's portrait not only followed that of her predecessor at Alexandria but her figure was also to be seen on Roman gold and silver coins. She is shown standing next to the emperor beside the inscription AVGVSTVS AVGVSTA.[8] On these issues she appears in the guise of the goddess Concord, a point which is elaborated by another series bearing the inscription CONCORDIA AVGVSTA. This conveys the

A young contemporary of Poppaea.

message that there is harmony in the imperial family, and that it matches
the universal harmony provided by the regime.

These markedly complimentary attentions, combined with those she
received from many communities and individuals aware which way the
wind was blowing, suggest that Nero was very fond of her; too fond, probably, to have murdered her son by an earlier marriage, as he was reported
to have done. He wrote a poem about her 'amber hair',[9] which created a
fashion for this intermediate shade between blonde and black; the coins of
Alexandria show that her coiffure was more pretentious than Octavia's,
but very like Agrippina's, with a sort of ponytail at the back. Otherwise we
know all too little about her, except that she was a few years older than Nero.
We are given quite a lot of information, it is true, but much of it has a fictitious ring. Her transfer from Otho to the Emperor was not only antedated
by the historians, but gave rise to many other myths as well; and the story of
her wooing of Nero, first coy and then insistent, is a corny traditional theme.

Tacitus, however, embroiders it with much gusto; and this is his summing-
up of her personality.

> She had every asset except goodness. From her mother, the loveliest woman of
> her day, she inherited distinction and beauty. Her wealth, too, was equal to her
> birth. She was clever, and pleasant to talk to. She seemed respectable. But her life
> was depraved. Her public appearances were few; she would half-veil her face at
> them, to stimulate curiosity (or because it suited her). To her, married or bachelor
> bed-fellows were alike. She was indifferent to her reputation – yet insensible to men's
> love, and herself unloving. Advantage dictated the bestowal of her favours.[10]

Probably this is, by and large, a true enough picture. But it is perhaps over-
dramatic, because there are suspiciously strong verbal and stylistic echoes
of what another great historian, Sallust, had written a century and a half
earlier about another sinister beauty, Catiline's patroness Sempronia.[11]

What else, then, are we left with for Poppaea, apart from the colour and
arrangement of her hair? We know that her father was a certain Titus
Ollius, who succumbed to Tiberius in a purge, but that she had preferred to
take the more glamorous name of her mother, the most beautiful woman of
her day and a victim of Messalina; the Poppaean family perhaps came from

147

Pompeii. We are given a report that she took great care about her personal appearance, since her face was her fortune. She invented the Poppaean face-cream which remained fashionable long after her time,[12] and she kept her skin soft by maintaining a herd of five hundred recently foaled she-donkeys, and bathing in their milk.[13] We also happen to know that, like her new husband, she was the friend of a comic actor called Alityrus, who was a Jew. Through his intervention, his compatriot Josephus, the historian, secured an interview with her at Puteoli and obtained the release of some rabbis who had been arrested,[14] and she also helped the Jews on another occasion.[15]

Poppaea shared this attention to eastern religions with Nero, who favoured the rather hysterical cult of the Syrian Goddess, otherwise known as Atargatis, and who also took the opportunity of the king of Armenia's visit to study the doctrines of the Persian wise men, the Magi. Otho, too, possessed similar exotic leanings, since he was a devotee of the Egyptian divinity Isis (like relations of Poppaea at Pompeii). He was also interested in astrologers, and so was Poppaea: one of her employees concerned with this subject, Ptolemaeus or Seleucus by name, went with Otho to Lusitania.[16] Agrippina was another who had been credulous about astrology, as were many other educated people of the time. It seemed self-evident that there must be some sort of harmony between the earth and the other heavenly bodies, and that the latter therefore regulated human lives. The leading contemporary exponent of these doctrines, Balbillus, who was of royal descent and may have been the son of Tiberius' court astrologer, wrote to one of Seneca's friends explaining why such influences existed;[17] and it is very probable that this man of much obscure learning[18] was a close friend of Nero and is identical with his governor of Egypt of the same name. There was a curious contrast between this fashion for astrology and the government's recurrent tendency to send its practitioners into exile – presumably the less stylish ones, who could easily become subversive, for example when they started talking about imperial horoscopes. The agricultural expert Columella wrote a treatise *Against Astrologers*,[19] but it is unfortunately lost.

As for Nero, his study of the Magi was due to a keen interest in the arts of magic. He used to carry about with him a little figure of a girl, as the sort of talisman we read about in magic papyri discovered beneath Egypt's sands; for soon after her image came into his possession he had discovered a plot against his life, and so thereafter it became his habit to sacrifice to the statuette three times every day. Lucan, too, is thoroughly familiar with eastern magic: the first poet, as far as we are aware, to possess such knowledge. The horrors in which Lucan, like his uncle Seneca, is fond of wallowing include a luxuriantly creepy account of necromancy – to which Nero, too, was passionately addicted. Contemporary gossip attributed his preoccupation to remorse for the murder of his mother. That is doubtful; but his refusal, later, to visit Athens may well have been due to that city's stories of how the matricide Orestes was pursued by the Furies. And for the same reason he did not dare to take part in the Eleusinian Mysteries – which were the most deeply revered ceremonies of Greek religion – because, before the rites started at Eleusis, a herald was accustomed to proclaim that all who have committed crimes must leave the place. Nero would not have dared to disobey such an order.

above: A young woman of the period. (Cf. p. 80.)

Nero on a coin minted at Alexandria.

148

An imperial lady
(Poppaea?). Found at
Olympia in Greece.

The emperor's superstition was no greater than that of his subjects, and perhaps less than the credulity of most of them. The appearance of comets was always a worry to the government: they caused people to surmise that there was going to be a change of emperor, and Seneca was not disposed to feel that they were completely without significance.[20] Prodigies, omens and portents were closely watched, widely reported and liberally invented. Historians, in accordance with tradition, still felt it worthwhile to record them; not necessarily because they credited individual reports (though they mostly believed they might, on occasion, be true), but because such stories reflected the state of popular sentiment and emotion. After the death of Agrippina, for example, many prodigies were spoken about. 'A woman', according to Tacitus, 'gave birth to a snake. Another woman was killed in her husband's arms by a thunderbolt. The sun suddenly went dark. All fourteen city-districts of Rome were struck by lightning. But these portents meant nothing. So little were they due to the gods that Nero continued his reign and his crimes for years to come.'[21]

And then, two years later, Nero was shown a child born with four heads and corresponding limbs.[22]

Whether, in 62, the emperor would have postponed his divorce and re-marriage if the omens had been unfavourable, we cannot tell. But, at all events, the appalling circumstances of Octavia's end presumably passed quite rapidly from his mind, since they had led to such a happy conclusion. His happiness was increased when, on January 21, AD 63, Poppaea presented him with a daughter.[23]

Born at his own birthplace, Antium (Anzio), the infant received the name of Claudia and was almost at once declared 'Augusta' like her mother. It was a somewhat ludicrous innovation to call a new-born baby by this revered name. But Augusta she is called on lead tokens which were issued in Rome and perhaps served as money-tickets for free distributions of gifts to celebrate the occasion. There was a great deal of rejoicing. Almost the entire Roman Senate turned out to visit Antium, and the town was presented with golden statues and endowed with Circus Games. More Games were established at Rome, where the foundation of a Temple of Fertility was also decreed; and the records of the Arval priesthood show that in April its members sacrificed to the spirits of both the Augustas together, Poppaea and Claudia.

But the celebrations came to an abrupt end in May, because the baby died. Tacitus' comment is unsympathetic. 'There followed new forms of syco-phancy. The dead infant was declared a goddess and voted a place on the gods' ceremonial couch, together with a shrine and a priest. The emperor's delight had been immoderate; so was his mourning.'[24]

Nero had achieved fatherhood by exceptionally squalid means. Yet he had achieved it all the same; and even a daughter, while she lived, was of some use as a potential dynastic advantage. But now the dream was over, and he never had another child.

9 The Great Fire and the Christians

The Romans attached great importance to anniversaries, natural or contrived. In AD 64 people noticed that a sinister one had come about by chance. 19 July was the day on which the Gauls had set fire to the city some four and a half centuries earlier. And now, on the night of 18 and 19 July, AD 64, the Great Fire of Rome broke out – the most terrible and destructive fire the city ever experienced. Tacitus tells the story:

It began in the Circus, where it adjoins the Palatine and Caelian hills. Breaking out in shops selling inflammable goods, and fanned by the wind, the conflagration instantly grew and swept the whole length of the Circus. There were no walled mansions or temples, or any other obstructions which could arrest it. First, the fire swept violently over the level spaces. Then it climbed the hills – but returned to ravage the lower ground again. It outstripped every counter-measure. The ancient city's narrow winding streets and irregular blocks encouraged its progress.

Terrified, shrieking women, helpless old and young, people intent on their own safety, people unselfishly supporting invalids or waiting for them, fugitives and lingerers alike – all heightened the confusion. When people looked back, menacing flames sprang up before them or outflanked them. When they escaped to a neighbouring quarter, the fire followed: even districts believed remote proved to be involved. Finally, with no idea where or what to flee, they crowded on to the country roads, or lay in the fields. Some who had lost everything – even their food for the day – could have escaped, but preferred to die. So did others, who had failed to rescue their loved ones. . . .

By the sixth day enormous demolitions had confronted the raging flames with bare ground and open sky, and the fire was finally stamped out. But before panic had subsided, or hope revived, flames broke out again in the more open regions of the city. Here there were fewer casualties; but the destruction of temples and pleasure arcades was even worse. . . .

To count the mansions, blocks and temples destroyed would be difficult. They included shrines of remote antiquity, the precious spoils of countless victories, Greek artistic masterpieces, and authentic records of old Roman genius.[1]

Nero was at Antium at the time, but as soon as the fire started he hastened back and organized relief. In addition to public buildings in the Field of Mars, his Vatican Gardens were thrown open to the refugees, and emergency accommodation was hastily put up. Food was brought in from Ostia

One of the earliest representations of St Peter and St Paul. Painted in gold on glass, *c*. 280 AD.

and neighbouring towns, and the price of corn was temporarily cut to one-sixteenth of its normal price.

But all these beneficent measures did not prevent the population from believing that it was Nero who had deliberately caused the fire. It was customary to praise the ruler of the world whenever the news was good, and so when disaster occurred it seemed right that the blame should fall on him. Besides, while the city was burning, it was rumoured that Nero had been so moved by the sight that he took his lyre, put on his singer's robes and sang through the whole of a tragic song of his own composition called the *Fall of Troy*, which was perhaps based on his epic *The Trojan War*. Such, then, is the famous story that Nero fiddled while Rome burned; though if he played any instrument it was a lyre and not a fiddle.

The historians agree that he played and sang, but there is a difference of opinion about where the scene took place. According to Tacitus, it was on the stage of his private theatre. Dio says he stood 'on the roof of the palace'. And Suetonius, more circumstantially, attributes the exhibition to the 'tower of Maecenas', presumably a tower connected with the mansions and gardens of Maecenas on the Esquiline, a property of Nero's which is likely to have been the headquarters of his relief activities. Wherever the scene may have been staged, it is all too probable that Nero did give such a display. A man of his artistic tastes and emotions, offered a background of such superlative fireworks, would have found the temptation irresistible. On the other hand, his effort was disastrous from the point of view of public relations: singing and playing the lyre when people were experiencing such hardships must clearly have given a callous impression. The performance does not make him the author of the fire. But the suffering population, when they heard the story, could very easily jump to the conclusion that, if he found the fire so exciting, he must have started it.

There were also other circumstances which whipped up suspicions that he had been the incendiary. First of all, efforts to fight the fire were seen to meet with obstruction. 'Nobody dared fight the flames. Attempts to do so were prevented by menacing gangs. Torches, too, were openly thrown in, by men calling out that they were acting under orders.' And Tacitus, who mentions this curious report, adds that, although these mysterious figures *may* just have been looters wanting to get on with their looting unhampered, it was also possible that they were acting upon instructions. If so, who had given them? Who else but the emperor? Another sinister happening was a *second* outbreak of the fire, after it had seemed to be at an end. The fact that this new conflagration started on an estate belonging to the guard commander Tigellinus made people think that he himself had started this new fire – in order to finish off a job which had been well begun (by the emperor) but not completed.

The rumours directed against Nero were stimulated by the knowledge, or suspicion, that he was glad to have a lot of ground cleared since he wanted to build a new palace. He had already greatly expanded his residence in the centre of the city. But, as people no doubt knew, this was quite a miniature affair in comparison with the Golden House that he had in mind. When, very shortly afterwards, it became clear that these forecasts about his building

An example of the magnificent brass coinage issued by Nero at Rome from AD 64 onwards. He is shown exercising with the Praetorian Guard (which he did very rarely, if at all).

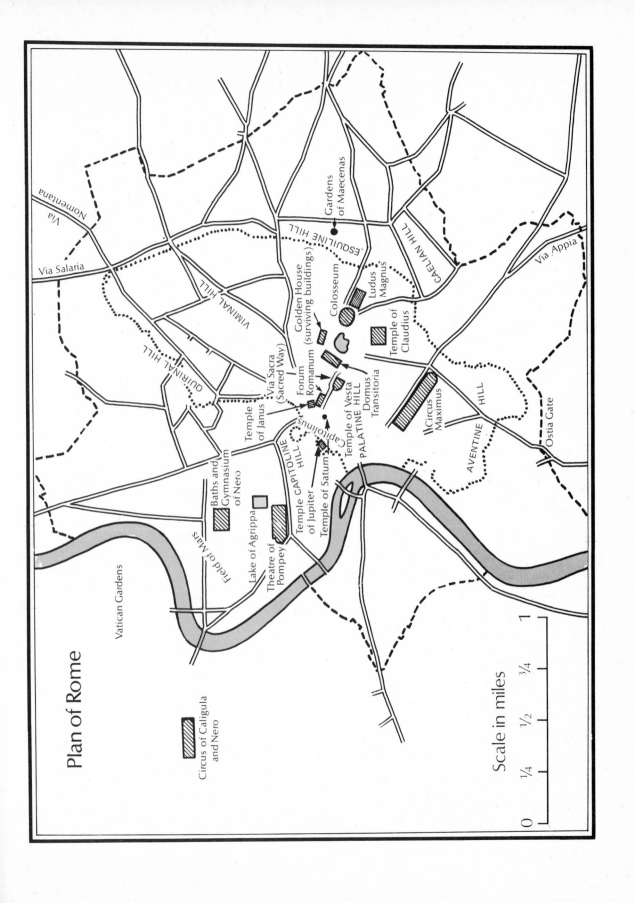

Plan of Rome

Circus of Caligula and Nero

Vatican Gardens

Via Nomentana

Via Salaria

VIMINAL HILL

QUIRINAL HILL

Baths and Gymnasium of Nero

Field of Mars

Lake of Agrippa

Theatre of Pompey

CAPITOLINE HILL

Temple of Jupiter

Temple of Saturn

Temple of Janus

Via Sacra (Sacred Way)

Forum Romanum

Capitolinus

Golden House (surviving buildings)

ESQUILINE HILL

Gardens of Maecenas

Colosseum

Ludus Magnus

CAELIAN HILL

Via Appia

Temple of Claudius

Temple of Vesta

PALATINE HILL

Domus Transitoria

Circus Maximus

AVENTINE HILL

Ostia Gate

Scale in miles

0   ¼   ½   ¾   1

intentions were correct, the belief that it was the emperor who had started the original fire seemed more convincing still. Nearly two generations later, Tacitus thought it best to suspend judgment on the matter, blending two versions, one of which blamed Nero, while the other stressed his energetic relief measures; as to the blame, he contents himself with typical innuendoes. But Suetonius directly incriminates Nero: and this view goes right back to contemporaries, including the elder Pliny, or someone who added a gloss to his text. Another writer of the time, who probably took the same view and was drawn upon by later historians, was a certain Cluvius Rufus, who wanted to erase people's recollection that he had been Nero's friend (see also Appendix 2).

In fact, however, the responsibility cannot be fastened on Nero. If he had wanted to demolish buildings for the Golden House, he would not have started the fire quite a distance away from the area in question. Furthermore, what the conflagration did reach and destroy was his own palace on the Palatine, which he had no desire to scrap since he had just redecorated it and clearly intended its incorporation into the new plan. Nor, surely, would he have got to work precisely when the moon was full – calculations have shown that this was the case – a full moon not being the best time for arson to escape notice. Nevertheless, the rumours that Nero was responsible raged among the distressed population. He had never been so unpopular, and a great burst of official, propitiatory, religious rites did nothing to distract public opinion from these perilous allegations. It had therefore become imperative to divert the charge to some other person or group.

An unknown woman of about the middle of the first century AD.

The victims the government chose for this role were the Christians, whose unhappy emergence on the stage of imperial history prompts Tacitus to one of his most famous and cryptic passages.

The public scapegoats

Neither human resources, nor imperial munificence, nor appeasement of the gods, eliminated sinister suspicions that the fire had been instigated. To suppress this rumour, Nero fabricated scapegoats – and punished with every refinement the notoriously depraved Christians (as they were popularly called). Their originator, Christ, had been executed in Tiberius' reign by the governor of Judaea, Pontius Pilatus. But in spite of this temporary setback the deadly superstition had broken out afresh, not only in Judaea where the mischief had started, but even in Rome. All degraded and shameful practices collect and flourish in the capital.

First, Nero had self-acknowledged Christians arrested. Then, on their information, large numbers of others were condemned – not so much for incendiarism as for their hatred of the human race.[2]

Jesus had been crucified in Judaea during the governorship of Pontius Pilatus, whose tenure as prefect of that minor province is recorded by an inscription recently discovered at his capital Caesarea, between the modern Nathanya and Haifa.[3] That was some thirty years before the Great Fire of Rome. Since then, the Church had spread from Jerusalem to Samaria and northwards to Antioch, and then on to Asia Minor and the Balkans and Italy. Before the middle of the century there were Christians at Rome itself. St Peter travelled to Antioch, Corinth and Rome, although, contrary to tradition, he probably found a church already existing in the capital on his arrival; and St Paul, a Roman citizen from Greek Tarsus in south-eastern Asia Minor, undertook his numerous journeys, preaching the faith, as others may have before him, to non-Jews as well as Jews. He too came to Rome.

Earlier, in Macedonia, Paul and his companion Silas had run into trouble at Thessalonica (Salonica) and Philippi.[4] They were probably accused of magic, which was illegal if it was of the wrong sort; and they were charged with attempting to convert non-Christians, which was widely felt to be improper and could easily lead to a situation in which criminal charges were brought. But Seneca's brother Gallio, who became governor of Achaea (Greece) in AD 52,[5] refused to consider an accusation by Jews that Paul had been trying to 'persuade men to worship God contrary to the Law'. Gallio prudently returned the charge into their own hands, declining to be the judge in such a matter.

About five years later, after Nero had come to the throne, another governor of Judaea, Festus, found himself in a similar dilemma. After a complaint by Asian Jews that he had profaned their precincts, Paul was detained by a Roman officer in the Judaean province in order to save him from being lynched. For two years he was interned at Caesarea, and then sent to Rome at his own request. Any Roman citizen could appeal to the emperor against a sentence that had been imposed on him. But this was apparently not quite the situation in the case of Paul, since the governor had not, as far as we know, ventured to try him at all. He could have done so if he had wished to, and there were some legal grounds for a charge of sedition. But he was only too glad to get rid of such an inflammable agitator. And so Paul was dispatched under military escort to Rome.

The voyage was eventful, and he was shipwrecked; but finally in 59 or 60 he arrived and was handed over to Burrus, as commander of the Praetorian Guard. Nevertheless, Paul was not detained, and we hear no more of the charge; but he spent two years in the capital, consorting very freely with all his fellow-Christians.[6] He recorded his intention of making a journey to Spain,[7] but we have no certain evidence that he went. Since he knew the Spaniard Gallio, he may conceivably also have been acquainted with Gallio's brother Seneca, whose philosophy contains, fortuitously, some of the same providential and moral conceptions as are to be found in early Christian ethics and theology, since these ideas were the common coin of contemporary thought. Later, an exchange of letters between the two men was forged. It also came to be believed that Peter and Paul were executed at Rome[8] – according to some accounts, both at the same time.[9] Relatively early versions of the story, dating from the third century, do not associate their deaths with the persecution following the fire, but the belief nevertheless grew that this had been the time when they were martyred.

Tacitus' version of the persecution veers between the notion that the Christians were convicted for arson and the view that they were attacked merely for being Christians. Even the most minute modern investigations of the historian's words – and such investigations have been numerous – do not clear up the confusion. Indeed, the same muddled attitudes existed among people in general at the time when the persecution took place. For the

obscurity was evidently exploited by the government, which tried to give the impression, in order to deal with this emergency, that the confession of Christian faith amounted to the same thing as an admission of arson.

Probably Nero and his advisers did not really believe that the Christians had set fire to Rome. But in order to divert attention from rumours that the emperor was to blame, they found it convenient to fasten on the most unpopular and defenceless group they could find. The Neronian persecution formed the prototype of others in later reigns. But it would be wrong to accept the implication, which might be deduced from Tacitus' words, that the Christians were attacked by Nero *because* they practised Christianity – that is to say, because they had failed to perform certain patriotic religious duties which it was normal for non-Christians to perform. It is improbable that Nero passed any measure which outlawed Christianity as such; legally the matter is likely to have remained indefinite.

Tacitus puts it concisely when he remarks that the Christians hated the human race. This was not a specific accusation in law, but in an inflamed situation it might very quickly lead to one. People who behaved with such suspicious strangeness could, at any time, find themselves accused of stirring up civil strife (*majestas*) or instigating public violence (*vis*).

What did this strangeness amount to? First of all, it was part of the strange-

above: St Peter and St Paul in a painting on wood of the eighth or ninth century.

The elegant stucco-work of the epoch, in an underground shrine (basilica) near the Porta Maggiore, Rome.

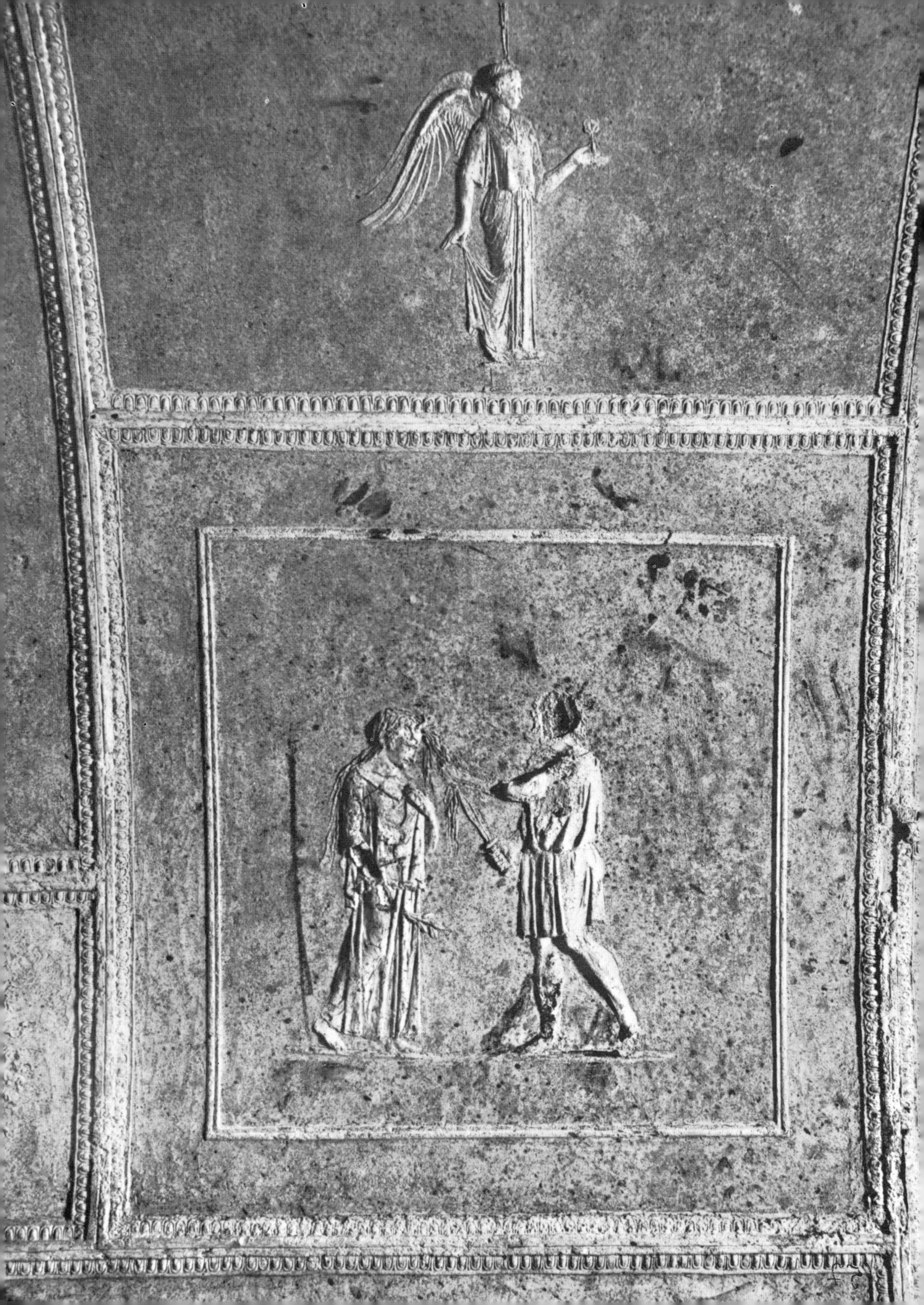

ness that clung to each and every foreign cult. There was a strong feeling that *only* the ancestral Roman gods ought to be worshipped, and that there was no proper way of doing this except according to the traditional procedures. Adherence to non-Roman religion was 'superstition': and that could easily imply crimes. It is true that throughout the centuries many eastern cults, even the most exotic and orgiastic ones, had been made respectable (or partially so) in Rome by being acclimatized there in temples of their own. It is also true that Nero, Poppaea, Otho and their friends freely exercised their personal tastes by favouring this or that oriental religion. But for others only slightly less privileged than themselves the peril was still not very far away.

There had been a *cause célèbre* on a charge of this kind only six years previously, when Pomponia Graecina, the wife of Aulus Plautius who had conquered Britain for Claudius, found herself arraigned for 'foreign superstition'.[10] The reasons for the accusation are not given. We are only told that after the murder of one of her relatives (an imperial lady) by Messalina, Pomponia had never stopped wearing mourning clothes and grieving. In other words she had shown herself 'different' from the community around her; and this alienation was made to look doubly suspicious by her interest in some eastern cult. The case was referred to her husband as head of the family: which rather suggests that the charge was the loose sexual behaviour attributed (sometimes rightly, sometimes wrongly) to oriental 'superstitions'. She was, as a matter of fact, acquitted; and went on wearing mourning for another thirty years. She may have been a Christian, for a century and a half later we hear of a Christian Pomponius Graecinus. But it is also possible that she was a Jew. The Jews too were 'different', because they could not subscribe entirely to the belief that the emperor was their one and only ruler. Indeed, it was a contemporary Jew, Josephus, who may have coined the word theocracy, the placing of all sovereignty and authority in the hands of God.[11] Thus the increasingly hostile emotions which the current wave of oriental religions inspired in the hearts of conservative Romans did not spare the Jews. And people knew who and what they were, because the capital contained a number of synagogues. Perhaps, by the end of the century, they totalled eleven or twelve; and the Jews, in the trans-Tiberine quarter where they lived, may have mustered a total congregation of some fifty thousand.

It was not only conservatives who disliked Judaism. Although a man of Jewish birth, Tiberius Julius Alexander, could reach the top of Nero's imperial service and the governorship of Egypt (admittedly after abandoning his religion), even the liberal Seneca speaks of the Jews in the same thoroughly hostile language that Tacitus and Suetonius use about Christianity. For he calls them 'that most criminal of races'.[12]

Why, then, did Nero, when he wanted scapegoats, not descend upon the Jews? One reason is likely to have been that they enjoyed the favour of Poppaea. But, in addition to that, an attack on the Jews of the capital would have had unfortunate repercussions on Roman administration in the east. This was because the flashpoint between Greeks and Jews was low. The governors of Egypt, Syria and Judaea were perpetually engaged in the delicate task of keeping the balance and the peace between these mutually and savagely hostile communities. And they by no means always decided in favour of the Greeks. As it happened, the discontents of the Jews in their homeland were at this very moment rising rapidly to a climax. To fall murderously upon their co-religionists in Rome would have been to invite the worst of troubles in Judaea and all the oriental provinces.

Jews and Christians   But the Christians were quite a different matter. The vast majority of Romans still did not distinguish them from the Jews. But those who were aware of the distinction could see clearly enough that to launch a persecution against this small group would not cause anything like the same adverse repercussions. There were, it is true, members of their faith in Nero's household;[13] he may even have had a Christian concubine.[14] But these were not people with anything like as much influence as the pro-Jewish empress, or Agrippa II, the Jewish client monarch of regions adjoining the Judaean province.

And the Jews themselves were most unlikely to sympathize with the Christians, or regret any misfortunes they might suffer. When Paul, a few years earlier, had arrived in the capital and requested support from the local Jewish leaders, they gave a non-committal answer – referring chiefly to

The version of Nero's portrait (showing him at about the age of thirty) favoured by his principal official mint in the western provinces (probably Lugdunum: Lyon).

all the reports they had heard against the Christians.[15] And then, after hearing him, they had been divided about whether to back him or not. But at Jerusalem, at just about the same time or slightly later, a fierce rift had developed between the Christians and Jews, whose high priest Ananus, profiting by an interregnum between Roman governors, arranged for James the Just, said to be the brother of Jesus, to be stoned to death (*c.* 62). And so now, only about two years later, the Jews would surely not make trouble if Nero persecuted the Christians.

In other respects, too, the latter made peculiarly suitable scapegoats. They kept themselves to themselves in an even more suspicious fashion than the Jews, indeed to a degree which, in an extrovert, nationally-minded community, must inevitably lead to hostile rumours. Their talk about universal love spread the belief that the religious services they conducted were orgies of sexual promiscuity and incest. The eucharist, with its symbolism of the body and blood of Christ, was widely regarded as a cannibalistic feast.

An unsolved mystery

But the worst suspicions of all were roused by the apocalyptic views passionately held by the early Christians. They still believed that the end of the world was very near, and that when it arrived the Second Coming of the Messiah would be accompanied by a general conflagration. 'The end of all things is at hand', wrote one of their leaders. 'Beloved, think it not strange concerning the *fiery trial* which is to try you. . . . But rejoice!'[16]

This attitude, of course, was known outside the community; and it made the Christians seem particularly suitable victims for the hysterical crowd. In the face of this belief in a universal holocaust – a much more imminent, indeed immediate, one than early pagan philosophers had believed in – it was little use for Paul, writing to the Christians in Rome some six years before the Fire, to remind them of Christ's instruction 'render unto Caesar', and reiterate that they should even bless their persecutors.[17] Although no one, on occasion, wrote more passionately about the Second Coming than Paul, he conceded that the doctrine of an imminent apocalypse might at times prove a dangerous liability to Christians, who were obliged, after all, to live their lives in the Graeco-Roman society of the day. But his impoverished audiences preferred to believe that their salvation was just round the corner; and that everything would then go up in flames.

Perhaps this happy process might be hastened on. Could it, then, have been the Christians who started the Great Fire, in the hope of achieving just this? Possibly. But it seems, on the whole, more probable that the whole thing was an accident, like all the many other fires that ravaged Rome every summer. Yet then we still have to explain the mysterious figures who appeared amid the flames and smoke, and prevented the fire-fighters from doing their job. Did these obstructors include not only looters but Christians: people who may not have started the fire, but now saw the hand of the Lord at work and sought to further its purpose? Again it could be so. But we shall never be sure.

One thing, however, we do know; or at least Tacitus tells us so, without there being, in this instance, any reason to doubt what he says. He reports that it proved possible to find people who admitted they were Christians –

and were prepared to implicate others. There are several tenable explanations of this, and they are not mutually exclusive. For one thing, any and every persecution finds out people who are too weak to withhold information under torture. Secondly, some of the confessions may also have been fakes, provided by secret agents of the government. But there was no doubt a third category also, consisting of Christians who were perfectly willing to die for their religion, as continued to be the case – to the never ending surprise and disgust of the Romans – in all later persecutions as well. Such martyrs could recall that, in spite of Paul's awareness of the need to keep in with the government, it was only a few years since he had extorted their own Roman congregation to 'present your bodies a living sacrifice',[18] though he did not at that time have the present appalling circumstances in mind.

For, whatever the emperor's personal objections to the death penalty may have been, his government executed the Christians in ways as unspeakably awful as any that Seneca had recently denounced.

Their deaths were made farcical. Dressed in wild animals' skins, they were torn to pieces by dogs, or crucified, or made into torches to be ignited after dark as substitutes for daylight. Nero provided his Gardens for the spectacle, and exhibited displays in the Circus, at which he mingled with the crowd – or stood in a chariot, dressed as a charioteer.[19]

Nero as Anti-Christ It is hardly surprising that later Christians believed that Nero had been the Anti-Christ (see Appendix 1). But the attitude of Suetonius was strangely different. Referring to the 'punishment inflicted on the Christians', he describes them as 'a class of men given to a new and mischievous superstition',[20] and he lists the persecution among Nero's good deeds.

As regards the immediate object of the executions, however, the government's tactics misfired. They had not reckoned with the fact that the populace of Rome, though revelling constantly in the most brutal gladiatorial displays and beast-fights, occasionally revealed a collective warm heart. They had shown it twice previously in Nero's reign, once when a lot of innocent slaves were going to be executed, and again when his guiltless young wife Octavia was being divorced. Now, once again, they felt sorry for the wretched victims. 'Despite their guilt as Christians, and the ruthless punishment it deserved, they were pitied. For it seemed that they were being sacrificed to one man's brutality rather than to the national interest.'[21]

10 The Golden House: Art and Luxury

Nero did everything possible to make good the damage caused by the fire. The buildings chosen for early reconstruction were a judicious blend of religious shrines and public amenities: the coinage of the year depicts the rebuilt Temple of Vesta[1] and the Provision Market. Nor was it forgotten that a good way to recapture popular favour was to rebuild the Circus Maximus and bring it into use again.

Enormous numbers of private houses had also been destroyed, and the emperor was ready with an ambitious urbanization scheme.

In such parts of Rome as were unoccupied by Nero's palace, construction was not – as after the burning by the Gauls – without plan or demarcation. Street-fronts were of regulated dimensions and alignment, streets were broad, and houses spacious. Their height was restricted, and their frontages protected by colonnades. Nero undertook to erect these at his own expense, and also to clear debris from building-sites before transferring them to their owners. He announced bonuses, in proportion to rank and resources, for the completion of houses and blocks before a given date. Rubbish was to be dumped in the Ostian marshes, by corn-ships returning down the Tiber.

A fixed proportion of every building had to be massive, untimbered stone from Gabii or the quarries near Alba Longa (these stones being fire-proof). Householders were obliged to keep fire-fighting apparatus in an accessible place, and semi-detached houses were forbidden – they must have their own walls.[2]

Tacitus adds that special guards were appointed to protect the public water-supply, hitherto encroached upon by illegal private enterprise. And the volume of water which poured into Rome was more abundant and extensive than hitherto, because Nero supplemented existing aqueducts by a number of extensions.

His residential Rome has vanished, but some idea of his intentions and ambitions can be obtained from the later apartment houses and blocks still to be seen at the harbour city of Ostia. Houses henceforward were not allowed to exceed a certain height – perhaps fixed at seventy or eighty feet – and the emperor proposed to do away with the rickety tenements which had long imperilled the capital.

'These measures', comments Tacitus, 'were welcomed for their practic-

ality, and they beautified the new city. Some, however, believed that the old town's configuration had been healthier, since its narrow streets and high houses had provided protection against the burning sun, whereas now the shadowless open spaces radiated a fiercer heat.'[3] Modern, northern commentators have been inclined to brush aside this criticism of the new broad streets as reactionary. But in a Mediterranean summer such avenues are only tolerable if there are trees, or alternatively the covered, colonnaded or arcaded sidewalks still to be found in many Italian towns. And Nero, too, was well aware of the value of covered galleries. For even if some of his new streets were unshaded, the most important of all, the Sacred Way, was flanked by roofed arcades on either side. At last Rome's narrow main street had a worthy setting.

But its setting was planned in relation to the imperial residence to which it led. Earlier in his reign, Nero had already constructed impressive edifices for his own accommodation. His elegantly decorated mansion on the Palatine had been joined to the imperial Gardens of Maecenas on the Esquiline. Remains of this linking Domus Transitoria, which spanned the Velian slope beside the Forum, have been found beneath the later Temple of Venus and Rome, where Nero erected a domed building intersected by barrel-vaulted halls in the shape of a Greek cross.

Now, however, the Domus Transitoria was to become the mere entrance hall to a new and vastly greater palace. This Domus Aurea, the Golden House, was to take in a very large area of Rome. For it included not only the

The Domus Transitoria and the Domus Aurea

Domus Transitoria and the mansions and gardens it had bridged but also the valley behind the linking building, where the Colosseum stands today, as well as a sizable region beyond – perhaps extending right up the Viminal hill as far as the present railway station. All this comprised a very substantial portion of the most thickly inhabited zone of the city. At the most modest estimate the park covered 125 acres, more than half as large again as the whole of the present Vatican, including its garden and St Peter's. But others believe that Nero's domain covered three hundred and seventy acres – the size of Hyde Park. And that is probably nearer the truth. No wonder nasty verses were going the rounds.

> The Palace is spreading and swallowing Rome!
> Let us all flee to Veii and make it our home.
> Yet the Palace is growing so damnably fast
> That it threatens to gobble up Veii at last.[4]

Whatever the exact size of the palace grounds may have been, it is clear that never before or since, in the whole course of European history, has a monarch carved out for his own residence such an enormous area in the very heart of his capital.

The new palace itself was not a single building, but many separate ones – and they were to be set among magnificent landscapes. This was to be the formula of Hadrian's Villa at Tibur (Tivoli), and then of the Sultans' Seraglio at Istanbul. But the same sort of thing was already familiar in the ancient world from Hellenistic palaces such as the Prytaneum of Antigonus Gonatas at Balla (Palatitsa) in Macedonia; and these complexes, in turn, 'th their landscape architecture of kiosks and pavilions and arcades and colonnades distributed round parks and framed in tasteful vistas, went back to the 'paradises' of Persian rulers, which themselves were derived (like Chinese palaces also) from earlier Iranian or Babylonian models. In Italy the same pattern had appeared on the Tyrrhenian coast, and then at Rome, in the extravagant villas of the late Republic. For example the notorious Clodia, Cicero's enemy, had left the elegant colonnades of her Palatine mansion open to the surrounding parklands, without Roman privacy – and, as critics were quick to point out, without Roman modesty either. Now Nero greatly enlarged this villa formula, transforming it by bold and spectacular planning into something altogether more impressive.

The architect-engineers whom he appointed to fulfil and excel this tradition were Severus and Celer, presumably Italian bosses presiding over an army of eastern technicians – the sort of people who were flocking profitably to Rome under Nero as never before. Tacitus is unenthusiastic about the whole project.

> Nero profited by his country's ruin to build a new palace. Its wonders were not so much customary and commonplace luxuries like gold and jewels but lawns and lakes and faked rusticity – woods here, open spaces and views there. With their cunning, impudent artificialities, Severus and Celer did not balk at effects that nature herself had ruled out as impossible.[5]

This was the romantic Italian pseudo-rustic ideal of contemporary painters, and of poets such as Petronius.

> The tall plane-tree disposes summer shade,
> Metamorphosed Daphne nearby, crowned with berries.
> Cypresses tremulous, clipped pines around
> Shuddering at their tops.
>   Playing among them
> A stream with wandering waters,
> Spume-flecked, worrying the stones
>   With a querulous spray.
>   A place fit for love.[6]

Suetonius further describes Nero's estate: 'An enormous pool, more like a sea than a pool, was surrounded by buildings made to resemble cities, and by a landscape garden consisting of ploughed fields, vineyards, pastures and wood-lands – where every variety of domestic and wild animal roamed about'.[7] The stretch of water to which he refers was a huge lake on the site of a former swamp at the bottom of the valley, where the Colosseum now stands.

As for the buildings, they were approached through the Domus Transitoria, between the Esquiline and Palatine Hills. This was now transfigured by the erection of what Suetonius describes as a mile-long 'triple' colonnade, that is to say perhaps a portico of three rows of columns, or more probably a colonnade divided into three parts where it was penetrated by the Sacred Way and New Way; its remains, mostly of travertine, are found scattered over the area. From now on, despite its huge size, the Domus Transitoria was to serve merely as a vestibule for the various buildings that comprised the Golden House – though admittedly a monumental vestibule, and indeed

An architectural fantasy, showing Neronian tastes, as the backcloth for a performance of the *Medea*. From Pompeii.

no other portion of the Golden House was designed on such a monumental scale as this earlier building that it incorporated.

As for the other buildings, the new ones, they were scattered about well behind the portico. In particular, there was one layout away on the right, and a large edifice to the left. To the right, upon the Caelian Hill, was a picturesque colonnaded retreat for plants, flowers and running water, adorned with grottoes and statues and related to the adjoining Temple of Claudius, in which Nero's interest was architectural rather than pious. Only heaps of masonry now record these various creations. But of the buildings to the left, standing roughly at right angles to the vestibule, much still survives today. Here, along the Oppian spur of the Esquiline Hill, stood the main residential section of the Golden House. It seems to have been some-what hidden away from the approaching visitor, whose eye it may only have struck when he came quite close and caught sight of its long and graceful colonnade.

But the sightseer today must be prepared for a great disappointment. It is true that these lofty, cavernous, brick-worked rooms and corridors show, dimly, something of Nero's architectural and decorative taste. However, they cast an impossible strain on our imagination, because they are so com-pletely shut in, and terribly dark. Originally they must have stood wide open to the sun and air, looking out over the artfully contrived landscape. But only half a century after Nero's death, the openings were all blocked up.

Although it is virtually impossible for the modern visitor to detect the fact on the spot, the Golden House was something of an architectural marvel. It consisted of unequal, asymmetrical, west and east wings, now only one but originally two or perhaps even three storeys high. It was a shallow build-ing with rows of small rooms facing on to a long, straight portico. But at the junction of the two wings this façade was broken and cut in two unequal portions by a five-sided, colonnaded courtyard (now inaccessible), with a larger sixth side open at the front. This attractive arrangement of two long wings divided by a courtyard, with their entire front consisting of a row of columns, was not new, because it is shown on a painting executed about a generation earlier for the house of Lucretius Fronto at Pompeii. But evidently the formula had never before been applied on so grand a scale.

Immediately behind the hexagonal courtyard is a central room known as the Hall of the Golden Vault. It leads back to a long corridor which ran the whole length of the building. Here at the rear there could be no second façade, because the back of the structure abutted directly upon the rising slope of the hill, from which it was insulated by the corridor in order to provide protection from landslides.

In the longer of the two wings, to the west of the courtyard, the front rooms include two similar suites, each containing a bedroom, two other rooms and a chapel. These suites have been tentatively identified as the personal apart-ments of Nero and Poppaea; though it must be regarded as more probable that the emperor and empress lived on the sumptuous second storey, now vanished, which corresponded with the *piano nobile* of Renaissance palaces. These rooms on the western side looked out on to the open air at the back as well as the front, because immediately behind them, adjoining or cut out of the slope of the hill, was a second courtyard (again invisible today), this time of oblong shape, and containing a fountain in the middle.

The east wing was both shorter and shallower, because the hill encroached more closely both on its flank and on its rear. Perhaps this wing represents a later stage in the plan, because it does not seem to have been finished in Nero's lifetime. Even so, he himself had already modified the original design, as certain inconsequences and walled-in spaces show. But the most important modification consisted of the interruption of the frontal rooms of this wing, at their central point, by an octagonal hall. Here, at last, is something which can still be seen. The hall is crowned by a dome, constructed by means of the revolutionary Roman invention of concrete, which architects were using with the ever greater confidence that would soon produce Hadrian's Pantheon. This octagon is one of the first known examples of the use of brick-faced concrete on an ambitious scale, and it possesses features which give it special interest in the history of architecture.

Like the circular Pantheon later on, the octagon was lit from a round hole in the centre of the cupola. Further lighting was provided by a series of small apertures (no longer to be seen) in the circular crown or rim between walls and dome. The walls were insubstantial, being broken at ground level by large openings separated by quite slender piers incorporating attached columns. The openings on the three southernmost faces of the octagon gave out onto the frontal colonnade, and the park beyond: which suggests that the octagon formed a kind of entrance hall. Four more of the openings, two on either side, radiated out into vaulted rooms, two cross-shaped and two square. And the eighth aperture, at the back, contained a flight of steps down which ran a stream of water channelled through the centre of the hall – an idea which had been tried out, on a smaller scale, in Roman coastal villas, and was to reappear in the sixteenth-century palaces and gardens of the Moguls.

Centralized, concrete-backed buildings invited experiments in vaulting, and here in the cupola we find a vault of the kind known as 'domical' or 'cloister'. Severus and Celer, as far as we know, were the first architects to

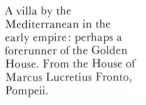

A villa by the Mediterranean in the early empire: perhaps a forerunner of the Golden House. From the House of Marcus Lucretius Fronto, Pompeii.

display and put into effect, on a large scale, an understanding of the uses of vaults. In addition, they were so fascinated by the manipulation of space that the masonry framework was pared down to a minimum and almost lost its traditional function. The spatial possibilities of the interiors of buildings spurred them on to an achievement which the architects of classical Greece had possessed neither the wish nor the technical ability to foreshadow. Nero's architects, writes John Ward-Perkins, 'came squarely up against the problem of interior space, in a context that demanded a solution from the inside outwards rather than from the outside inwards'. Structures such as this octagon were revolutionary achievements which set the pattern for later Rome and Europe.

In addition to all these architectural features, the Golden House was full of technical novelties, mechanical wonders, and curious gadgets. The baths

The frontage of the Golden House, overlooking its great park, must have been rather like these façades on paintings from Pompeii.

The octagonal hall of the Golden House.

were served by a flow of both salt and sulphurous water. The music room contained the largest and most powerful hydraulic organ that had ever been built. There were dining rooms with ceilings of fretted ivory, containing moving panels which showered down flowers on the diners, and squirted them with scent from hidden pipes. Seneca knew other mechanical ceiling devices of a similar kind, consisting of movable parts which could present a different pattern for every course of a dinner-party.

The main banqueting-hall of the Golden House, which has not survived, is described by Suetonius as 'circular, and constantly revolving, day and night, like the heavens'.[8] It has been much disputed, without any clear solution, whether the whole room was constructed to revolve, like a merry-go-round, or whether the spherical ceiling and dome were all that moved. In any case, the motive power must have been provided by some considerable source of energy, probably combining the principles of water-mill and water-clock. Whatever the exact method used, it was clearly the last word in technical progress, the final luxury product of centuries of research by the scientists of Alexandria.

'*Lover of the incredible*' Some contemporaries, men like the elder Pliny, were pessimistic about the possibilities of any real scientific progress at all. But these technical developments in the Golden House are closer to the spirit of Seneca, who at about this very time, in his retirement, was expressing an extremely hopeful attitude on the subject – though it must be added that one of his literary letters, written around this time, contained criticisms of just the sort of luxuries that were displayed in the Golden House. As for Nero, he adored these innovations and discoveries, especially if there was something sensational about them. Tacitus aptly called him 'a lover of the incredible';[9] and the

A model showing the vault of the octagonal hall.

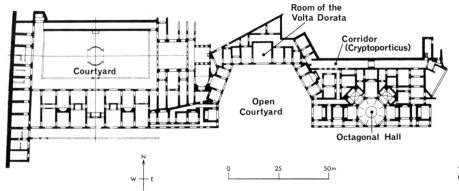

Courtyard

Open
Courtyard

Octagonal Hall

N
W—E
S

0   25   50m

A plan of the
Golden House.

architects and engineers of the Golden House had a wonderful opportunity
to satisfy this taste.

So had the other artists employed on the project. Again there was an
emphasis on novelty. Inventions of the time included marble stained in
artificial colours or given artificial spots;[10] and such tricks were no doubt in
evidence at the Golden House. A temple of Fortune, in its grounds, was made
of a stone recently discovered in Asia Minor which was transparent and
enabled light to enter the building even when the doors were closed. In the
palace itself, walls were studded with precious stones, and rooms set aside
for love-making were adorned with pearls.[11] There were also said to be rooms
where the walls and ceilings were covered with plates of gold. But that may
be an exaggerated description of the gilt stucco which was used, for example,
in the Hall of the Golden Vault. The Vault is a sad and poignant sight today,
but fortunately, before deterioration, its beauties were investigated by
artists at the sixteenth-century court of Pope Leo x and made the subject of
a detailed water-colour reproduction by Francesco d'Olanda.

Above all, the Golden House provided a fabulous opportunity for mural
painters. Most Romans did not enormously admire artists; and even Seneca,
as an educationalist, refused to allow art a place in the curriculum at all,
following the tradition which down-graded its practitioners to the status of
artisans. His pupil Nero, however, is known to have been interested in
painting, and the Golden House and its frescoes surely owe a very great deal
to his own personal initiative (the term fresco, implying work on damp
mortar, is used loosely, since other techniques that permitted more careful
retouching were also involved). Many of these paintings, and the stucco
patterns with which they alternated and blended, have survived on the spot;
and although they are now deprived of the airy, gay light in which they were
intended to be bathed, their delicate *chic* can still be discerned amid the
encircling gloom.

In contrast to Pompeii, where the basic colour is red, here it is white.

*The mural paintings
of the Golden House*

Expanses of white ground on walls and ceiling are covered with an open, widely-spaced network of painted panels, framed by plain lines or fragile, filigreed trellises. Often the centres of the painted panels form leafy squares occupied by groups of birds or animals, or by tiny free-standing human figures, realistic or fantastic. When they came to light in the early sixteenth century, these elegant decorative schemes profoundly affected Raphael and his school. They are echoed in the painting and stucco on the Vatican Loggia (by Giovanni da Udine) and many another Italian building, as well as in the Gallery of François I at Fontainebleau. The Hall of the Golden Vault was especially influential, and so were paintings in the rear corridor: high up on its walls are the signatures of numerous Renaissance artists who came to see the place. Our word 'grotesque' is derived from the term *grottesca* ('belonging to a cave') that they applied to these paintings and stuccoes because the Golden House, which they found far beneath the ground, seemed like a subterranean cavern.

One tall, vaulted gallery contains panel paintings of imitation windows revealing romantic landscapes like the parks of the Golden House itself. Elsewhere there are large mythological scenes, such as 'Hector's Parting from Andromache' (is this the room where Nero recited his epic *The Trojan War*?) On the whole, however, the artists preferred to subordinate their panels to the general design of wall and vault, and to blend human bodies impressionistically into the painted architectural frameworks of their designs. The ceilings are particularly successful – though it must be regarded as a lapse of judgment that even at this great height the pictures have the same miniature scale as others lower down; and large rooms are treated in just the same way as small ones.

This kind of decoration was inspired by the discovery of the Golden House in the early sixteenth century. These paintings by Giulio Romano and Primaticcio are in the Palazzo del Te, Mantua (Casino della Grotta).

These styles have many forerunners, notably at Pompeii and in a little Roman 'columbarium' on the Appian Way which lodged the ashes of the household of Livia, the wife of Augustus. But the Neronian climax is delightfully crisp and vivid. Presumably the main part of the achievement must be credited to Nero's chief painter, whose name has come down to us as either Famulus or Fabullus. A specialist in combining painting with stucco, he was famous for his fresh colours, and also, we are told, for a picture of Minerva whose eyes seemed turned to the spectator from whatever side she was viewed. Pliny remarks that it was bad luck for him to be tied down to the Golden House, which became the prison of his art.[12] On the other hand, the chance the job gave him was something few artists have ever known before or since. One cannot say for certain which of the paintings are by him and which by his helpers. But it is possible to hazard the guess that he was not quite as outstanding as the architects of the building; he was not one of the world's greatest painters, but an inspired interior decorator. Even while painting on the scaffold, we are told, he still worked in his formal Roman toga. This was to emphasize the importance of his role, as a Roman directing a team of Greek or oriental assistants. The toga may also have been intended to assert the dignity of the Artist, against the deprecatory view held by Seneca and many others. If so, Famulus, or Fabullus, no doubt enjoyed his emperor's support.

An eighteenth-century drawing of a ceiling of the Golden House which has now disappeared.

The collection of sculpture

Nero had long been as greatly interested in sculpture as in painting; and for the Golden House he commissioned an enormous statue of himself. Its sculptor Zenodorus is known to have been paid a huge sum for another statue, an image of Mercury he made for the Gallic town of Augustodunum (Autun); and he was also a well-known copier of antique cups. His effigy of Nero, which stood between 110 and 120 feet high, was erected as the centre-piece for the vestibule of the palace (the rebuilt Domus Transitoria) where it probably stood within a central colonnaded court overlooking the Forum. The emperor's brow was crowned with rays, suggesting a comparison or identification with the Sun-god. Later, Vespasian took off the head altogether, replacing it with another which represented the Sun without any resemblance to Nero. And then Hadrian in the following century, to make room for his Temple of Venus and Rome, had the statue moved down into the valley – mobilizing twenty-four elephants for the purpose. This Colossus, as it was called, long continued to be regarded with superstitious awe as a guarantee of Rome's eternity: every year, on a certain day, its pedestal was heaped with offerings of flowers. Now it is no more, though the building which still towers up beside its site is named after it, the Colosseum.

Nero's interest in sculpture also led him to collect as many of the world's masterpieces as possible in his own residence. Some were lodged in his other mansions at Sublaqueum (Subiaco) and Antium, and excavations at both places have yielded famous antique statues. But the majority of the acquisitions were destined for the suitable niches which abound at the Golden House. It is there, for example, that the representation of Laocoon and his two sons wrestling with a serpent – now to be seen in the Vatican museum – was found in 1506. This group, it is true, may not have been brought to the Domus

Aurea until after Nero was dead, but the importations for which he himself was responsible comprised equally or even more famous statues by Praxiteles and other Greek sculptors, who at this time fetched enormous prices.

In order to get hold of such works, the emperor sent two envoys all round Greece and Asia Minor. Tacitus dates their mission to the time after the Fire, when the Golden House was being built. But he also happens to reveal that one of them, the freedman Acratus, had already been engaged on this job a few years earlier, because he mentions that the governor of Asia was Barea Soranus (61–62), who refused, according to the historian, to punish the city of Pergamum for failing to hand its treasures over. Acratus, then, had begun his mission before the Fire, though after it he was probably given an even more comprehensive commission. His colleague was Secundus Carrinas, probably a well-known rhetorician's son, who was able to console the plundered Greeks by philosophic sayings culled from their own literature.

The remains of Nero's villa at Sublaqueum (Subiaco), forty-six miles east of Rome. At a banquet here his table was struck by lightning. The substructures of the villa are still visible on the sides of the valley of the River Anio (Aniene). The extensive lake he created by damming the valley vanished when the dam was destroyed by a flood in 1305.

It was imputed against Nero that he committed sacrilege by seizing works of art from temples, including famous shrines not only in Greece but at Rome itself. This sacrilege, it was said, caused Seneca such pain that he sought permission to retire to a distant country retreat, and, when that was refused, feigned a muscular complaint and took to his bedroom. Whether the story about Seneca is true or not, Nero certainly must have taken objects from temples, because that is where many of the best things were. The ancient writers state or imply that he paid nothing for what he took, either now or on the later occasion when he visited Greece himself. But that is doubtful, since it is part of the hostile tradition represented, for example, by the traveller Pausanias who quoted the unlikely report that he removed five hundred statues from Delphi alone. The city of Rhodes, in whose interests Nero had delivered a speech when he was a youth, was evidently more or less spared, because we happen to know that it still possessed three thousand pieces of sculpture in the following decade.

When the Golden House was dedicated, the emperor remarked: 'At last I am able to live as a human being should!' It was his refuge, his paradise, the masterpiece he had created himself and for himself, an exemplar of fashion

right: The Baths of Trajan: the approach to what is left of Nero's palace.

overleaf: The Golden House – two of the surviving rooms, of which the original appearance is greatly altered owing to the masses of masonry that have been superimposed and now block the openings.

left: The Laocoon group, a Rhodian work perhaps of *c.* 175–150 BC, was found in 1506 on the site of the Golden House to which Nero (or one of his successors?) brought it. Laocoon (whose right arm has recently been changed from the straight position in which it was restored by Giovanni Montorsoli in 1531) was the priest of Apollo who warned the Trojans against the Wooden Horse and was strangled with his sons by snakes sent by his god.

The garden of the House
of the Vettii at Pompeii
gives some idea of the life
of the rich under Nero.

and taste. The project gave point and spice to his further remark that no
ruler, ever before, had really appreciated what power he possessed. And
indeed, the realization of the project may have helped to unhinge his mind
and character, illustrating the verdict of Josephus that he became unbalanced
owing to an excess of riches and pleasures. This was the process of deterioration later worked out in detail by Tacitus. He saw Nero as just another of
the sinister members of the dynasty, who all in turn went to the bad in one
way or another.

The fate of the Golden House

Some of the paintings in the Golden House may belong to slightly later
reigns. For, however much its novelties and pretensions must have scandal-
ized many Romans, the palace was still in occupation during the year after
Nero's death, when his former friend Otho, emperor for a few months, was
voted fifty million sesterces for its upkeep. However, Otho's equally short-
lived successor Vitellius disliked the Golden House, and his wife ridiculed
the decoration, which was presumably too graceful for her taste. Or perhaps
they found the whole place not grandiose enough, no doubt recalling that
even mansions of the later Republic, more than a century earlier, had been
designed on a more monumental scale; and in their day the habit was about
to return, in accentuated form.

So the objection to the Golden House was not its splendour. The trouble
was rather that these vast domains, in the words of the poet Martial, had
'robbed the poor of places to live'[13] – not to speak of grave encroachment on
the highways and amenities of the city. It was indefensible that so large a
central portion of the capital should be the dwelling of one man, even if he
was the emperor himself. For that reason, Vespasian (69–79) demolished
most of the Golden House, retaining just a relatively small section in which
he himself lived, as did his son (who built Baths nearby). That is why the
Laocoon group, later found on the site, was said by Pliny the elder to belong
to the 'palace of Titus'.[14] Finally Trajan, building his own Baths – through
which lies the modern access to the Golden House – closed the openings
with huge heaps of rubble so that now its daring architectural forms and
brilliant paintings can only dimly be glimpsed.

Pompeii and Herculaneum

As we can tell from Pompeii and Herculaneum, the styles of painting to be
seen in the Golden House were not entirely novel; while they in turn
exercised a reverse influence on the subsequent art of those cities. Pompeii
and Herculaneum, both a few miles from Neapolis (Naples), were destroyed
by an eruption of Vesuvius eleven years after Nero's death. But while he was
still on the throne they were attacked by an earlier, premonitory disaster,
the earthquake of 5 February, AD 62. This upheaval, which is graphically
described by Seneca[15] and represented on two marble reliefs at Pompeii,
partially destroyed both these towns, as well as inflicting slighter damage at
Neapolis and Nuceria (Nocera). But the earthquake also performed the
same sort of cultural service as the Great Fire of Rome, which followed two
years later. That is to say, the reconstructions that ensued gave artists an
extraordinary opportunity – which they promptly and abundantly took.[16]

Some of the work at the Vesuvian cities which was done during the years

immediately after the earthquake shows the direct influence of the Golden House. But careful inspection suggests that a good many pictures of similar styles at Pompeii and Herculaneum antedate the earthquake. Seen in this light, the subsequent paintings in the Golden House turn out to be not so much innovations as stages, important but not wholly original. For its so-called Fourth or Fantastic or Intricate Style is also characteristic of Neronian frescoes at these towns, where it had started more than a decade earlier – even before the accession of Nero, who thus appears as its stimulator rather than its originator. But the spirit of Nero and his age is often to be seen. Sometimes architectural fantasies depicted on Pompeiian walls are reminiscent of stage sets. Moreover, actual performances are recalled by panel pictures which portray fashionable, mythological, theatrical scenes of just the kind in which the emperor liked to sing and act himself. There is a discreet reference to him in repeated depictions of the infant Hercules strangling a snake that had been sent to kill him; Nero liked being compared to Hercules (and there was a story that, when he was a little boy, thugs sent by Messalina to slay him had been scared away by a serpent).[17]

In the House of Pinarius Cerealis at Pompeii, a whole wall is painted as a stage, on which Euripides' tragedy *Iphigenia in Tauris* is in the process of being acted. Nero took many of his parts from the morbid, pathetic Euripides; and there is also much of the baroque melodrama of Seneca in these paintings. The ancient myths, far from dead, are given new thrust and movement, with crowded groupings and complicated spatial effects. Thus a picture of *Theseus and the Athenian Captives* from Pompeii displays a sharply vivid contrast between calm Theseus and the eager huddle of prisoners. Nero's own special poetic interest in the Trojan War has its counterparts in many a fresco. One of them, in the House of the Cryptoporticus at Pompeii, is a frieze with scenes from the *Iliad* in white on a blue ground; they may have been derived from

above and below: The two reliefs of the household shrine of Lucius Caecilius Jucundus showing the earthquake which partially destroyed Pompeii in AD 62.

some illustrated manuscript now lost. The fight beside the ships at Troy was another theme which painters, like contemporary poets, never tired of.

There is also a dramatic, eerie picture of the Trojan Horse insinuated into the doomed city.[18] In a flickering light behind the urgent figures is a dim landscape, amid towers and walls. Neronian artists felt the same love of landscape which prompted their emperor to create the parklands of his Golden House, and the frescoes of the time not only comprise part of the architecture of the buildings they adorn, but form an annex to the gardens as well. The paintings at Pompeii and Herculaneum range from realistic or romantic parks, rugged hills, pastoral compositions, and views of sea coasts, to the favourite, traditional theme of sacred enclosures with rustic shrines and holy trees.

Often these landscapes, like the architectural fantasies, display pygmy human beings. These are not the familiar, monumental personages of the big mythological scenes, or the skilful portraits at which these painters also excelled. They are smaller, more insubstantial and more light-hearted figures. As in the Golden House, little human forms are inserted, with grace and irony, into these dream-like frameworks, floating and flitting on their lofty cornices, or balancing on an architrave to play with a peacock.

The taste of the age There was also in Rome, we are told (though examples do not seem to have survived), a following for a famous and expensive painter called Piraeicus, who in about the third century BC had specialized in depicting commonplace objects, barbers' shops, cobblers' stalls, donkeys and food.[19] We can do without another artist, a freedman of Nero's from Antium, who painted realistic pictures of gladiatorial shows.[20] This distasteful theme has survived from later epochs, in the more durable medium of the floor mosaic. But so have Pompeian mosaics of about Nero's time which correspond with surviving descriptions of a mosaicist of the second century BC, Sosus of Pergamum. One of his masterpieces, according to Pliny the elder, was a realistic depiction of the refuse lying about on a dining-room floor;[21] and we have a mosaic showing just such a scene. Another of Sosus' famous efforts, we are told, portrayed a pigeon drinking, and mosaics on this theme, too, have survived; Neronian Pompeii provides examples, and a copy from Hadrian's villa at Tibur (Tivoli) shows one bird drinking while others stand.

Such studies, like artistic manifestations of any age, were subjected to the usual sort of ultra-conservative, uncomprehending Philistine criticism. Thus Petronius quotes his fictitious, fatuous professor Eumolpus as declaring that the current art 'copies only the faults of antiquity, not its merits'. Yet, even if Sosus and the like encouraged frivolities, the age of Nero was a time of genuine artistic achievement. And for this the taste of the emperor was in large part responsible.

Luxury and extravagance However, there was also a reverse side of this attractive picture. For if Nero's interests stimulated the arts, they also caused him to indulge in staggering luxury and extravagance.

He had always been surrounded by people who encouraged him in this direction. Otho, before he was sent away so as to leave Poppaea available for

Nero, had done a lot to show his emperor how to live in the grand manner. And then came the turn of Petronius:

Petronius spent his days sleeping, his nights working and enjoying himself. Others achieve fame by energy, Petronius by laziness. Yet he was not, like others who waste their resources, regarded as dissipated or extravagant, but as a refined voluptuary. People liked the apparent freshness of his unconventional and unselfconscious sayings and doings.

It is true that, as governor of Bithynia and later as consul, he had displayed capacity for business. But then, reverting to a vicious or ostensibly vicious way of life, he had been admitted into the small circle of Nero's intimates, as Arbiter of Taste: to the blasé emperor, smartness and elegance were restricted to what Petronius had approved.[22]

For example, Petronius appears to have given the *coup de grâce* to the fashion for roses. It had been customary, in stylish circles, to spend a very great deal of money on roses for banquets. On one occasion a friend of Nero spent four million sesterces on the roses for a single meal. Winter roses were greatly in demand. Often they were shipped from Egypt, but some were cultivated in Italy under glass. A fresco in the House of the Vettii at Pompeii shows the manufacture of attar of roses in that town. But then Petronius, in the *Satyricon,* decreed that roses were unfashionable; and so, therefore, they are quite likely to have become.

> Wives are out of fashion. Better get a girl friend –
> A little more expensive but really very nice.
> Rose leaves are out of date,
> Cinnamon's the thing now.
> Anything hard to get is well worth the price.[23]

However, as purveyor of the imperial amusements, Petronius had to compete with the guard commander Tigellinus, who owed much of his influence over Nero to his reputation as a giver of parties.

Nero gave feasts in public places as if the whole city were his own home. But the most prodigal and notorious banquet was given by Tigellinus. . . . The party took place on a raft constructed on Agrippa's lake. It was towed about by other vessels, with gold and ivory fittings. Their rowers were degenerates, assorted according to age and vice. Tigellinus had also collected birds and animals from remote countries, and even the products of the ocean. On the quays were brothels stocked with high-ranking ladies. Opposite them could be seen naked prostitutes, indecently posturing and gesturing. At nightfall the woods and houses all around echoed with singing and blazed with light.[24]

The emperor obviously loved that kind of entertainment. Yet he was by no means an imperial gourmand of the calibre of his step-father Claudius. We are not told if Nero was amused by the famous contemporary glutton Arpocras, who ate four tablecloths at a time, and broken glass as well. As regards drink, there are a number of references to his doing quite well himself. However his own contribution to the pleasures of the table, in the shape

above: Portrait of a lady, from Hawara, Egypt. Third quarter of the first century AD.

right: A stucco relief of Dionysus (Bacchus) with Ariadne, at Pompeii, symbolizing an age of sumptuous banquets and of the cult of Dionysus, with its promise of an after-life.

overleaf: One of the major paintings of the Neronian age: the horse in the doomed city of Troy. The Trojan War was a theme dear to the emperor, and the air of sinister mystery in such pictures recalls the contemporary poetry of Lucan and Seneca.

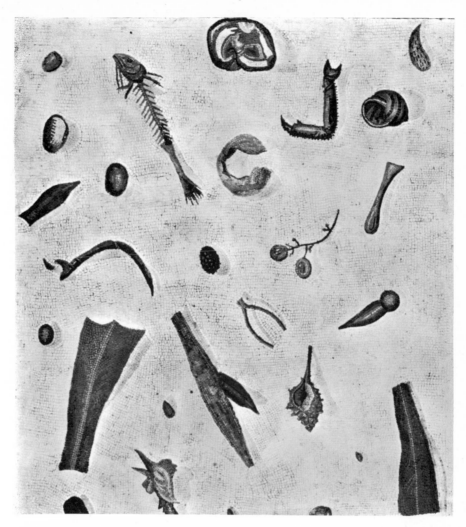

of a drink he personally invented, was neither gross nor even alcoholic. For this *decocta Neronis* consisted merely of water, first boiled, and then cooled in a glass vessel which was plunged into snow.[25]

All the same, in spite of the requirements of vocal and athletic training, he did spend a tremendous amount of time reclining at meals and banquets – sometimes from noon (instead of the usual afternoon hour) continually until midnight. The job of the emperor's cupbearer was evidently an important one. Nero's occupant of the office, Pythagoras, with whom he perhaps had a homosexual association, was still spoken of as a famous cupbearer twenty-five years later. Another very responsible post was that of imperial taster of food and wine, an office which went back to the time of Augustus. Halotus, holder of this office at the death of Claudius (which he was suspected of having hastened), seems to have made a good subsequent career, reaching the position of imperial agent under Nero's successor. It is strange to find that a young prince like Britannicus, even when dining in the company of the emperor, took his taster with him, and let him taste everything first; though in Britannicus' case that did not prevent him from being poisoned, since

above: The Portland Vase, dating from the time of Augustus, is made of relatively cheap paste or cameo glass: but it suggests the appearance of the precious cups and vases which Nero loved.

nobody tasted the water which was added to his wine. We have inscriptions of one of Nero's food tasters, a man who also served on his bedroom staff.[26] Another inscription refers to the association *(collegium)* to which these men belonged.[27] If they did their job well (and survived), they could be promoted to chief butler, or superintendent of the imperial table.

Even if Nero was not a great eater or an exceptional drinker, the appurtenances of his meals were tremendously luxurious. They included 'myrrhine' cups and bowls, which were made of some very rare material, perhaps fluor-spar, obtained, for the most part, from Carmania (south-east Persia). These vessels were said to possess a delicate scent. Fragile and sometimes iridescent, they were prized for their colouring, which was white or purple or dark red. Nero paid a million sesterces for one cup of this sort. He also very much wanted to get hold of another worth a mere three hundred thousand that belonged to Petronius, but the latter, when at last he fell out with Nero and was forced to commit suicide, displayed a final piece of retaliatory bitchiness and broke the cup to prevent the emperor from getting hold of it. Nero himself, when he flew into a temper on hearing of the rebellion at the end of his reign, knocked over the table by his side and broke two extremely valuable crystal cups, engraved with scenes from Homer. The Portland Vase in the British Museum may give some idea of what they were like.

Nero never wore the same robe twice. Even his fishing-nets were made of gold, threaded with meshes of purple and crimson silk. He paid four million sesterces for embroidered Babylonian sofa coverlets. He also possessed a famous emerald which he was said to have used as an eye-glass for watching gladiatorial shows,[28] but the jewel must have been ill-adapted to such a purpose, and an alternative reading of Pliny's text suggests that the emperor instead used it as a mirror or reflecting stone, to save his weak eyes. He was also particularly fond of pearls, which he not only distributed round the love-nests of the Golden House but employed to stud actors' wands and masks,[29] just as he decorated the equipment of gladiators with amber. Poppaea, not content with bathing in asses' milk, shod her mules in gilded shoes.

There were many stories of Nero's generosity. He was very ready to summon a doctor all the way from Egypt for a friend who was sick. The principal beneficiaries of his gifts, however, were actors and athletes, to whom he was said to have dispensed 2,200 million sesterces,[30] as well as vast properties. Poets also did well out of him,[31] and so, among others, did a moneylender of humble origins who took his fancy. Agrippina had once remonstrated with her son for presenting ten million sesterces to his minister Doryphorus, but Nero, when he saw it all piled up in a heap, said it looked very little.[32] The men at the head of the government, including Seneca, got even more enormous sums of money out of him.

At the Circus Nero used to throw down tokens into the crowd. Those who picked them up, no doubt after an amusing though possibly lethal scuffle, might find themselves entitled to gifts of birds, food, tickets for the grain dole, clothing, jewellery, pictures, slaves, cattle, trained animals, ships, apartment blocks and plots of land.

A mosaic at Pompeii, adapting another masterpiece of Sosus.

II The Official Image of Nero

If Nero was lavish, it was because he had a lot to be lavish with.

This was an age of immense estates. Seneca, on the usual moral grounds, objected to absentee landlords,[1] yet he himself possessed very large estates, particularly in Egypt. But the emperor's domains everywhere vastly exceeded those of everyone else. They were run by a host of agents – whose numbers swelled greatly during the course of Nero's reign.

The imperial possessions increased rapidly through inheritance. It was imperative, for the sake of one's family and dependents, to leave the emperor a substantial legacy, even if he had condemned you to death. Those who instead bequeathed insults, like Petronius, were so rare that the historians regarded such incidents as worthy of a special mention. In hunting for legacies Nero was only doing, on a larger scale, what most eminent Romans had always done. Agrippina, for example, after witnessing her lady-in-waiting's violent death by the collapsible ship meant for herself, did not forget – even when she had had to swim for her life – to look for the woman's will and have it sealed. And when she herself was assassinated the same night, no doubt Nero laid hands on her huge possessions, as he seized those of anyone else who was liquidated. For example, he was said to have poisoned his aunt Domitia, old though she was, because he could not wait for her estates at Baiae and Ravenna, on both of which he subsequently built a fine gymnasium. The rumour that he killed her may not be true, since such gossip was current coin; but in any case he got her Italian properties, and extensive lands she possessed in north Africa likewise passed under his control. This was the territory in which Nero was said to have killed six people who owned half the province.[2] Although that was no doubt a rhetorical exaggeration, the imperial domains in the grainlands of Tunisia were henceforward particularly extensive, and employed whole armies of slaves. And Nero owned almost innumerable holdings and concerns elsewhere. To take a single example, he possessed a tile factory near Calleva (Silchester),[3] in recently conquered Britain.

The emperor's gigantic financial interests were divided into a variety of categories, and these personal resources were hard to disentangle from the national finances.[4] One of the promises which he proved least able to keep was an early assurance to the senators that his private affairs would be kept quite separate from those of the state. Ever since the time of Augustus it had become increasingly unclear which funds were public and which belonged to the emperor. The confusion between the state Treasury, in the Temple of Saturn, and the emperor's private fortune was massive and inextricable. Emperors before Nero had already begun to appoint what were, in effect, their own nominees as directors of the national Treasury, and so did Nero – strengthening his control over the Treasury still further by choosing directors who were more senior in rank than before. Secondly, following a precedent already established by Augustus, Nero boasted of the subventions, both annual and special, which he was accustomed to pay into the Treasury. But since no accounts were published, who could discover whether he was telling the whole truth? For one thing, there were probably hidden movements of funds in the opposite direction as well: no one would be able to say, for example, to what extent Treasury funds were used to pay for the Golden House.

What was clear, however, even before the Golden House was begun, was that even the combined resources of the national income and imperial possessions had become inadequate to defray Nero's extravagant expenditure. His loyal, unobtrusive Greek finance minister Phaon must have found it more and more difficult to balance the accounts. In AD 62, therefore, the emperor appointed three former consuls, including Seneca's brother-in-law, to supervise the use of the national revenues. This may not have been a serious contribution to the situation; but at least it was calculated to allay senatorial alarm. On the same occasion, since attack is better than defence, Nero criticized his predecessors for their wicked practice of allowing expenditure to anticipate income.

Financial problems

Additional funds clearly had to be raised. In 65 he was fooled and disappointed by a lunatic Carthaginian who claimed to have found huge quantities of gold bullion in Africa. But, already a year before that, the emperor had begun to extract a considerable quantity of new revenue by manipulating the coinage. In particular, the gold and silver currency was tampered with. The Roman public, simple-minded in its economic ideas, could not be told that the metal of which these coins were made by no means came up to the value of the denominations they officially stood for. Successive emperors, however, had already quietly debased the silver; and Nero did the same. But he also, officially, lightened the weights of silver and gold issues alike. Peoples beyond the imperial frontiers, such as the Germans, did not like this, for hoards show that henceforward they preferred the old silver. But within the empire, which was what mattered, it appears that Nero got away with it – though what explanation he may have offered is unknown. The profit to the state – and no doubt to himself, since he owned and controlled most of the mines – must have been very large indeed. The old weights were never restored.

At about the same time, in AD 64, an attempt was made to tamper with the base metal coinages of brass and copper. Unlike the gold and silver, these had been issued since the times of Caesar and Augustus at fictitious token values, without anyone, as far as we know, disapproving – presumably because their golden and red colours were so attractive.[5] Nero had so far not issued any token coinage at all, since enough still existed from previous reigns. Now, however, he experimented with a purely brass coinage; no doubt because he possessed a monopoly of its constituent zinc, and could, therefore, make a good profit. But evidently the change proved unacceptable, for joint issues of brass and copper were soon resumed, at Rome and a second western mint which has been identified as Lugdunum (Lyon).

The beauty of these brass and copper pieces, and the messages and designs stamped on their surfaces, played a major part in Nero's publicity. They were, artistically, the finest coins ever produced by Rome and among the finest the world has ever seen. The large brass sesterces in particular, which aroused immense admiration in the Renaissance, represent an enormous improvement on the coins of Claudius. Although, for century after century, the designs and slogans on many a Roman coin reflected, in their own traditional way, the successive nuances of official policy, it can never be determined for certain whether or when an emperor intervened personally to decide what they should be at any given moment. But it surely cannot be fortuitous that this sudden improvement coincided with an emperor who was, above all else, artistic. The remarkable appearance of Nero's coinage surely owed much to Nero himself.

In the first place the new coin portraits are superb. Hitherto, coin-engravers, like sculptors, had varied between two main conceptions of how emperors ought to be shown. One of these theories favoured a more or less

The personification of Rome, in the guise of the warrior-goddess Minerva, on the brass coinage of Nero. The design appears to refer to the rebuilding of the city after the fire.

realistic depiction, on the principle that the tens of thousands of communities among which these coins circulated should be shown what the emperor looked like, so as to obtain some idea of his personality. The alternative theory was that he ought to be depicted in the traditional grandiose style of some ideal, godlike Hellenistic monarch.

Nero's early portraits, on his first gold and silver coins, had tended to the former conception, and give not too bad an idea of his appearance as a young man. But now, from about 64 onwards, artists of an altogether different and superior calibre were employed. They decided that the thing to do was to make the emperor's portraits both realistic *and* idealistic at the same time – to aim at the exuberant splendour of a mighty Greek monarch, but to endow this magnificent ruler with the heavy, not to say bloated, features that the twenty-seven-year-old Nero actually possessed: thus producing a masterpiece of grand individuality.

His hair-style on certain coins looks peculiar. The forehead seems to display a series of parallel, uniform curls. Their points lie flat on the brow, while the curls above are waved or crimped, and stand up stiffly in a sort of cliff above the face, reflecting Suetonius' assertion that his hair was 'arranged in steps'.[6]

Nero's coinage

Beautiful long hair on a young male was much appreciated in Neronian Rome, especially for handsome slaves.[7] Free-born boys, on the other hand, normally removed their long curls when they assumed the toga of manhood, and from that time onwards their hair was relatively short. But it had been part of the traditional get-up of the great Greek monarch to dispense with this austerity and display the waving, leonine locks which had become fashionable with Alexander the Great. However, that is not quite what Nero now did. Although his portraitists were influenced by Lysippus' head of Alexander – which was among the sculptures he had brought to Rome – his own new hair-style was by no means exactly in the leonine tradition of Alexander. Instead it was based on a current, low-class Roman fashion: on the way in which charioteers and actors set and dressed their hair before appearing in the Circus and on the stage. A bust of a charioteer, which is now in the National Museum at Rome, shows a very similar arrangement.

Just occasionally the strong personal taste of a ruler peeps through the conservative conventions that usually governed Roman coin designs; and so it has here. Nero's coiffure, though later affected by respectable professional men, was essentially the style of beat or off-beat, deliberately anti-conventional, youths. Although his general appearance is rendered with noble splendour, his hair-style created the sort of impression that would be produced if a monarch of 1971 appeared on a coin with shoulder-length hair. Indeed Nero himself, two years later, opted for precisely that style himself. His barber, Thalamus, enjoyed a reputation which was still spoken of a generation later.

The efforts of Thalamus can also be seen on some fine marble heads of Nero, but very few of those that survive date back to his lifetime (see Appendix I). Among them is a portrait in the Palatine Museum in Rome: and there is another contemporary bust in the Art Museum at Worcester, Massachusetts. On the latter the deep-set eyes look slightly upwards, a

right: Nero in his late twenties, on a brass coin issued in the western provinces and generally attributed to Lugdunum (Lyon).

Overleaf
left: A view of Ostia, the chief grain-harbour, on a brass *sestertius* of Nero, to remind the people of his care for their food supply. A new harbour had been built by Claudius and may have been completed by Nero. A crescent-shaped mole and row of breakwaters are shown on the coin, with Neptune reclining beneath; the statue on the column represents the lighthouse.
right: A Campanian harbour bearing Italy's trade, *c.* AD 60. Probably Puteoli (Pozzuoli).

spiritual heaven-gazing convention which came into vogue again one and a half centuries later. But some of the coin-designers are not afraid, on occasion, of giving Nero a much grosser appearance, almost justifying Strindberg's comment that in the end he looked like 'the landlady of a Melbourne gambling house' (why Melbourne?).

While it was the function of the obverses of the coins to project an image of the emperor, great use was made of their reverse designs and inscriptions to put across messages which were in the interests of the imperial regime and those members of it who directed publicity: men who surely included some of the topmost officials, and who sometimes, as has been suggested, consulted the emperor himself.

The reverses of the coinage launched in 64 include a judiciously selected series of compositions, some of considerable artistic merit, though the more elaborate scenes and groupings do not appeal to modern taste. First of all, the Romans are pressingly reminded of the emperor's continuing attention to their food supply. One design brings together Ceres and Annona, the goddesses who presided over this activity. Reference has already been made to a map-like view of the harbour of Ostia, enlarged by Claudius and perhaps completed by Nero, which ensured the maintenance of the supply (p. 62); and to pictures of special imperial largesses, accompanied by inscriptions recalling that this exceptional generosity had been exercised not once, but twice. The reminder of this munificence was worth making, because it

right: The Worcester (Massachusetts) portrait of Nero: his hair is brushed up in front like a charioteer's, but from certain angles he has a spiritual expression.

left: In this coin, Annona, the personification of the grain harvest – labelled 'of the Augustus', i.e. presided over by the reigning emperor – stands before Ceres (Demeter) who carries a torch and ears of corn. The garlanded stern of a ship is in the background.

might help to distract attention from the unfortunate need to suspend regular free doles for a time after the Fire. Another coin shows the Provision Market – restored by Nero after it had been burnt down during the same conflagration.

Foreign affairs are represented on these issues by the Temple of Janus, labelled with an indication that it had been closed by Nero because the Roman people were at peace. The doors of this temple could only be closed when there was no war anywhere in the empire – which meant that throughout all the centuries of its existence they were nearly always open. But Nero closed them,[8] his brilliant settlement of the problem of Armenia having made this possible. And so another coin depicts an Altar of Peace. We do not know where this altar was – the coin was issued outside Rome – but evidently it was erected on the same occasion, and it deliberately recalled a famous Altar of Peace which had been set up by Augustus.

Other issues carefully stress the military qualities by which it was claimed that the Peace had been won (diverting notice from the diplomatic achievement, which was less popular). One coin shows Nero taking part in the military exercises of the praetorian guardsmen (p. 152), another displays him addressing them – both being activities which he engaged in all too rarely, from the standpoint of conventional opinion, and which it was therefore desirable to emphasize. And these warlike allusions, like the references to Peace, were presented with echoes of Augustus.

The Augustan flavour is particularly apparent in another series of coins, issued in gigantic quantities, which display an elegant figure of Victory carrying a shield dedicated to the emperor by the Senate and Roman People (SPQR). The design was exactly, though much more artistically, imitated from a type of coin that had originally been issued in memory of Augustus, representing the golden Shield of Valour (or Virtue) which Senate and People had dedicated to him in his lifetime. The original coin had been issued on the tenth anniversary of his death and deification. Now, in 64, the fiftieth anniversary of the same occasion had arrived. In other words the population was being invited, by the designs on this coinage, to regard Nero

far left: Nero's full name and title – NERO CLAVD(*ius*) CAESAR AVG(*ustus*) GER(*manicus*) P(*ontifex*) M(*aximus*) TR(*ibunicia*) P(*otestate*) IMP(*erator*) P(*ater*) P(*atriae*). On the reverse – ADLOCVT(*io*) COH(*ortium*): the emperor addressing the cohorts (battalions) of the Praetorian Guard, accompanied by one of its prefects, Tigellinus or Faenius Rufus. It seemed advisable to distract attention from Nero's unwarlike tastes by reviving this design (from the coinage of Caligula).

This picture of Victory, echoed from a coinage in memory of Augustus fifty years after his death, was shown on millions of copper *asses* circulating throughout the empire. The golden shield had been dedicated to the imperial founder by the Senate and People (SPQR).

as a worthy descendant of the imperial founder. The memory of Augustus was ever-present. The monetary issues of towns in Asia Minor often still bore his head, alternating it with the emperor of the day. And the issues of the governor of Egypt address Nero specifically as 'the new Augustus'.[9]

Another of his issues deliberately copies a design that had figured on Augustus' own coinage. This depicts the laurel-wreathed god Apollo playing his lyre. But, as Suetonius or his sources realized, the figure must unmistakably be identified with Nero himself, whose habit and delight it was to do the same. Here, as in the hair-style of his portraits, is another reference to the emperor's personal tastes. Traditionalists might find the allusion a shocking one, but it is tactfully framed right in the Augustan tradition; and reference is made to the *respectability* of this lyre-playing owing to its traditional patronage by Apollo, to which Nero himself was accustomed to refer. He was constantly compared with the god,[10] and his great statue, the Colossus, wore Apollo's sun-ray crown; it also appears encircling Nero's brow on coins.

Would it have been wiser for those who chose the coin designs to say or hint nothing at all about his lyre-playing? Evidently they thought otherwise; presumably because the scandal was too public to be ignored. And so they did the best they could, facing the awkward facts but glossing over them by allusions to Augustan precedent and Apolline sanction.

Apollo, the lyre-player – a tactful reference to the divine sponsorship of the emperor's own playing and singing – appears from AD 64 on the coinage of Nero, as well as on this medallic piece. (Since it lacks the formula SC, 'by a decree of the senate', which appears on normal token issues, it was probably intended for private distribution.)

12 The Upper-class Backlash

Indeed the scandal of Nero's performances had reached monumental proportions. Hitherto they had been limited to private, invited audiences. But it had now proved impossible to prevent him from appearing on the public stage; perhaps the set of advisers who now surrounded him had never tried. He quoted a Greek proverb: 'music unheard has no charms'.[1] Private gatherings did not seem large enough to do justice to his voice.

For his private début he chose not Rome but Greek Neapolis (Naples), since, as he observed: 'Only the Greeks have an ear for music – they alone are worthy of my efforts.' The great Neapolitan festival, held every four years in memory of Augustus, had been attended by that emperor in person. He had not performed in it; Nero did.

above: A special portrait of Nero on the medallion-like issue which showed Apollo on the reverse.

His first stage appearance was at Neapolis where, disregarding an earthquake which shook the theatre, he sang his piece through to the end. He often performed at Neapolis, for several consecutive days, too; and even while giving his voice a brief rest, could not stay away from the theatre, but went to dine in the orchestra where he promised the crowd in Greek that, when he had downed a drink or two, he would give them a fine high note.[2]

Worried senators were aware that the time was coming for the second of the five-yearly Neronian Games at Rome (65). And they were reminded of this by a special issue of coinage, which referred to the occasion by name and displayed the victor's wreath and judge's urn. The Games were held in the Theatre of Pompey; and it was now that Nero took the decisive and ominous step of making his first personal appearance before the Roman public.

The Senate tried to avert scandal by offering the emperor, in advance, the first prize for song, and also conferring on him a crown 'for eloquence' to gloss over the degradation attaching to the stage. But Nero declared that there was no need for favouritism or the Senate's authority; he would compete on equal terms and rely on the conscience of the judges to award him the prize he deserved.[3]

The chairman of the Games, who had the delicate task of organizing the imperial début, was Aulus Vitellius, the son of a subtle and influential counsellor of Claudius. Vitellius, who later became emperor for a few months, was enjoying a prominent career, but had an unenviable reputation for gluttony, sycophancy, a passion for charioteering and throwing dice, and

Nero in about AD 65, aged twenty-seven.

sodomy with the late emperor Tiberius. Now, according to Suetonius, 'when Nero wished to compete among the lyre-players, but did not venture to do so although there was a general demand for him, and accordingly left the theatre, Vitellius called him back, pleading that he came as an envoy from the insistent people and wanted to give Nero a chance to yield to their entreaties'.[4] Elsewhere, Suetonius gives a slightly different and more detailed description of what happened.

When the crowd clamoured to hear his heavenly voice, he answered that he would perform in the Palace gardens later if anyone really wanted to hear him; but when the guards on duty seconded the appeal, he delightedly agreed to oblige them. He wasted no time in getting his name entered on the list of competing lyre-players, and dropped his ticket in the urn with the others. The guard prefects carried his lyre as he went up to play, and a group of military tribunes and close friends accompanied him. After taking his place and briefly begging the audience's kind attention, he made Cluvius Rufus, a former consul, announce the title of the song. It was the whole of the tragedy *Niobe*; and he sang on until two hours before dusk. Since this allowed the remaining competitors no chance to perform, he postponed the award of a prize to the following year, which would give him another opportunity to sing. But since a year was a long time to wait, he continued to make frequent appearances.[5]

Security arrangements were very strict and embarrassing.

While he was singing, no one was allowed to leave the theatre even for the most urgent reasons. And so it is said that some women gave birth to children there, while many who were worn out with listening and applauding secretly leapt from the wall, since the gates at the entrance were closed, or feigned death and were carried out as if for burial.[6]

left: Vitellius, during his brief reign in AD 69.

right: Probably Vitellius.

Tacitus also remarks that unsophisticated visitors had great difficulty in keeping up with the claque, earning many cuffs from the guardsmen in attendance; and that listeners to the emperor's songs had to watch their expressions, which were carefully noted by spies.[7]

These threatening manifestations formed part of a general picture: Rome was gradually turning into a police state. Nero, being so suspicious and easily frightened, readily fell in with the views of the praetorian commander Tigellinus, who believed in savage security measures. We have already seen him at work cooking up charges against Octavia; now the death-roll of men with imperial connections, by blood or marriage, increased. Moreover, in the year of Tigellinus' promotion (62), the old, indefinite charge of high treason (*majestas*), which earlier emperors had extended to cover alleged threats against their own persons, was revived.

The senators, as well as the emperor, had their own law-court; and on his accession Nero had promised to safeguard their independence – though senatorial proceedings all too often turned into sycophancy. This did not happen, however, in 62, when the Senate decided that a man accused of reciting satirical verses about the emperor at a dinner-party should be sentenced to nothing more severe than banishment. Nero was reported to have been indignant at such leniency, since it was assumed that he had hoped for a harsher sentence, which he could then gain credit by mitigating. However, a certain amount of licence was still possible, at least among unimportant people. A comic actor Datus, while reciting lines 'goodbye Father, goodbye Mother', ventured to make gestures of drinking and swimming, with reference to the fates of Claudius and Agrippina. Then he recited 'Hell guides your feet', and waved towards the senators to indicate that he was referring to their destination under Nero. However, he too was only exiled; as was a philosopher who shouted rude remarks at the emperor in the street.

But Datus' sick joke about the senators was becoming no joking matter. How soon genuine threats against the emperor's life materialized we cannot

A determined attempt by an artist to give Nero a noble, heroic appearance, though without rejuvenating his chin.

say. But a secret police menace was now developing quite rapidly. One result was a crop of informers,[8] including sinister figures like Vatinius, a crippled, malicious shoemaker from Beneventum of whom Nero was fond. More dangerous still was the rise of a considerable number of formidable prosecution lawyers. Oratory had always been the principal civilian occupation of the Romans, and young men had made their names as accusers. Nowadays this had become the only important role left to an ambitious or talented public speaker. Consequently, prosecuting lawyers abounded; and a great many leading figures suffered from their attentions. The peril had already been gradually increasing during the previous years, and in the prevailing atmosphere it was sharply accentuated. The expert prosecutors were personages like the blustering and fanatical Eprius Marcellus and the bland, facetious Vibius Crispus, a table companion of Vitellius. Such men, in spite of their humble origins, were enormously rich and powerful, and, what is more, they had now joined Tigellinus among the emperor's most intimate advisers.

As for Tigellinus himself, he appears to have presided personally over the intelligence service which provided these men with their weapons. We have seen it at work in the amphitheatre, where agents noted the expressions of people watching the emperor's performances. The roving philosopher Apollonius of Tyana declared that Tigellinus had made Rome into a city all eyes and ears; and Seneca, though before his retirement he must have used spies himself, lamented the situation as one in which 'things could neither be heard nor told in safety'.[9] For example, there were agents in the brothels, with frequently fatal results for visitors. And public lavatories, too, were unsafe. In one of them Lucan, suffering from flatulence, was unwise enough to quote part of a line written by Nero himself: 'You might suppose it thundered 'neath the earth'.[10] Everyone else got up and left hastily, and the joke, duly reported to the emperor, had a bad effect on his relations with the young poet.

The Pisonian conspiracy Tigellinus' security measures misfired, because they increased the very threat they were intended to stamp out. That is to say, they contributed directly to the genuine, dangerous plots against Nero's life which were hatched in 65 and 66. No doubt the horror of the upper class at Nero's un-Roman stage tastes and appearances had something to do with these conspiracies. But the main reason was because the plotters understandably felt afraid that they themselves would be the next to fall.

The Pisonian conspiracy, discovered shortly before the Neronian Games of 65, was designed to assassinate the emperor and to set a certain Gaius Calpurnius Piso on the throne in his place. Piso was aristocratic, generous, handsome and eloquent. He was also famous for his skill at a game resembling draughts or backgammon.[11] He was superficial and ostentatious. Like Nero, he sang and played the lyre – which confirms the view that the plotters' motive was terror on their own accounts rather than disapproval of the emperor's tastes, since otherwise they would scarcely have chosen a man with such similar interests as his successor. Tacitus gives us a long story of the plot, with many fine rhetorical themes. But it is very hard to know how far they reflect the truth. The same applies to nearly all conspiracies; and in the case of this one, there is an alarming variation between the accounts of one historian and another.[12] For the rest, we have to rely too much on the subsequent accounts put out by the emperor himself, who, with Tigellinus to help him, personally conducted the investigations.

Nero reported that the plan had been to murder him in the Circus Maximus, while Games were being held. As a result of leakages, which are variously described, fifty-one people were charged with complicity, including nineteen senators, seven knights, eleven officers, and four women. Nineteen executions followed and thirteen sentences of banishment; four officers were cashiered. Other leading men succumbed later, and indirectly. Popular talk at the time seems to have been doubtful about whether there had ever been a plot at all. But Tacitus vouches for its authenticity: and, to that extent at least, he must be believed, since he was able to appeal to the testimony of survivors, who may well have had their own special pleas and versions which they wished to commend to posterity, but are unlikely to have invented the whole thing.

A perilous feature of the affair, from the emperor's point of view, was the involvement of so many senior military men. One of them proved to be Tigellinus' popular colleague Faenius Rufus. After the plot had been discovered, he set himself up as one of the inquisitors. But, like a general who made a similar attempt after the 1944 conspiracy against Hitler, he was betrayed and executed.

It is curious that Dio Cassius, in his description of the plot, makes no mention of Piso at all. According to him, one of the leaders of the enterprise was Faenius Rufus: and the other was Seneca. After the whole thing came out, Seneca was compelled to commit suicide. Tacitus' over-long account credits him with a traditional philosophical end, carefully modelled on the death of Socrates, and including a last message to the world which was only published later on. Tacitus also assumes that he had not really been involved at all. But had he? Much play was made with something he was supposed to have said to Piso. The latter, it was claimed, had suggested that he and Seneca should meet: whereupon Seneca had replied that 'frequent meetings and conversations would benefit neither, but that his own welfare depended on Piso being safe'.[13] That might be a sign of guilt. But equally, according to the courteous terminology current at the time, it might not. What seems very likely is that the important officers who were supposedly involved in the plot had their eye on Seneca, rather than Piso, as the next emperor. The increasing personal menaces from Nero's informers, spies and prosecution lawyers weighed less heavily on them than on senators, because the soldiers were on the whole in less danger; but the scandals of Nero's artistic tastes loomed larger, and Piso would not have been the right replacement because his own inclinations were so similar. Tacitus claims to be quoting the actual words of one of the principal officers involved, Subrius Flavus.

Asked by Nero, in the course of the investigation, why he had forgotten his military oath, Flavus replied: 'Because I hated you! I was as loyal as any of your soldiers as long as you deserved affection. I began hating you when you murdered your mother and wife and became charioteer, actor and incendiary!'[14]

Piso may not have been a murderer, but he was certainly another actor and singer. The officers would rather have had Seneca. And it is not impossible that he did join their plot: he may have felt impelled to do so by Tigellinus' hostility, which threatened his life. He is on record, as we have seen, as observing that the time may come when a tyrant becomes so intolerable that he must be killed. And perhaps he now believed that this moment had finally arrived. His writings, for some time, had been deeply preoccupied with death; and even if the histrionics accompanying his end may contain an element of pious invention, there is no reason to suppose he was unready to meet his last hour. Nero prevented Seneca's wife Pompeia Paulina from committing suicide with him, but, a little later on, Seneca's brother Gallio was forced to kill himself. Another, earlier, victim was their nephew Lucan – a Republican at heart, but a Republican who had won a prize at the first Neronian Games in 60 for a poem in praise of the emperor, and whose epic the *Pharsalia* had again, amid Republican sentiments, managed to flatter him. His fate was sealed, perhaps, when his unfortunate joke in the public lavatory was reported back – or else, it was said, when Nero began to veto his publicity. Fortunately it does not seem necessary to accept the story that Lucan, before dying, incriminated his own mother Acilia. If that had been so, a later poet, Statius, could hardly, in verses addressed to Lucan's widow, have had the tactlessness to refer to Nero as a matricide.[15] At all events, Acilia survived. But, after a time-lag, her husband Annaeus Mela was compelled, like his two brothers, to die.

So was Petronius, whom Tigellinus disliked as rival entertainer of Nero; Petronius managed his suicide with typical panache, involving a good deal of nonchalant malice towards Nero. And so another of the emperor's old friends had gone. Petronius' wife poisoned their two children, and then died herself.

There was also, after an interlude of doubt, an imperial casualty. This was Claudius' daughter Claudia Antonia – the half-sister of Britannicus and Octavia. Nero was induced to believe that, if Piso had carried out his plan of proceeding to the camp of the praetorians, he intended to take Claudia Antonia with him.[16] Piso loved his own wife Satria Galla (whom he had stolen from a friend), but the rumour about Claudia Antonia – with the implication that he intended to make her empress – seemed possible all the same, because Galla, although beautiful, was too low-born to be likely to enjoy any popular or senatorial favour if her husband gained the throne. But Piso did his best to save Galla's life by flattering Nero grossly in his will; and she apparently survived.

A new pattern of power began to emerge from the débris, and we can see who the men were who helped Nero to put down the conspiracy. They included one of his current secretaries of state Epaphroditus, who had succeeded Doryphorus as Minister of Notes. This was his revenge because he had been sneered at by one of the plotters as a lackey. An honorary Triumph was awarded to Petronius Turpilianus, the man who had introduced a peace policy in Britain after the rebellion; evidently he had now become useful again. A similar honour was sent to a thirty-five-year-old lawyer and poet called Cocceius Nerva (the future emperor), so that he too must have helped to stamp out the plot. Nero put up his statue in the Forum, and another in the palace itself. Statues of Tigellinus were erected as well.

In addition an honorary consulship went to the man who now replaced Faenius Rufus as Tigellinus' colleague in the praetorian command. This was Nymphidius Sabinus. His mother, child of a dressmaker by the former minister Callistus, had been an attractive freedwoman and prostitute who drew her clientèle from the slaves and ex-slaves of the imperial household. The supposed father of Nymphidius was a gladiator, but Nymphidius himself claimed to be the son of the emperor Caligula. His height and ferocious expression gave some plausibility to this claim. 'And perhaps', as Tacitus remarks, 'his mother had indeed participated in the amusements of Caligula, whose tastes extended to whores.'[17] Tacitus, like other leading Romans, was prejudiced against Nymphidius for his peculiar origins; so that if there were any points in his favour, we are not told what they were. Since the discovery of the plot was the occasion of his promotion, it may well be that, like Tigellinus, he was a security expert. Nevertheless, whatever services he may have rendered now, he was later on, as we shall see, to prove unreliable. Nero had evidently saddled himself with two pretty nasty praetorian commanders.

Once the plotters had been eliminated, the official coinage hastened to honour Jupiter the Guardian (CVSTOS) and two appropriate goddess-personifications, Welfare or Well-Being (SALVS) and Security – the Security of the Emperor.[18] A temple in honour of Salus was voted by the Senate, and the Arval Priesthood sacrificed to the welfare of Nero and the Commonwealth. Threats to the lives of emperors were frequent, but it is not very common for the coinage to call attention to them. In fact it was perhaps rather unsophisticated to do so, since such reassurances suggested that the situation must be unsafe indeed, if so much fuss had to be made about insisting that the opposite was the case.

The death of Poppaea

Nero tried to throw off such anxious thoughts by concentrating on his first public appearance at the Neronian Games – described in the previous chapter. But a little later he suffered a tragic blow. For soon after the Games, Poppaea died. She had become pregnant for the second time. Tacitus rightly rejects the story that the emperor poisoned her, commenting that he wanted children and loved his wife. Yet in spite of this, says the historian, he kicked her, in a chance fit of anger, and this was what caused her death. The other historians agree; and Suetonius adds that she was ill at the time, and offers the rather bourgeois additional detail that he was cross because she had scolded him for coming back late from the races. Who can say how badly he may not have behaved on such occasions? But if it is true that he kicked her, it is very unlikely that he meant to kill her.

Her body was embalmed like an oriental queen's, and the quantity of spices burned at her funeral was the equivalent of an entire year's supply from the whole of Arabia. Nero delivered the funeral oration, praising her beauty and her parenthood of a deity – since that is what their baby Claudia had been declared after her death. And now Poppaea, too, was pronounced a goddess; and she and her daughter were celebrated together, with their

Nerva, who helped Nero suppress the Pisonian conspiracy. Here he is portrayed after he became emperor thirty-one years later.

NERVA

divine titles, on a coin of the Jewish king Agrippa II, in whose faith she had been interested.[19] Nero never forgot her; one of the last acts of his reign was to dedicate her shrine. Henceforward, whenever he sang a female part, he liked to wear a mask with her features. His fancy fell on the eunuch Sporus because his looks reminded Nero of Poppaea, and indeed he was accustomed to address the boy by her second name, Sabina.

None the less, in AD 66 the emperor embarked on a third marriage. His new wife was the fashionable and lovely Statilia Messalina, who had been married four times already.[20] Her latest husband Vestinus was out of the way, having been got rid of for complicity in Piso's plot, when he held the consulship. The imperial executioners called at his house while he was giving a dinner party. They kept his guests under guard all night, until Nero laughingly remarked that they had suffered enough for their dinner at the consul's. Perhaps Vestinus' real mistake was that he had married Statilia when she was already Nero's mistress. But there were other reasons, also, why he was accident-prone. In particular, he was an outspoken sort of man, with the extraordinarily risky habit of making crude jokes about the emperor to his face.

top: Nero's third wife Statilia Messalina, on a recently discovered base metal (billon) coin issued by the Imperial prefect of Egypt at Alexandria. The obverse shows Nero crowned with Apollo's sun-rays.

In 66 Nero turned against another group of noblemen. These were the ultra-conservatives, the men who went as close to being Republicans as they dared – a good deal further than Lucan ever had. Their most prominent member was Thrasea Paetus, from Patavium (Pavia), one of the leaders of a rising group of important north Italians. After being in favour during the early part of the reign, Thrasea had lost faith in Nero and thereafter devoted himself to passive resistance and a policy of absenteeism from the Senate, where he was much respected. During a senatorial debate after Agrippina's death, he walked out of the Senate-house. He had also shown a lack of enthusiasm about the Youth Games; and this had particularly wounded Nero since Thrasea himself, at his own birthplace, had appeared in public and sung tragic songs. In 62, when a man was charged with writing rude verses about Nero, it had been Thrasea who annoyed the emperor by persuading the Senate to be lenient. Now, after Poppaea's death, he stayed away when she was voted divine honours; he also stayed away from her funeral. And his grim schoolmasterly expression, for which Suetonius vouches, must have been a further source of irritation to the emperor.

Disfavour had already begun to fall on Thrasea in 63, when he was forbidden to join his fellow-senators at Antium to congratulate the empress on the birth of her daughter. But then Nero made an effort to become reconciled to him. For, after all, Thrasea was probably the most influential of all the senators. And he was famous for his impeccable integrity: Nero himself spoke of it with admiration.[21] When he attempted his reconciliation with Thrasea, he was congratulated on the move by Seneca – which did neither Seneca nor Thrasea any good. Now the end had come for Thrasea, and the blow fell also on a whole set of men who were his relatives or thought in the same way as he did.

The Greek philosophical schools adopted varying attitudes towards monarchy. The Cynics (going back to the fourth-century BC philosopher

Diogenes) disapproved of all autocrats, whereas the Stoics only disliked bad ones. When Thrasea died, a Cynic philosopher, Demetrius – the man who had objected to Nero's Baths – was present to offer him consolation. But Thrasea had been an adherent of the Stoic sect, and had sought to model his life on its doctrines. There was a tincture of Greek philosophy in all the group of Romans who were his kinsmen and friends. It was a tradition which the imperial government had tried to incorporate in the moralizing self-praise of its own propaganda, as the coins of successive rulers show.[22] Nevertheless, the philosophers themselves, at least as long ago as Caligula's time, had shown signs of opposing the regime[23] – and they had recently suffered a casualty after the Piso plot.[24] Seneca felt it necessary to refute the charge that philosophy was a subversive study. Ordinary Romans, naturally enough, felt nothing but contempt for the whole subject; and Nero's intellectual interests did not really extend to philosophy, though he found it a good joke to listen to professionals squabbling after dinner. But the philosophical aura which surrounded Thrasea evidently exercised considerable glamour. For it was responsible for a vast and truth-obscuring saga,[25] much of it reminiscent of other pagan martyrdoms, and anticipatory of Christian ones to come.

The interest which Thrasea and his friends felt for philosophy, and their desire to live up to its precepts, must not be underestimated. Yet they were Romans, and what they stood for, above all else, was the old uncompromising dignity of their own ruling class, full of prickly personal honour and insistent on absolute freedom of speech. Later on, even the easy-going Vespasian was to find this group intolerable (in the person of Thrasea's son-in-law); and during the highly charged later years of Nero it was the easiest thing in the world to find formidable and malignant prosecutors to accuse them – with the emperor's own friend Eprius Marcellus enthusiastically in the lead. Accordingly Thrasea died. So also, though Tacitus and Dio may be wrong to link the two cases directly,[26] did an almost equally distinguished public servant and Stoic, Barea Soranus. Like Thrasea, he had at one time collaborated with the regime; he had seen fit to flatter the former imperial minister Pallas. But now Barea was charged with encouraging the great cities of Asia Minor to start a rebellion – and their richest man, who was his friend, was ruined in his fall. Another victim was Barea's teenage daughter Servilia, who had rashly paid magicians to advise her how to save her father's life. Her death was pathetic and unnecessary. But the men who chose to show their lack of sympathy with Nero clearly did not have much prospect of survival. And Tacitus, while praising the nobility of their behaviour, makes it clear elsewhere that he regards such martyrdoms as fine gestures – but useless waste.[27]

The downfall of Thrasea and Barea was probably not the result of their participation in any actual plot. There is no reason to suppose that they had gone to such lengths. But in the same year a second plot, the successor to the Pisonian conspiracy, did apparently occur. Our knowledge of what happened is exceedingly fragmentary. The surviving manuscript of Tacitus breaks off at this point; and so we do not possess his account of the last years of the

Statilia Messalina on a local bronze coin of the Greek town of Thyatira (Akhisar in Turkey).

reign. It is Suetonius alone who tells us of the 'Vinician conspiracy', which was launched unsuccessfully at Beneventum: and this, evidently, is the 'nefarious plot' mentioned in the records of the Arval Brethren, when on 19 June, AD 66, they gave thanks for its suppression and for the preservation of the emperor's life. The leader of the movement seems to have been a certain Annius Vinicianus, the son of a man who had conspired against Claudius and perhaps possessed marriage links with the imperial house. Vinicianus had served with distinction on the staff of Nero's greatest general Corbulo, and had married Corbulo's daughter. His brother had been exiled after Piso's conspiracy; and they were related to Barea, who had lost his life soon afterwards. The removal first of the brother and then of Barea were perhaps the causes which led Vinicianus, in fear for his own safety, to conspire against Nero. Barea had been a prominent provincial governor, and governors played a large part in Vinicianus' plot, or at any rate in the carnage that followed its detection.

Corbulo was apparently unemployed at this time, but at about the end of 66 Nero, who had now gone to Greece, summoned him to join the imperial party there. On arriving at Cenchreae, the port of Corinth, Corbulo was handed orders from the emperor to kill himself. Before dying, he uttered the Greek word *Axios*. This was the term customarily used in acclaiming a hero or winner in the Games, meaning 'you deserved it'. Corbulo was saying 'this serves me right'. But did he mean 'I was a fool to have come' or 'I was a fool to have served Nero for so long' – or 'I am guilty'? At all events, whatever the correct interpretation of Corbulo's utterance may be, it is extremely likely that Vinicianus and his fellow-plotters had intended to place him on the throne – though they did not necessarily let him into the secret in advance.

At about the same time two brothers, Scribonius Rufus and Scribonius Proculus, who commanded the two provinces of Germany bordering on the Rhine, were also summoned to Greece. They too were forced to kill themselves, without being heard in their own defence or allowed to see Nero. Their family could claim descent from imperial personages and from Pompey, and had produced suspects in imperial eyes before now. If the brothers were guilty of conspiring, this was indeed a serious matter for the government, since in their provinces they had each controlled a substantial force of three legions. Evidently Nero and his advisers were under the impression that the rot had spread to the great generals and governors. And they may have been right. If so, the situation was perilous.

A later, almost baroque, interpretation of Nero: only a fragment of the face is antique.

13 Rebellion and Triumph

above: A bronze coin of Felix, Nero's prefect of Judaea, issued at the provincial capital Caesarea in AD 59.

The reverse of this coin of Nero shows a Triumphal Arch – either the monument erected for eastern victories in AD 58 (according to Tacitus), or another to celebrate the visit of Tiridates in 66 (when the coin was issued).

The government's increasing preoccupation with plots or possible plots by distinguished Romans coincided with a subject people's rebellion which far exceeded the British revolt in gravity. Its scene was Judaea, the Roman province that approximately corresponded with Israel. Although the Romans, all over the east, tried to keep the peace fairly between Greeks and Jews, in Judaea itself they had failed completely with the Jews: their Israel was the British Empire's Ireland – with additional complications, owing to class-hatred among the Jewish inhabitants themselves. Under Roman governors (prefects or procurators) who were of fairly junior status and sometimes found things too much for them, troubles rapidly multiplied; and Poppaea's pro-Jewish attitude could do nothing to help.

The final disaster was brought about by the prefect Gessius Florus (64–66), who abandoned his predecessor's mild policy and endeavoured to extort a large sum from the Temple treasury, claiming (perhaps rightly, though without tact) that it was due to him as tax arrears. When rioting broke out, Gessius allowed a Roman unit to plunder parts of Jerusalem (May, 66). But he had to retreat from the city, and the nationalist leaders (Zealots), who controlled a powerful terrorist wing, had the Roman population massacred. Meanwhile, large silver shekels were issued, proclaiming the sacredness and redemption of Zion; Greeks in neighbouring countries were deeply disturbed; and all over the Levant and in Egypt as well, they and the Jews began killing one another.

In Judaea itself, the rebels rapidly won support. They received enormous encouragement when Cestius Gallus, the governor of Syria, intervened only to receive a sharp setback. For when this official, who was far senior to the prefect of Judaea, entered that province, he was obliged to call off his attempt to recapture Jerusalem. Harassed by irregular bands, he recoiled from its walls, and while retreating to Beth-Horon suffered damaging losses (November, 66). When this became known, the revolt spread to the east of the River Jordan, and south into the Negev.

Meanwhile, at the turn of the year, Nero appointed the fifty-seven-year-old Vespasian to take command in Judaea. Vespasian, who at the time was with him in Greece, had originally become important because his mistress was the freedwoman of an imperial lady, and because he himself paid court

This silver shekel commemorates the Jewish Revolt or, as the Jews call it, the First Roman War of AD 66 – 'year one'. The obverse shows a chalice and on the reverse is a sprig of myrtle or a bunch of pomegranates. The inscriptions read 'Shekel of Israel' and 'Jerusalem the Holy'.

Vespasian.

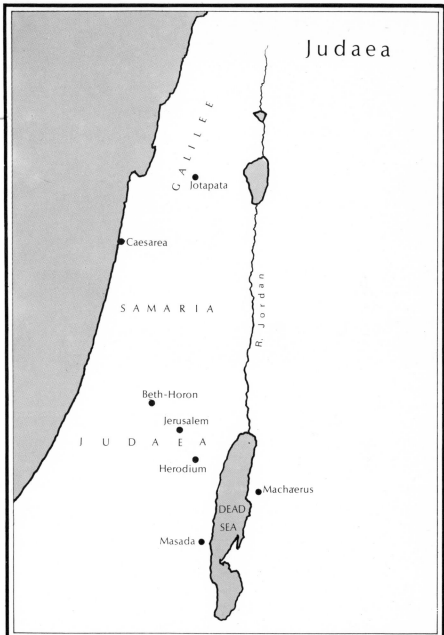

Judaea

GALILEE

Jotapata

Caesarea

SAMARIA

R. Jordan

Beth-Horon

Jerusalem

J U D A E A

Herodium

Machærus

DEAD
SEA

Masada

to Caligula. Under Nero he had imperilled his career and his life by leaving the theatre while the emperor himself was performing; according to another version he stayed, but fell asleep. It was also awkward that he had been a friend of Thrasea and Barea, both of whom had been struck down. Nevertheless, he got the Judaean appointment. For not only was he a good soldier, he also entirely lacked social distinction – after recent plots, or rumours of plots, Nero was deeply suspicious of dashing figures.

In 67 Vespasian started his campaign against the rebels. Moving south from Syria, he invaded and occupied Galilee. The historian Josephus, who

An aerial view, seen from the south, of Masada, which held out against the Romans for three years after the fall of Jerusalem. Thus the Jewish insurrection, begun under Nero, lasted for seven years.

had been appointed the Jewish commander in this area, deserted his compatriots at Jotapata and became a collaborator with Rome – prudently and accurately prophesying that Vespasian was destined to become emperor. After spending the winter of 67–68 at the capital of the province, Caesarea, Vespasian proceeded to reestablish Roman rule almost everywhere. Only a few hill-fortresses still resisted (Herodium, Machaerus and Masada, which has now been excavated), as well as Jerusalem itself, in which the rebel command was split by savage factional strife. But the capture of Jerusalem by the Romans, and then the conclusion of the whole campaign, had to wait until Vespasian's supreme commander, Nero, was no more.

As the Jewish rebellion began, the emperor, still in Rome, had been preparing to receive King Tiridates of Armenia, in pursuance of the diplomatic agreement reached with Corbulo three years before: according to which, although the Parthian nominee, he should ostensibly receive his crown from the emperor of Rome. The visit symbolized Nero's supreme success in foreign affairs – the peaceful, durable Armenian settlement. However, since the Roman public liked victories, it was important to make Tiridates' visit look as much of a military triumph for Rome as possible, although – as both he and the king of Parthia insisted – nothing whatever must be done to humiliate him.

A royal visit

Tiridates was treated with the greatest honour. The journey of his entourage, including a large bodyguard both of Parthian and of Roman soldiers, cost the unprecedented amount of eight hundred thousand sesterces a day, a sum which was apparently paid by the Roman state treasury. And they were no less than nine months en route. Except for the unavoidable crossing of the Hellespont (Dardanelles), Tiridates came entirely by land, because, as a Magian priest, he was not permitted to pollute the sea by travelling on its surface. As far as Italy he rode all the way, accompanied by his wife, who had to wear a golden vizor as a veil since, according to the custom of their country, her face must not be seen. After entering the Italian peninsula from the north-east, the royal party took their places in a two-horse carriage sent for them by Nero. Finally, Tiridates was conducted into the imperial presence at Neapolis.

Moving on to Puteoli, he attended gladiatorial Games. These were organized, with the utmost splendour, by an imperial minister named Patrobius, who had imported Nile sand for the gymnastic exercises. In order to show gratitude for these arrangements, Tiridates expressed the desire to have a shot at some of the wild beasts in the arena: and he got two bulls with a single arrow – if one can believe it, adds Dio Cassius. Another special feature of the display was the appearance of female as well as male fighters of every age, from childhood upwards – and all of them Ethiopians.

Then the emperor escorted him to Rome.

The guards battalions paraded in full armour round the temples of the Forum, while Nero occupied his official chair on the Rostra, wearing triumphal dress and surrounded by military insignia and standards. Tiridates had to walk up a ramp

Nero, on the obverse of
the coin on p. 222.

and then prostrate himself in supplication; whereupon Nero stretched out his hand, drew him to his feet, kissed him, and replaced his turban with a diadem.[1]

A Latin translation of Tiridates' speech was read aloud. He handed over, as hostages, his own sons and those of his royal kinsmen – including the off-spring of his half-brother the Parthian king himself. Then Nero addressed him in reply. The text of the emperor's speech, which has come down to us, strikes an authentic, inflated note.

You have done well in coming here in person to enjoy my presence yourself. Your father did not leave you this kingdom; your brothers, though they gave it to you, could not guard it for you; but that is my gracious grant to you, and I make you King of Armenia, in order that both you and they may learn that I have the power both to take away kingdoms and to bestow them.[2]

After this imposing scene, Games were held in the Theatre of Pompey, the interior of which was specially gilded for the occasion; the stage properties, too, were plastered with gold, so that people looked back on this afterwards as the Golden Day. Even the purple awning stretched overhead was covered with golden stars – amid which was embroidered a figure of Nero driving a chariot. And indeed the emperor, after ushering Tiridates to a seat at his right hand, promptly translated the picture into fact by actually mounting a chariot and riding in a race himself, as well as playing the lyre. The king was said to have been disgusted; but the crowd hailed Nero as 'Imperator', the salutation of victorious generals, and he permanently assumed the designation as his first name – which only Caesar and Augustus had done before. Next he went in solemn procession up to the Capitol, where he dedicated a laurel wreath in the Temple of Jupiter. Then, descending to the Forum again, he closed the double doors of the Temple of Janus for a second time, in order to reiterate that peace had truly come. In honour of the occasion, a commemorative column was erected at Moguntiacum (Mainz), where it can still be seen.[3]

above: A coin of Nero recording the closure of the Temple of Janus during Tiridates' visit, to celebrate the arrival of peace. The little Temple was beside the Forum, but its exact site is still not certain.

Finally, Tiridates left Rome, loaded with magnificent parting presents. He had announced his intention of renaming his capital Artaxata as 'Neronia' and rebuilding the town on a magnificent scale. Consequently, his retinue was now still further swelled by large numbers of workmen. On the return journey he took a different route, overcoming his religious scruples sufficiently to cross the Ionian Sea. Then, after traversing the Balkans, he visited the cities of Asia Minor before returning to Armenia, to govern it henceforward as a joint Parthian and Roman nominee.

Nero in Greece

But the emperor was now thinking of a far more elaborate festival – and a prolonged one too, since it was going to last for a whole year. Nero decided that the time had come to make his long-projected visit to Greece (Achaea). He had intended to go two years before, and had actually left the capital – only to turn back at Beneventum, we do not know why. Now, in 66, probably at the end of September, he set out again. He was accompanied not only by his third wife Statilia Messalina but by the pretty eunuch Sporus. Tigellinus

The column of Nero at Moguntiacum (Mainz), to commemorate the settlement with Parthia at the other end of the empire, and the visit of Tiridates.

was also a member of the party, and it was arranged that in Greece there should be a ceremony at which he should give the bride Sporus away to his imperial bridegroom; the Greeks celebrated the occasion with a party. According to a current joke, it was a pity Nero's father had not been satisfied with a wife like Sporus. During the trip the boy was put under the care of a rich, thieving, beautiful woman called Calvia Crispinilla, who now emerges as guide to the palace pleasures, with special responsibility for Sporus' extensive wardrobe.

To the Roman senators, on the other hand, Nero showed marked coolness. So many of them, nowadays, seemed unable to appreciate him: not surprisingly, since the groups round Piso and Thrasea had recently been liquidated, and the conspiracy of Vinicianus lay just ahead. Nero's favourite Vatinius, the crippled shoemaker turned informer, used to amuse the imperial table by a significant joke: 'I hate you, Nero, because you are a senator!'[4] The emperor had taken the point; for it was noted that, when setting out for Greece and again when returning to Italy, he refused to give senators the usual ceremonial kiss, or to return their salutations. The control of affairs at Rome was left not with his council, since its guiding spirit, Tigellinus, accompanied him to Greece, but with two Graeco-oriental freedmen serving as his ministers: Helius, who had been the comptroller of his Asian estates, and Polyclitus, whom he had earlier entrusted with a mission to Britain.

And so, with these arrangements made, Nero felt able at last to turn to the people who really understood what good art was: the Greeks. For this was to be an artistic tour. After taking part in festivals at Corcyra (Corfu) and Actium, the emperor proceeded to Corinth, the capital of the province, where he probably spent the winter. Then, in the following year, he participated in a festival at Argos and in the four national Games of Greece, the Olympic, Pythian, Isthmian and Nemean. All these five occasions are commemorated on contemporary Greek-inscribed coins issued by the governor of Egypt. The dates of the various Games had been altered to follow one another closely, so that Nero could compete in the whole lot. The programmes were altered, too. Tragic acting was introduced at the Isthmian Games at Corinth, where Nero also sang a hymn and a short song about divinities of the sea.[5] At the Olympic Games (later declared invalid), a musical contest was exceptionally arranged, so that the emperor could appear not only as a herald but as lyre-player and tragic actor as well. At Olympia, too, he drove two teams of four horses and one of ten. While racing with the team of ten, he was hurled from his chariot; he climbed back, half-dazed, but could not manage to finish the course. Nevertheless he was awarded the prize, a decision which earned the judges a gift of a million sesterces.

At all the Games in which he competed he gained prizes, eighteen hundred and eight of them in all. In the musical contests, he defeated the most distinguished musicians of the day, including his own teacher Terpnus. His victories were proclaimed in the following terms: 'Nero Caesar wins this contest, and crowns the Roman people and the inhabited world, which is his.' He had declared beforehand that it was his ambition to become

229

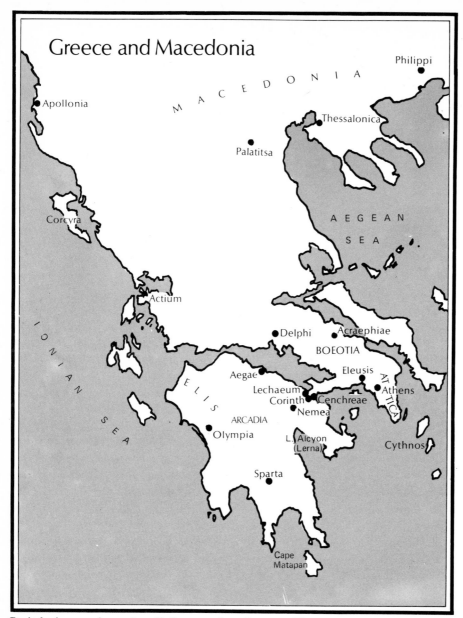

Greece and Macedonia

Periodonices – victor in all four major Games. The various sets of judges ensured that this ambition was fulfilled. But although Nero ensured that their appreciation should not go unrewarded, he did not altogether forget the bad financial situation at home; for he did not see fit to waive his claim to the money-prizes that went with the victors' wreaths. Another problem for the Greeks, which had already given them cause for anxiety but was even more serious now that the emperor was present in person, was his insatiable taste for acquiring works of art.

Nero found time to enter not only the famous national competitions but smaller local ones as well. However he avoided visiting Sparta or Athens. The traditional Spartan discipline failed to appeal to him; and Athens perhaps repelled him, as was mentioned earlier, because of all its myths about

The Pythian Apollo: one of a series of five designs on coins issued by the governor of Egypt to celebrate Nero's successes in the Greek Games.

the Furies chasing Orestes after he had murdered his mother. Nor could he be tempted to enter Athenian territory to take part in the Eleusinian Mysteries, from which people with bad consciences were excluded by public order of the herald.

However, his gift for adventurous and imaginative projects was seen at its best in a plan to construct a canal through the Isthmus of Corinth – a plan which had been launched, without effect, on three previous occasions, and most recently by the emperor Caligula. If such a canal could be built, ships would be able to avoid the stormy journey round Cape Matapan, which every year took a heavy toll of life and property. Vespasian, now commander in Judaea, sent six thousand Jewish prisoners to help with the job, and a musical programme was arranged for the official inauguration of the work. But traditionalists declared that the omens were discouraging, since the plan was an offence against heaven. So Nero himself grasped a golden spade and threw up a little of the soil, and then the others had to do the same. It was said that when the canal was ready, he was going to rename the Peloponnese 'Neronnesus', the island of Nero.

But the sage Apollonius of Tyana pessimistically declared that the emperor would never sail through the Isthmus; and he was right. Only one-fifth of the canal was cut, starting at the port of Lechaeum at the western end, and then Nero's successors abandoned the scheme. The Corinth Canal was not opened until 1893. (Nero's project for another and much longer canal, in Italy itself, extending from Neapolis and Puteoli to Ostia, proved equally abortive; all it did was to ruin the famous Caecuban vineyards.)

The liberation of
Greece

At the end of his Greek tour he performed an action which brought him immense popularity throughout the east. For on 28 November 67,[6] he appeared in the stadium of Corinth and declared Greece free. Cities in various parts of the empire were already 'free', meaning that they were allowed to retain special prestige and usually a somewhat enhanced degree of self-government. But for a whole Roman province to be declared free was something new. Since the province in question was Greece, the joy caused by the gesture was disproportionate, for all its people were sentimentally immersed in its past glories. But it was far from being a matter of sentiment only, because Nero simultaneously declared the country exempt from Roman tribute.[7] The 'freedom' of a city by no means always carried immunity from taxes. But now the whole assemblage of cities that made up the province of Achaea were given both; and this was, obviously, a tremendous practical advantage, especially as most Greeks had little money to spare.

Nero's oration announcing his gift to them is preserved on a bronze tablet found at the little town of Acraephiae (Karditsa) in Boeotia, northwest of Athens. Like his address to Tiridates shortly before leaving Italy, it is a fine illustration of the emperor's grandiloquent, complacent style.

Unexpected is the gift, men of Greece, with which I present you – though perhaps nothing can be thought unexpected from munificence such as mine – and so vast that you could not hope to ask for it. Would that I could have made this grant when

Hellas was in its prime, so that there might have been more men to enjoy my grace. Not through pity, however, but through goodwill I now make you this benefaction, and I thank your gods, whose watchful providence I have always experienced both on sea and land, that they have afforded me the opportunity of so great a benefaction. Other emperors have freed cities; Nero alone a whole province.[8]

Nero at Smyrna (Izmir): one of the bronze coins issued in his honour by the Greek cities of the empire.

At the town where this inscription was found, and no doubt at every other Greek town as well, a decree was passed thanking Nero for his generosity. The motion at Acraephiae was proposed by the bearer of a great Boeotian name, Epaminondas, the son of Epaminondas. He identifies Nero with the New Sun; the emperor is a reincarnation of Apollo, and of Zeus the Liberator as well. This flight of fancy echoed, or was echoed by, an imperial coinage displaying IVPPITER LIBERATOR; the deity, by an unfortunate coincidence, to whom Seneca and Thrasea had poured libations before they died. 'Hail to the patron of Greece!' pronounces a contemporary coinage of Apollonia on the Ionian Sea,[9] and even a gloomy ascetic like Apollonius of Tyana was impressed. A Nero legend was in the making (see Appendix I).

Meanwhile, however, the general euphoria was by no means shared by the two ministers whom Nero had left behind to run Rome, Helius and Polyclitus. Morale in all quarters was uncertain. The population of the capital had become irritable because grain-ships were not arriving regularly. Either they had been requisitioned for the Jewish War, or perhaps some were diverted to transport Nero's enormous suite to Greece. The soldiers, too, were grumbling because financial stringency had caused their pay to fall into arrears.

Nor could the upper class be expected to feel very happy or loyal after the ravages Nero had recently caused in their ranks, not to speak of his obvious mood of alienation from the Senate as he departed from Rome. In his absence, Helius had continued with the executions of possible recalcitrants. But soon he took fright, and repeatedly pressed the emperor to come back. Finally, in about January 68 – after Nero had been absent from Italy for longer than any other ruler since the days of Tiberius' retirement to Capri – Helius went over to Greece himself in great haste, and begged him to return. He asserted that another great conspiracy had been discovered. Whether this was true or not, it is easy to believe that the intelligence reports reaching his ears were causing him alarm.

In any case Nero now delayed no longer, and he started back across the Adriatic at once – indeed so precipitately that he set out during a storm, which nearly wrecked his ship. But when he arrived in Italy, apart from a few death sentences, all such unpleasant matters were forgotten. For his attention was entirely concentrated instead upon a whole series of spectacular parades, which had been arranged to welcome the returning hero. With his hair now hanging down to his shoulders, he made a triumphant entry into his beloved Neapolis in a white horse chariot, entering through a breach in the wall after the custom of victorious Greek athletes. Then on to Antium and Alba Longa, reputed to be the mother-town from which Rome had originally been colonized, and so to Rome itself, where a similar special gate was inserted in the city wall.

The Romans then witnessed a startling variant of the traditional triumphal procession: startling, because the triumph was one of peace not of war, of the arts not of arms. Decked out in a purple robe and a cloak glittering with gold stars, crowned by the wild olive that was the prize of the Olympic Games and brandishing the bay-leaves of their Pythian counterpart at Delphi, the emperor stood in a gilded chariot with the lyre-player Diodorus, who was one of the famous performers he had defeated during the Greek competitions. In front marched men carrying the emperor's 1,808 wreaths and crowns, together with banners which enumerated all his victories and emphasized that he was the first Roman ever to have won them. Down the Sacred Way he paraded, and on into the Forum, amid waving streamers and fragrant clouds of saffron, while the crowds cheered him as the greatest of all conquerors since the beginning of time. 'Hail, Victor of Olympia!' went their litany. 'Hail, Pythian Victor! Augustus! Augustus! Nero Apollo! Nero Hercules! The one and only all-victorious! The one and only Lord! Augustus! Augustus! Voice divine! Blessed are those who are thy listeners!' This was the moment of Nero's supreme jubilation; and it was indeed something to have converted the classic, bloodthirsty Triumph to peaceful purposes.

Then, like the great battle-winners of bygone days, he proceeded onwards up to the Capitol. But, whereas that had been the final, climactic destination of the traditional processions, Nero wanted the emphasis to be different. This time the parade was to finish up instead on the adjacent Palatine Hill; for it was there that Augustus had built his magnificent shrine of Apollo, divine patron of the arts. And so it was to Apollo, on the Palatine, that the new Augustus dedicated all his wreaths. Later he kept many of them in his own bedroom, since he could not bear to be without them. But others were seen crowning an obelisk in the Circus Maximus – where he graciously accepted invitations to compete in person.

He also gave a variety of other public performances – even, on occasion, voluntarily allowing himself to be defeated, though that must have been a ticklish question for his fellow-competitors and the judges. At this point certain enterprising individuals began to cherish hopes that they might also be able to entice Nero to give private shows for a fee, as a professional performer. A man called Larcius, from Lydia in Asia Minor, had the nerve to offer him a million sesterces to play the lyre on such an occasion.[10] Larcius failed to get his performance, but he lost his money all the same, because Tigellinus collected it as the price of his life.

Nero stayed on in Rome for a few weeks. Then he retired to the more congenial, Hellenic atmosphere of Neapolis.

14 The End

The emperor's advisers, already worried about rumours of discontent which were reaching them through their intelligence services, must have been made even more nervous by the fantastic spectacles which accompanied Nero's return and whipped up still further his increasingly obsessive passion for the stage and Circus. But they do not seem to have allowed this to discourage them, for plans were now under way for what would have been the most far-reaching military expedition of the reign. The scheme envisaged, as a first step, the occupation of the Dariel (Krestovy) Pass through the Caucasus range, north of Tiflis. All through Nero's reign a series of efforts had been made to convert the Black Sea into a Roman lake. With the Caucasus occupied, this would be achieved. The base for the operation would be the Cimmerian Bosphorus (Crimea), where the regime of a client king had been replaced by direct Roman rule a few years earlier. And the immediate target was a fierce tribe, the Alani,[1] who were threatening a Caucasian client state of Rome and endangering the Greek cities along the coast.

But where, having achieved these objectives, Nero's government intended to establish the empire's new boundary remains difficult to imagine. The whole project seems linked up with the government's keen interest in exploration, which had already led to notable expeditions to the Baltic and central Africa; and recently a preliminary survey of the Caucasus, too, had been undertaken on Nero's instructions. Knowledge of the remoter areas of southern Russia was still fragmentary. But it was known, for example, that the north end of the Caspian received the waters of a great river, the Volga;[2] and an eventual move in that direction was possibly contemplated. Alternatively, the Caucasus might have been envisaged as a springboard for movements further south and east, against Parthia; but after the hard-won and much proclaimed settlement with that power over Armenia, this seems unlikely. Perhaps Nero, at this stage, merely intended to occupy the Caucasus, and then to see how things developed. It is possible also that his ministers, with their oriental trade connections, had an eye on commercial expansion, especially as this was the time when Romans were learning, through intermediaries, about Chinese trading operations in the Himalayas.

But Nero's personal interest, like that of Caesar before him and other

Galba, who after hesitation came out against Nero in April 68 and succeeded him in June, reigning for seven months.

235

Roman rulers later on, was probably enlisted by people who compared him flatteringly with Alexander the Great. Seneca and Lucan had been taking a highbrow, minority attitude, a few years earlier, when they saw Alexander as a mad, unhappy, restless man.[3] For he was, above all, a glorious legend, and a legend which Nero, with his Greek tastes, was likely to find more powerful even than the distaste he had earlier felt for war. And evidence that the Alexander myth appealed to him was provided by the new legion which he now began to raise, composed of Italians six feet tall; for he named it 'the Phalanx of Alexander the Great'.

Other legions for the expedition could be drawn from Rome's eastern armies, now that peace had been established on the Parthian frontier. And Nero also ordered recruitment in Germany and Britain and on the Danube. These extensive preparations were signalized by a silver coinage, displaying a legionary Eagle and two standards. The design was a traditional one, having been issued exactly one hundred years previously, on a famous coinage which was still in circulation. Its original issuer had been Antony, from whom Nero through his paternal grandmother was directly descended. The occasion for that first coinage had been the campaign of Actium, won by Nero's other ancestor Augustus. Both men had aspired to eastern conquests, and Nero intended to outdo them both: though it is unlikely that he would have taken the field himself, for he had never done so yet. However it would be satisfactory to be an Alexander by proxy, and then to celebrate an appropriate Triumph.

Revolt in Gaul   But the proposed expedition never materialized. For on the anniversary of his mother's death – that is to say, a few days after the middle of March 68 – Nero received news that one of his provincial governors was in revolt. He was Gaius Julius Vindex, governor of one of the provinces of Gaul – probably its central area, Lugdunensis, of which the capital was the important city of Lugdunum (Lyon), at the junction of the Rhône and the Saône. Although Gaul enjoyed great prosperity, Vindex, who himself claimed royal Gallic origin, was joined by large contingents, especially from the rich central tribes. These made up, to some extent, for the fact that he had no legionaries under his command. For, in spite of this lack of regular troops, he collected a force estimated at one hundred thousand strong. Lugdunum, with its marked loyalist tradition,[4] did not rally to him; but he was joined by another settlement of Roman citizens which was its rival, namely Vienna (Vienne), lower down the Rhône in the adjoining province of Narbonese Gaul, the southern part of France.

Vindex is described as a brave, daring and clever man; the only thing recorded against him (unless he was playing a practical joke) is that he painted his face white so that the throngs of legacy hunters who surrounded eminent men should be particularly respectful and assiduous. Nero's government accused him of fanning the flames of seditious Gaulish nationalism, but the coinage Vindex now issued, without inscribing it with his name, at Vienna, bears slogans which deny any connection with narrow Gallic interests. The principal motifs are Freedom and Vengeance (which was what the name of Vindex meant), that is to say the liberation of Roman citizens

Nero shortly after his accession to the throne, on a silver coin issued at Ephesus in Ionia.

239

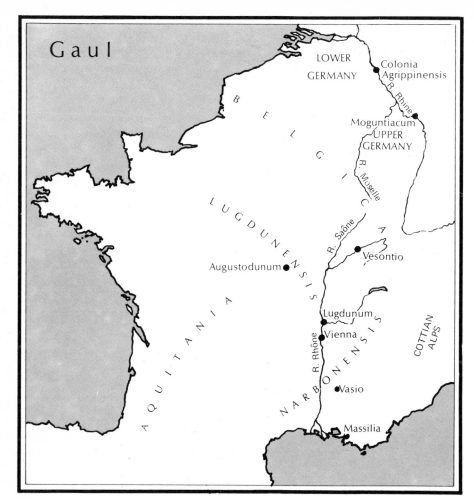

Gaul

LOWER GERMANY
Colonia Agrippinensis
R. Rhine
Moguntiacum
UPPER GERMANY
R. Moselle
BELGICA
LUGDUNENSIS
R. Saône
Vesontio
Augustodunum
Lugdunum
Vienna
R. Rhône
NARBONENSIS
AQUITANIA
COTTIAN ALPS
Vasio
Massilia

Mars the Avenger (MARS VLTOR) – one of the slogans of Vindex and Galba when they rose against Nero.

and other imperial subjects, wherever they might be, from Nero's allegedly arbitrary and tyrannical rule.[5]

Vindex issued a proclamation denouncing the emperor's extravagances, but what he no doubt had particularly in mind was the peril from Nero that now beset every one of his provincial governors each day of their life. Yet although his official language smacked of Republican tradition, Vindex did not envisage that Rome could do without an emperor at all. It was not possible for the Republic to be restored. The old system had vanished more than three generations ago, and was now irrecoverable. What he wanted instead was the replacement of Nero by some other emperor: a constitutional ruler like Augustus – or like Nero as he had been in the first years of his reign.

Vindex did not, however, aspire to this position for himself. Instead, he offered the leadership of his movement to another and much more eminent figure. This was Galba, the seventy-three-year-old governor of Nearer Spain (Hispania Tarraconensis). Galba was a very wealthy, though avaricious, member of one of the few surviving families of the old Republican aristocracy. He had been greatly liked, long ago, by Augustus' wife Livia. Thirty-five years previously he had held the consulship; and then, after a long and distinguished career, he had been appointed to his present post by Nero in AD 60. Galba had tried to keep very quiet in Spain, since he knew that the emperor was capable of turning against hustling governors. But he had managed, all the same, to get on bad terms with Nero's personal agents in the province, so that there was some reason to fear that the next to be struck down might be himself. He knew he could rely on popular support inside Spain, especially as Nero's destruction of Seneca's family the Annaei must have left many of their feudal clients disaffected.

Still, Galba was old and in weak health, and he only had one legion; and so he procrastinated. But further delay became impossible when the governor of south-western France (Aquitania) wrote to invoke his help against Vindex on Nero's behalf.[6] As the commander of Galba's legion remarked, even to discuss such a request amounted to treason towards Nero: a decision simply had to be reached one way or the other. And so, on 2 April 68, in a proclamation at Carthago Nova (Cartagena), Galba came out openly against the emperor. But he still did not agree to be hailed as his successor, calling himself instead the general and representative of the Senate and Roman People. He and Vindex were now virtually allies. Galba was also supported by Otho, who had held the governorship of Lusitania (Portugal) ever since he had been obliged to depart from Rome in a hurry, leaving Poppaea with the emperor. But Otho, too, could contribute only very few men. So Galba started enrolling a further legion among the Spaniards. Yet that would still not be nearly enough.

The only large concentration of troops in the entire western half of the empire was far away on the Rhine; and it was on them that everything now depended. The Rhine armies were divided into two commands, Lower and Upper Germany. The governor of Lower Germany was not only vicious but incapable of making up his mind what to do. The master of the situation was therefore his colleague in the Upper province. The holder of this com-

Galba.

Galba looked (and is carefully made to look) like an austere old-fashioned Roman. His legionary eagle and standards copy one of Nero's last issues. The design had first appeared just a hundred years earlier, on a famous series issued by Antony (Nero's ancestor) before the battle of Actium. Antony's enemy, Nero's other forbear Augustus, had later issued variants of the type.

mand, who had his headquarters at Moguntiacum (Mainz), was Lucius Verginius Rufus, a highly respected figure from Mediolanum (Milan) and one of the chief leaders of a group of prominent men from north Italy. And now, after an interval, Verginius moved. With at least three legions, and corresponding auxiliary troops, he left the Rhine and marched south: but by no means with the intentions for which Galba hoped, since, in the event, Verginius did not back Vindex but fought against him.

Our knowledge of his actions is almost wholly clouded by the anti-Neronian political attitudes which leaders like himself found it convenient to adopt in later reigns. Less than the truth, for example, is told by his own epitaph, in which he or his heirs make no mention of Verginius helping Nero but suggest that in fighting Vindex he was patriotically suppressing a Gaulish nationalist menace.[7] In fact, however, not only was this description of the aims of Vindex inaccurate, but Verginius himself had acted in loyal support of Nero. It is true that there may have been moments when he did not intend to do this. In the first place, he had been slow to get going: although not many days' march away from Vindex, he had taken two months to react. And when he did move, he made contact with Vindex and arranged a meeting with him, at which no one else was present. Presumably they discussed whether Verginius might transfer his allegiance to Galba. But, if so, nothing came of the idea, for, at about the end of May, the two armies clashed and fought. The battle was at Vesontio (Besançon): Vindex was defeated, and died – probably by his own hand. Subsequently it was said that the two armies had insisted on fighting against the wishes of their commanders.[8] But this was an attempt to pretend that Verginius had not decided to fight in defence of Nero: which was, in fact, what he had done.

In this considerable crisis, then, a very senior commander did not see fit to desert the emperor; and the legionaries did not desert him either. Nero has often been blamed for never visiting his legions, and as for the Rhine garrisons, he had recently removed and executed their last pair of commanders. Yet in spite of this, and in spite of the slowness with which he was giving them their pay, and in spite of his artistic tastes, the armies on the German frontier remained loyal to the descendant of Augustus. As for Verginius, either now or a little later – or possibly already earlier – there were suggestions that he should declare himself emperor. But instead he retired to his province, dutifully or at least noncommittally. Galba, when he heard of the death of Vindex, sent Verginius an appeal for cooperation, then withdrew to the remote Spanish town of Clunia in despair.

Nero's response to the crisis Nero had the situation well in hand. Or, rather, he could have had it in hand. When news of the rebellion of Vindex had originally been brought to him at Neapolis, at first he paid no attention and took no action – for eight days continuing his daily visits to the gymnasium; though a particularly disturbing dispatch, which arrived while he was having dinner, did cause him to utter an irritable threat of punishment. Finally he wrote a letter to the Senate, excusing himself for his absence on the grounds of a throat infection, and asking them, on behalf of himself and Rome, to put Vindex down.

But the first thing that really stung the emperor was a report that came in soon afterwards indicating what Vindex had said about him. He did not so much mind that the rebel had called him by his own family-name Domitius Ahenobarbus instead of by his adoptive imperial designation Nero. Indeed he himself, he said, was thinking he might bring his old name back into use. But Vindex's assertion that he played the lyre badly hurt him very much, and he made the rounds of his friends asking if they did not agree that this was utterly outrageous. Finally, he returned to Rome; but still he did not appear before the Senate or people. When his leading advisers, at his own urgent request, paid him a visit, he cut the meeting short, and spent the rest of the day showing them a newly invented type of organ run by hydraulic power, and announcing that he had discovered a way of making such organs produce louder and more musical tones.

On hearing of Galba's proclamation at Carthago Nova, Nero fell into a faint. But a woman who had once been his nurse offered words of comfort, and he recovered sufficiently to dash off some poems making fun of the leaders of the revolt. Then he went to the theatre. An actor was receiving loud applause, but Nero sent the man a message protesting that he was taking unfair advantage of the emperor's own preoccupation with other matters.

The Senate duly declared Galba a public enemy, and Nero seized as much of his property as he could lay his hands on, while Galba reciprocated. Then at the end of April, before Vesontio, the emperor made a gesture of defiance by assuming the consulship, without a colleague, as Pompey had done in the previous century at another critical time. He also began recruiting a new legion from the sailors at Misenum, the naval base near Neapolis. Moreover, two generals were appointed to take command in north Italy: Petronius Turpilianus, the former governor of Britain – who had helped him to put down Piso's conspiracy – and another ex-consul, Rubrius Gallus. To provide them with a striking-force, Nero held back a group of three legions, derived partly from the Danube area and partly from Britain, which had been intended for the Caucasus expedition; and the new Phalanx of Alexander the Great, which he had raised for the same purpose, was dispatched to Gaul in order to strengthen loyal Lugdunum. To Africa, where his commander in Numidia (eastern Algeria) was beginning to play a lone and piratical hand,[9] he sent the woman Calvia Crispinilla who looked after Sporus – unless, as is

This soft, Greek portrayal of Nero was deliberately counteracted by the artists of Galba's coins.

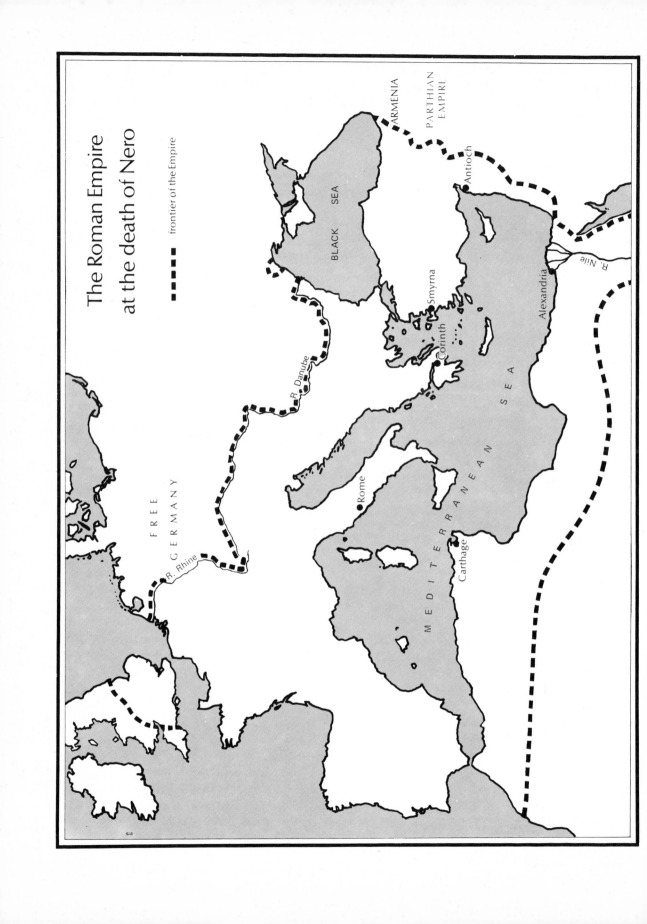

The Roman Empire
at the death of Nero

▬ ▬ ▬ frontier of the Empire

ARMENIA

PARTHIAN
EMPIRE

Antioch

BLACK SEA

Smyrna

Corinth

Alexandria

R. Nile

R. Danube

MEDITERRANEAN SEA

FREE
GERMANY

R. Rhine

Rome

Carthage

also possible, she fled there on her own account a little later.

The emperor also tried to raise money. But none of these measures were very effective, since his personal attitude was far from reassuring.

> One day he left the dining room with his arms round two friends' shoulders, and remarked that when he reached Gaul he would at once step unarmed in front of the embattled enemy and weep, and weep. This would soften their hearts and win them back to loyalty; and on the next day he would stroll among his joyful troops singing paeans of victory – which he really ought to be composing now.[10]

And then, he declared, he would hold Victory Games, at which he himself would perform on the pipe and flute, and on his new water organ. Besides, even if he did lose the throne, he said, he would still be able to live by his art.

The end At some stage during this period the two praetorian commanders, Tigellinus and Nymphidius Sabinus, decided it was no use trying to help Nero any longer. Even the news of Vesontio, which must have reached Rome within a few days, evidently did not make them change their minds, because by now things were too far gone.

The exact role played by Tigellinus is uncertain. He may have actively deserted Nero;[11] or he may not. He was suffering from an incurable disease,[12] and perhaps he left Rome altogether. In any case he took no action on the emperor's behalf. The initiative, then, lay in the hands of his colleague Nymphidius.[13] And he evidently came to the conclusion that Nero had so completely lost touch with reality that military oaths of loyalty no longer applied. Support for the emperor had dwindled in all quarters. Members of the upper class, gravely disaffected because of executions in their ranks, had received a secret visit from an envoy of Galba, his freedman Icelus Marcianus. The soldiers of the German garrison had remained loyal, but with so much back pay owing how long could the legionaries be relied upon? As for the people of Rome, Nero believed that they still loved him, and a draft appeal to them was later found among his documents. But they were suffering from a shortage of grain – and ships were seen arriving full of sand for some court performance of wrestlers! An outbreak of offensive *graffiti* showed that the

Nero.

emperor's reputation in the capital was going through a bad period. Yet it was none of these sections of the community that ruined him. As far as Senate, army and people were concerned, he could still have saved the situation if only he had acted energetically. It was his failure to retain the personal fidelity of the guard commanders, and particularly of Nymphidius, that proved fatal.

The report of Vesontio was more than counterbalanced by a piece of bad news which sharply increased Nero's natural tendency to panic. For on 8 June there arrived a report, according to Suetonius, that 'the other armies had revolted'.[14] This probably refers to the fact that Rubrius Gallus – one of the two generals sent to command the army in north Italy – had now decided to desert to Galba, thus immobilizing his colleague Turpilianus, who apparently remained loyal but could do nothing.[15]

It was at this point that Nero decided to get away. How long the idea had been brewing in his mind we cannot tell. But now, at any rate, he planned to leave instantly, without the loss of a single day. His destination was to be Egypt, the only major province that was habitually governed by the emperor's own agent, always a non-senator (at this time the renegade Jew, Tiberius Julius Alexander, was in charge). Nero, who had already planned to visit the country on a previous occasion, believed it to be loyal.[16] So he gave orders to his most trusted ministers to hasten to Ostia to get a fleet ready; and he would join it forthwith.

He left the Golden House on the same day, and travelled a short distance to his mansion in the Servilian Gardens, on the way to Rome's Ostia Gate. There he rested. But after a short sleep, he woke: only to find that the unit of the Praetorian Guard which had been on duty outside was no longer there. For although it had been Nymphidius himself who advised him to stop at the Servilian Gardens, as soon as Nero left the Golden House the commander had hastened to the praetorian camp and told the guardsmen that the emperor had already fled to Egypt. Nymphidius, who was accompanied by a group of senators, then offered the praetorians a gift of thirty thousand sesterces a head, and induced them to proclaim Galba emperor.

The situation was now desperate for Nero. Without his praetorian bodyguard and their commanders, he was lost.

What followed must be told in the words of Suetonius, though his narrative differs from the account of Dio Cassius and leaves many questions unanswered. In particular, the course of events, as outlined here, suggests that there was treachery among the men who accompanied Nero in his last hours: though Suetonius does not actually say this in so many words. Nevertheless, the description is his masterpiece.

Nero was roused about midnight, and when he learnt that the troops on guard-duty had vanished, he leapt out of bed and sent round to his friends; and because he received no reply from any of them, he visited their lodgings in turn, with a few attendants. But all their doors were closed and no one answered. He returned to his room, to find his bodyguards had also fled, having plundered his bedclothes and removed his box of poison as well. At once he asked for Spiculus the gladiator, or someone else who would kill him. When he could find no one, he said, 'Have I

A gold coin of Vindex, issued in Gaul during his rebellion of AD 68. Instead of the emperor's head appears the 'Genius of the Roman People' (GENIVS *Populi* R*omani*). (Cf. p. 240.)

246

neither a friend nor an enemy?' and rushed out, as if to throw himself into the Tiber.

But, recovering his spirits, he wanted some more secret hiding-place to collect his thoughts; and when his freedman Phaon offered him his suburban residence between the Salarian and Nomentan roads about four miles out, just as he was, with one foot bare and wearing a tunic, he threw on a cloak of faded colour and mounted a horse, holding a handkerchief in front of his face, with only four companions, including Sporus.[17] At once he was thrown into panic by an earthquake and a flash of lightning, and heard from the camp nearby the shouts of the soldiers, promising trouble to him and success to Galba. He also heard a traveller who met them saying, 'These fellows are after Nero', and another asking: 'Any news of Nero in the city?' Moreover, his horse reared at the smell of a corpse lying by the road, so that his face was uncovered and he was recognised and saluted by a retired guardsman.

When they reached the side turning, he sent the horses away and made his way with difficulty among the bushes and brambles along a path in the reeds, having a coat thrown down for him to walk on, until he reached the rear of the house. There, when Phaon urged him to withdraw for the moment into a cave where sand had been dug, he said he was not going to be buried alive. He waited a little while, until a concealed entrance to the house should be made; and, wishing to drink some water from a pool close at hand, he took some in the hollow of his hand and said 'So this is Nero's famous drink!'[18] Then, tearing his cloak on the brambles, he pushed himself through the twigs across his path and crawled through a narrow tunnel into a cellar which had been dug out and lay down in the adjoining store-room on a bed fitted with a moderate mattress and an old robe laid on it. And feeling hungry and thirsty again, he refused to touch some grimy bread that was offered him, but drank a little lukewarm water. Then as each of his attendants in turn pressed him to save himself as soon as possible from the indignities that threatened him, he ordered a grave to be made in his presence, measuring it by his own body, and some bits of marble to be arranged, if they were to be found, and water and firewood for dealing with his corpse forthwith, weeping at every juncture and repeating over and over again: *What a loss I shall be to the arts!*

A runner brought him a letter from Phaon. Nero tore it from the man's hands and read that having been declared a public enemy by the Senate,[19] he would be punished in 'ancient style' when arrested. He asked what the 'ancient style' meant, and learnt that the executioners stripped their victim naked, thrust his head into a wooden fork, and then flogged him to death with rods.

In terror he snatched up the two daggers which he had brought along, and tried their points; but threw them down again, protesting that the fatal hour had not yet come. Then he begged Sporus to weep and mourn for him, but also begged one of the other three to set him an example by committing suicide first. He kept moaning about his cowardice and muttering: 'How ugly and vulgar my life has become!' And then in Greek, 'This certainly is no credit to Nero, no credit at all – one should be tough in such situations – come, pull yourself together, man!'

By this time the troop of cavalry who had orders to take him alive were coming up the road. Nero gasped: *Hark to the sound I hear! It is hooves of galloping horses.* Then, with the help of his minister Epaphroditus, he stabbed himself in the throat and was already half dead when a centurion entered, pretending to have rushed to his rescue, and staunched the wound with his cloak. 'Too late', Nero muttered, 'how *loyal* you are.'[20]

Nero as he seemed to a later age: his hair-style 'in steps', as described by Suetonius and suggested on certain coins.

His former mistress Acte, and his two nurses, were allowed to give him an expensive funeral.[21] Then his ashes, in a porphyry urn, were taken to the burial-place of the Domitian family, beneath the Pincian Hill.

Appendix 1

The Legend of Nero

When Nero died, Suetonius says the people were glad, but Tacitus believed they were sorry. In the words of the next emperor Galba, 'Nero will always be missed by the riff-raff'.[1] Otho, who murdered Galba in January, 69, and ruled until his own death three months later, had been one of Nero's betrayers, but when he became emperor he showed various signs of favour to his former friend,[2] as well as to Poppaea whom they had both loved. Then Vitellius, who occupied the throne thereafter until December of the same year, paid similar tributes to his own friendship with Nero, calling out to a lyre-player at a banquet: 'now let us have one of the Master's songs!'[3]

An eighteenth-century Nero.

Nero's memory also continued to be cherished in the east. For one thing, he was remembered for his eastern settlement – remembered gratefully by the Parthians and their friends, since it had worked in their favour; and he was remembered, too, for the grandeur with which the settlement had been celebrated during Tiridates' visit to Rome. After his death, therefore, King Vologases of Parthia requested the Senate to revere his memory. Furthermore, Nero was one of a select body of rulers including King Arthur, Frederick Barbarossa, Frederick II 'Stupor Mundi' and Hitler – men cut off by sudden or mysterious deaths which people refused to believe had ever really happened, weaving 'return' sagas round their memory.

Almost immediately after Nero had died, a pseudo-Nero appeared, much to the excitement of people in Greece and Asia Minor. Either a slave from Pontus or an Italian freedman, he was an accomplished lyre-player who looked very like the dead emperor; at about the time of Otho's accession, he declared that he was indeed Nero, and a gang of supporters gathered round him. However, he was soon cornered on the Aegean island of Cythnos and was killed. Then in 79, a certain Terentius Maximus came forward in his native country of Asia Minor, and announced in his turn that *he* was Nero, having presumably been in hiding for eleven years. He was welcomed by many credulous people, and made his way to the Parthian king Artabanus who, being angry with Titus who was Roman emperor at the time, seriously considered trying to 'restore' him to the Roman throne. Finally, however, Terentius was recognized as a fraud and was handed over to the Romans who probably put him to death: but not before he had stimulated Jewish seers to prophesy of a king who would come back westwards across the Euphrates with tens of thousands of men. Probably there was also a third pseudo-Nero in 88, who likewise fled to a welcoming Parthia.[4]

The Greek orator and philosopher Dio Chrysostom of Prusa, who had been wandering about the east at the time, felt able to declare, early in the next century, that there was no certainty about how Nero killed himself – and that most people believed he was still alive.[5] He was speaking as a Greek: for Nero's memory was revered by Greeks because of his liberation of their country. The gift, it is true, was very quickly rescinded after Nero's death, because of disturbances under Vespasian. And yet when Plutarch, himself a Greek, later pictured Nero's soul awaiting torture and reincarnation, he imagined a voice coming out of a great light and declaring: 'Some good thing is owed him by the gods! For he has freed the race of men which is the best and most beloved by the gods among all the subjects of the empire.'[6]

Nero's act was again praised by the traveller Pausanias (*c.* 150), and later still by another Greek savant Flavius Philostratus, who also had a good word to say about the project for a Corinth canal.

However, if Nero was remembered as a saint he was also remembered as a devil. When the unknown author of the *Book of Revelation of St John the Divine*, writing towards the end of the first century AD, talks of 'the Beast whose number is 666',[7] he is probably speaking of Nero, because the Hebrew numerals comprising that figure are the same as the letters of Nero's name. This was 'the Beast which was wounded to death, but whose deadly wound was healed: the Beast that was, and is not, and yet is'.

The popular belief that Nero would one day return caused Christians to think of this expected event as the sinister counterpart of the Second Coming of Jesus, and to believe that Nero himself was Christ's rival who stood for wicked earthly joys against the blessings of the life of self-denial. And so, while pagan games-tokens[8] and gems[9] honoured him as charioteer and sportsman, Christian writers of the third and fourth centuries denounced him as the Anti-Christ himself: 'Some suppose that Nero will rise again as Anti-Christ. Others think that he is not dead, but was concealed, so that he might be supposed to have been killed, and that he still lives on as a legendary figure, of the same age as that at which he died, and will be restored to his Kingdom.'[10]

Nero and the Circus Maximus. This prize or memento of the public Games was issued more than three hundred years after his death, in *c.* AD 390.

Heads of Nero continued to be made long after his lifetime, with a brisk production in the Renaissance and the baroque age. *Far left:* here the head and the cuirass are of different dates. *Left:* Nero in the Italian Renaissance.

Pope Paschal II (1099–1118) used to listen to crows cawing in a walnut-tree near the tomb of the Domitii, and he dreamt that they were demons serving Nero. So he tore down the tomb and erected in its place the chapel which became the present church of Santa Maria del Popolo. The crows went away, but throughout the Middle Ages they were believed to be still serving the emperor's wandering spirit. For it would continue to wander until the time came for its return to earth, when Christ himself would come again and Nero Anti-Christ be hurled down into the bottomless pit. As late as 1900, sagas of Nero's diabolical evil were still being told in the Marches behind Ancona.

During the Renaissance, Nero had been remembered for another reason as well, because the spectacular fashion in which ancient artists had portrayed him appealed to the sculptors of the day. And then his features inevitably caught the fancy of baroque artists, for if anyone ever looked baroque it was he. But the result is that only a minute proportion of all his busts that we can see today go back to his own time.

As with these sculptural portraits, so with the literary record; and the next Appendix will discuss the acute difficulty of trying to get back to contemporary accounts and find out what really happened.

A baroque Nero; probably second century AD.

NERONE

Appendix 2

The Sources of Information

Instead of the superfluity of material which awaits the biographers of modern personages, the evidence about people who lived some two thousand years ago is often very slight indeed, and sometimes very contradictory as well. Ancient writers often leave out 'background', because, although we may need it now, their contemporaries did not.

Besides, in the Roman empire, as in autocratic states today, there is the additional difficulty that the government often did not *want* people to discover what had happened. The point was put clearly in the early third century AD by the historian Dio Cassius, a Greek from Nicaea (Iznik) in Asia Minor, who was also a Roman senator and knew the position only too well.

From now on [the time of Augustus], most things that took place began to be kept secret and confidential. Even when public announcements are made, they are distrusted because they cannot be confirmed; for there is a suspicion that all sayings and actions are related to the policy of the rulers and their staffs. As a result there are many rumours about things that have never happened at all – and many things that have certainly happened are quite unknown.[1]

As for the rumours, they were made the subject of some verses by Nero's friend Petronius:

> People would rather swallow a lighted candle
> Than keep a secret that smacks in the least of scandal.
> The quietest whisper in the royal hall
> Is out in a flash buttonholing passers-by against a wall;
> And it's not enough that it's broadcast to the nation –
> Everyone gets it with improvement and elaboration.[2]

Tacitus pinpointed another problem. Every historian, he said, for reasons of his own, either flattered emperors grossly (in their lifetimes) or detested them and wrote malignantly about them (after their deaths).

Truth suffered in more ways than one. To an understandable ignorance of policy, which now lay outside public control, was in due course added a passion for flattery, or else a hatred of autocrats. Thus neither school bothered about posterity, for the one was bitterly alienated and the other deeply committed. But whereas the reader can easily discount the bias of the time-serving historian, detraction and spite find a ready audience. Adulation bears the ugly taint of subservience, but malice gives the false impression of being independent.[3]

Another remarkable historian Josephus, a Jew writing in Greek about Rome, explicitly states that Nero received both these treatments, favourable and unfavourable alike.[4] But if this was so, as it evidently was, we are ill-served, because such a very large proportion of the literary evidence that has come down to us is of the unfavourable sort. There must have been pro-Neronian versions as well; and rightly so. Nero was obviously in many ways an abominable man. But it is perfectly clear from pieces of information which emerge through all the dirt that he and his government had solid, and indeed sometimes extraordinary, achievements to their credit.

His own presentation of these achievements can be seen on the Roman coinage. There is, of course, a total contrast between all the offensive literary accounts and the great array of publicity slogans that he himself or his administrators selected for his coins. Naturally one cannot *believe* all the slogans, any more than one can believe the propaganda of any government, even one far less autocratically run than Rome's. On the other hand, really good propaganda – and the astute, hard-headed Roman efforts certainly deserve to be placed in this category – does not normally say anything that is a complete lie. It is true that complete lies *are* feasible in very tightly controlled modern states; but in ancient Rome, which lacked the necessary totalitarian machinery, the rulers would never have been able to get away with it. So the designs and inscriptions on the coinage need to be studied with care, not necessarily as a true account but as an account of what the authorities had some hopes of getting people to believe. In any case it quite often provides a useful counterblast to what the writers say on the other side.

The ancient authors who have left us any considerable narratives of Nero's life and reign are only three in number; and one of them, Dio Cassius, has to be regarded as less 'primary' than the others, because, as far as this period is concerned, he is only represented today by a boiled-down version dating from the Middle Ages. Of the two authors who remain, one, Suetonius, would have been too modest to say he was a historian at all: he would have called himself a biographer, recalling the ancient view that this was a humbler activity than history. His biography of Nero is, in fact, full of fascinating historical information, but it is collected indiscriminately, un-critically and sometimes self-contradictorily from every kind of source, including those of a thoroughly scandalous nature.

The only full-length story of Nero's reign which survives comes from the *Annals* of Tacitus: or rather we have twelve out of its fourteen years. Unlike the other writers who have been mentioned, Tacitus was a historian of portentous talent. Indeed, he possessed the greatest historical brain that ever applied itself to Rome. But, for that very reason, he cannot resist stamping its imprint on events, and the imprint of his strongly Roman conservatism, and perhaps, if as some believe he did not complete his *Annals* until the reign of Hadrian (117–138), the imprint of the early crises of that reign. I have recently said a little about the results of these processes in my book *The*

Ancient Historians. But we have also had occasion to see something of his methods in the course of this present study of Nero. The general picture of that emperor which emerges from Tacitus' marvellous pages is plausible enough as far as it goes, indeed almost obsessive in its plausibility. But it is often one-sided and sometimes self-contradictory as well. His narrative is also garnished, according to the ancient tradition, with dramatic dialogues and speeches and situations, many of which were quite clearly invented by himself, or brilliantly built up from material too inadequate to justify their acceptance as factual truth.

But much the most serious problem we have to confront still has to be mentioned. It consists of the long time that elapsed between Nero's death and the dates when these surviving historical accounts were written. Tacitus composed his *Annals* something like fifty years after Nero died, and Suetonius' *Life* was slightly later still: while yet another hundred years had passed before Dio Cassius wrote. It is extraordinarily difficult to see what someone like Nero was really like when you are relying on authorities as late as that. And the writers in question were all, in various ways, coloured by what was happening in their own times. One example of how this may have affected Tacitus has been mentioned; but many such influences, of an entirely indisputable character, could be listed in all three cases.

Of course they had their contemporary sources. But like every ancient historian and biographer, they only cited them in the most wayward and occasional fashion. And in any case each of these original authorities had again possessed his own set of slants and biases, which can sometimes be guessed today and sometimes cannot. One of these authorities was Pliny the elder, thirty years old when Nero came to the throne. We have his vast *Natural History*, a mine of information; but the thirty-one-book history he wrote about his own times has not survived. Although it was not published until after his death in 79, the period it dealt with perhaps covered the years 41–71, and in any case included the whole of Nero's reign. There was also the wealthy Cluvius Rufus, who acted as Nero's herald at the second Neronian Games and wrote a history which centred upon his reign;[5] it must have been a delicate job to perform, since Cluvius was a champion turncoat, transferring his allegiance to each of the rulers in turn during the Year of the Four Emperors (69). Another history was written by Fabius Rusticus, a Spaniard who may have been dining with his fellow countryman Seneca on the evening when the officer came from Nero to order his death.[6] Modern scholarship has taken considerable steps towards discovering what parts of these men's accounts have been reproduced in the various sections of Tacitus, Suetonius and Dio. But of their own histories nothing has come down to us.

And the memoirs and dispatches of the great general Corbulo, well known in ancient times,[7] likewise exist no longer. Nor does the auto-biography of Agrippina.[8] It was apparently pretty strong stuff, seeing that she indicated that she did not at all mind having old scandals shown up.[9]

All these losses mean that what we are told has to be supplemented by every possible means. We can pick up a great deal of priceless material, far more than is generally realized, from a study of surviving contemporary works that do not purport to be histories of Rome at all: notably Pliny's

Natural History, of which mention has just been made, and the surviving writings of Seneca and Petronius. I have tried in this book to make some use of these works.

It is also advisable to devote extensive attention to archaeological sources. In addition to the official coins of Rome and the west, which I have often had occasion to cite, a great many coins were struck in the eastern provinces, mostly with Greek inscriptions. Some of these were minted by the governor of Egypt; but the great majority were issued by cities, in Asia Minor and elsewhere. They are of particular value because they take a less cautious view than the mint of Rome. For example they deify the emperor more freely, and unlike the metropolitan coinage they sometimes provide portraits of his successive wives. Before the reign began, too, their estimates of the relative chances of Nero and Britannicus supply valuable evidence of public opinion. Moreover, as in previous reigns, they continue, especially in Asia, to demonstrate the amount of attention that was still being paid to the memory of Augustus. But since a pioneer endeavour of 1917–20, no attempt has been made to survey the empire-wide coinage collectively for this reign.

For epigraphy we are better off; and, although Nero's is by no means a rich period in this respect, certain surviving inscriptions are invaluable. For example, the records of the Arval Brethren's sacrifices show keen awareness of current political events.[10]

Finally, the art and architecture of the period are immensely important historical sources – especially as art was one of the major loves of Nero's life. The Golden House at Rome, and the frescoes of Pompeii and Herculaneum, are all remarkable testimonies to Neronian taste; and perhaps, in the last resort, they are the best guide that we possess to what Nero himself felt and thought.

Appendix 3

Sums of Money

It is, unfortunately, quite impossible to give any reliable modern equivalent of the Roman *sestertius*. In terms of the salaries of the period, it has been suggested that sixpence or 2·5 new pence (6 cents) may not be too far from the mark.[1] In writing of the previous century, however, I preferred (as the roughest of approximations) twice that amount – though it was also suggested to me that having an *as* (one-quarter of a *sestertius*) in one's possession probably felt like having a two-shilling piece (ten new pence; twenty-four cents).[2] The overall movement of prices during this epoch cannot be reconstructed.

References

In the following references, Pliny *HN* = Pliny the elder, *Historia Naturalis*. Translations from Tacitus, *Annals*, are by myself, in the Penguin Classics.

CHAPTER 1

1 Pliny *HN*, XI, 144
2 Suetonius, *Nero*, 51
3 Velleius Paterculus, II, 10, 2; II, 72, 3
4 Others prefer 35, 36, 38 or 39
5 Scholiast on Juvenal, IV, 81
6 Not a very honest man: Josephus, *Antiquitates Judaicae*, XX, 8, 9
7 Pliny *HN*, XXXIII, 63; cf. Tacitus, *Annals*, XII, 56, 5
8 M. Grant, *Roman Anniversary Issues*, pp. 78f., n.7 (Hippo Diarrhytus); (the second known specimen was presented by the writer to the British Museum). Cf. Ilium (Troy)
9 M. Grant, *Essays in Roman Coinage presented to Harold Mattingly*, p. 105; *Roman Imperial Money*, p. 109.
10 I now prefer to consider this a sister-coinage to the Nero piece, and not post-humous (reign of Titus) as Mattingly, *Coins of the Roman Empire in the British Museum*, II, p.lxxviii
11 Tacitus, *Annals*, XII, 67, 1–68, 1
12 Josephus, *Antiquitates Judaicae*, XX, 8, 1 ('some said'). Pliny *HN*, XXII, 192, was certain.
13 Juvenal, VI, 620–623 (trans. P. Green)

CHAPTER 2

1 Suetonius, *Vespasian*, 9, 1
2 Tacitus, *Annals*, XIII, 3, 2
3 Tacitus, *Histories*, IV, 8
4 She and Nero also owned property jointly, e.g. in Greece, *Corinth*, VIII, 2, p. 50, n.68
5 Dec. Silanus, L. Silanus; Junia Silana was exiled in 55.

6 Suetonius, *Nero*, 29 (trans. J. C. Rolfe, slightly amended)
7 Lucilius, *Anthologia Palatina*, XI, 68 (trans. W. Cowper)
8 Petronius, *Satyricon*, 132 (trans. J. Sullivan)
9 *Latomus*, XX, 1961, pp.821–5
10 Tacitus, *Annals*, XV, 37, 9
11 Id., XIV, 63, 4, is ambiguous on this point.
12 Plutarch, *Galba*, 9 (trans. A. Clough)
13 Pliny *HN*, XIII, 22
14 Tacitus, *Annals*, XIII, 15, 2–4. His song may have come from the *Andromache* of Ennius.
15 Tacitus, *Annals*, XIII, 16, 3–17, 2
16 Suetonius, *Titus*, 2
17 Josephus, *Antiquitates Judaicae*, XX, 8, 2, believed it, but Plutarch, *Galba*, 17, does not list the murder of Britannicus among Nero's crimes.
18 Tacitus, *Annals*, XIII, 18, 5

CHAPTER 3

1 Dio Cassius, LXI, 9, 2f.
2 Juvenal, III, 58ff. (trans. P. Green)
3 L. Servenius Cornutus of Acmonia: Balbillus, C. Caecina Tuscus, Ponticus
4 Seneca, *Apocolocyntosis*, 13. Dio Cassius, LXI, 34, 4, agrees with Tacitus that he outlived Claudius.
5 Pliny the younger, *Epistulae*, VII, 29
6 Seneca, *Epistulae Morales*, XLVII, 12
7 Though the text of Tacitus, *Annals*, XIII, 26 and 50, is in both cases uncertain.
8 Seneca, *De Clementia*, II, 1, 2
9 *Latomus*, VIII, 1949, pp.229–254; cf. Dessau, *Inscriptiones Latinae Selectae*, 1321
10 *Digest*, XXXVI, 1, 1, 1
11 Seneca, *De Clementia*, loc. cit.

12 *Ibid.* I, 26 (trans. M. Hadas)

13 Calpurnius Siculus, *Eclogues*, I, 59

14 Seneca, *De Clementia*, I, 4, 3; I, 8, 5; cf. *Consolatio ad Polybium*, 7, 2; *De Beneficiis*, II, 20, 2

15 Calpurnius Siculus, *Eclogues*, I, 147ff. (trans. E. J. L. Scott)

16 Pliny *HN*, XIV, 51

17 Juvenal, V, 108

18 Suetonius, *Nero*, 15

19 Scholiast on Lucan, I, 319

20 Seneca, *Epistulae Morales*, 77, 1

21 Petronius, *Satyricon*, 44

22 Tacitus, *Annals*, XV, 36, 3–6 (AD 64)

23 Seneca, *Epistulae Morales*, 7, 3; 93, 33; cf. 70, 20

24 Petronius, *Satyricon*, 119 (trans. W. Arrowsmith)

25 Calpurnius Siculus, *Eclogues*, VII, 66; III, 57

26 *Ibid.* VII, 135ff. (trans. E. J. L. Scott). Perhaps written in *c*. AD 58–59.

CHAPTER 4

1 Tacitus, *Annals*, XIV, 5, 1–7

2 Memnon, XI, 4: C. Müller, *Fragmenta Historicorum Graecorum*, III, 529–32

3 Quintilian, VIII, 5, 18

4 Suetonius, *Nero*, 39 (trans. R. Graves); cf. *Oracula Sibyllina*, V, 145, 363ff.

5 For a message from Gaul, cf. Quintilian, VIII, 5, 16

6 E.g. Seneca, *Troades*, 258f., *Thyestes*, 446

7 Seneca, *De Ira*, III, 18–19

8 Seneca, *Phaedra*, 215ff.

9 Seneca, *De Beneficiis*, VII, 20, 4

10 Seneca, *De Ira*, II, 28. His play the *Hercules Furens* seems to dwell on the futility of action, e.g. 955ff., 1267ff.

11 Seneca, *De Ira*, II, 33

12 Seneca, *De Beneficiis*, VII, 20, 3

13 Dio Cassius, LX, 35

14 Pliny the younger, *Panegyricus*, 11

CHAPTER 5

1 Lucian, *De Saltatione*, 64a

2 Pliny *HN*, VII, 184. Or his name may have been Mythicus.

3 Seneca, *Naturales Quaestiones*, VII, 32, 3

4 *Digest*, XII, 4, 3, 5; cf. Tacitus, *Annals*, XIII, 19, 4

5 Suetonius, *Nero*, 20 (trans. R. Graves)

6 Quintilian, XI, 3, 171. On Nero's voice see Suetonius, *loc. cit.*

7 E.g. Seneca, *Oedipus*, 184ff.

8 Pseudo-Plutarch, *De Esu Carminum*, II, 2; cf. Quintilian, I, 10, 31

9 Flavius Philostratus, *Vita Apollonii*, IV, 39

10 Servius on Virgil, *Aeneid*, V, 770. Perhaps Nero got some hints from Euripides' *Alexandros* (now lost). Petronius' poem on the same subject, *Satyricon*, 89f., is a skit, but probably not on Nero's epic (the metre is different).

11 Juvenal, VIII, 222ff. (trans. P. Green)

12 Seneca, *Naturales Quaestiones*, I, 5, 6: *colla Cytheriacae splendent agitata columbae*

13 Scholiast on Lucan, *Bellum Civile (Pharsalia)*, III, 261

14 Persius, *Satires*, I, 99ff. (trans. W. S. Merwin)

15 Martial, *Epigrams*, VIII, 70, 8. The flattery is in the *Einsiedeln Eclogues*, I, 48–9

16 Tacitus, *Annals*, XIV, 16, 1–2

17 Suetonius, *Nero*, 52 (trans. R. Graves)

18 Suetonius, *Augustus*, 85, 2

19 Tacitus, *Annals*, XIV, 15, 2–5. According to Juvenal, VIII, 194, Nero forced nobles to act.

20 *Ibid.* XIV, 15, 7

21 II Samuel, VI, 16

22 Josephus, *Bellum Judaicum*, II, 13, 1; Plutarch, *Galba*, 17

23 Tacitus, *Annals*, XIV, 14, 2

24 *Ibid.* XIV, 15, 8

25 Suetonius, *Nero*, 23 (trans. J. C. Rolfe)

26 *Ibid.* 24

27 Tacitus, *Annals*, XIV, 14, 1, 5

28 The Neronian Games bore no relation to the 'quinquennia' of Nero's reign, with which the festivals did not coincide.

29 Tacitus, *Annals*, XIV, 20, 4

30 Seneca, *De Brevitate Vitae*, 12, 2; cf. Lucan, *Bellum Civile*, VII, 270; and both Plinies

31 Tacitus, *Annals*, XIV, 21, 6

32 *Ibid.* XIV, 21, 8

33 Seneca, *op. cit.*, 12, 3. In this period Julius Cornutus and his family built a wrestling school at Perga in Pamphylia.

34 Martial, *Epigrams*, VII, 34, 4f. Jerome and Cassiodorus, who date the Baths of Nero to 64, are contradicted by the historians. The Baths were rebuilt in the third century by Severus Alexander.

35 Flavius Philostratus, *Vita Apollonii*, IV, 42

36 *Inscriptiones Graecae ad Res Romanas Pertinentes*, IV, 1086

37 Galen, *Methodus Medendi*, I, 2, 3, 10; cf. Pliny *HN*, XXIX, 9

CHAPTER 6

1 Tacitus, *Annals*, XIV, 42, 1
2 Seneca, *Ad Marciam*, 20, 3
3 Seneca, *Epistulae Morales*, 14, 5
4 *Ibid.* 47, 1 (trans. R.Campbell)
5 Cf. Seneca, *De Clementia*, I, 18, *De Ira*, III, 40
6 Petronius, *Satyricon*, 71
7 *Digest*, I, 12, 1
8 Tacitus, *Annals*, XIV, 44, 5–7
9 *Ibid.* XIV, 45, 3
10 *Corpus Inscriptionum Latinarum*, VII, 11
11 Tacitus, *Annals*, XIV, 29, 3–30, 3
12 Tacitus, *Histories*, IV, 54, 3
13 Dio Cassius, LXII, 2, 3f. (trans. E.Cary)
14 The accounts of Paetus' terms in Tacitus, *Annals*, XV, 16, 2f., and Dio Cassius, LXII, 21, 2, do not quite agree.

CHAPTER 7

1 Dessau, *Inscriptiones Latinae Selectae*, 986. *Ibid.*, 985: a Pannonian governor is also pacifying his part of the frontier.
2 Josephus, *Bellum Judaicum*, VII, 89, 94. In winter 67–8 the Sarmatians killed the governor of Moesia, Fonteius Agrippa, and destroyed two cohorts.
3 Pliny *HN*, XXXVII, 45
4 Suetonius, *Galba*, 12. There is an inscription of one of these guards, the Batavian Indus, *Notizie di Scavi*, 8th series, IV, 1951, pp.86ff.
5 Tacitus, *Annals*, XIII, 54, 4–7
6 Seneca, *Naturales Quaestiones*, VI, 8, 3–4, Pliny *HN*, VI, 181ff., cf. XII, 19
7 Petronius, *Satyricon*, 76 (trans. J.Sullivan)
8 Seneca, *Medea*, 371ff. (trans. J.M.Todd)
9 Seneca, *Naturales Quaestiones*, VII, 30 (trans. F.H.Sandbach)
10 *Ibid.*, prologue, 13

CHAPTER 8

1 Scholiast on Juvenal, *Satires*, I, 55
2 Tacitus, *Histories*, I, 72
3 Tacitus, *Annals*, XIV, 56, 6
4 Cf. Dio Cassius, LXII, 13, Seneca, *De Beneficiis*, III, 16, 2; he disapproved of easy divorce.
5 Anon., *Octavia*, 699ff. (trans. G. and H. Highet)

6 Plutarch, *Galba*, 20
7 Suetonius, *Otho*, 3
8 Cf. H.Mattingly, *Coins of the Roman Empire in the British Museum*, I, p.clxxiii, against E.A.Sydenham, *The Coinage of Nero*, p. 126, who relates the issue to Statilia Messalina (AD 67)
9 Pliny *HN*, XXXVII, 50
10 Tacitus, *Annals*, XIII, 45, 2–3
11 Sallust, *Catiline*, 25
12 Juvenal, VI, 462
13 Dio Cassius, LXII, 28, 1
14 Josephus, *Life*, 3
15 Josephus, *Antiquitates Judaicae*, XX, 8, 11
16 Tacitus, *Histories*, I, 22, 2
17 *Catalogus Codicum Astrologiae Graecae*, VIII, 3, p.103 (to Hermogenes)
18 Seneca, *Naturales Quaestiones*, IV, 2, 13
19 Columella, *De Re Rustica*, XI, 1, 31
20 Seneca, *Naturales Quaestiones*, VII, 1, 5; cf. Anon., *Octavia*, 231ff.
21 Tacitus, *Annals*, XIX, 12, 3f.
22 Phlegon, *Mirabilia*, 35; cf.49
23 *Acta Fratrum Arvalium*, 24
24 Tacitus, *Annals*, XV, 23, 4–5

CHAPTER 9

1 Tacitus, *Annals*, XV, 38, 2–41, 2
2 *Ibid.* XV, 44, 2–8
3 *L'Année Epigraphique*, 1963, no. 104 (Caesarea in Palestine)
4 *Acts*, XV–XVII
5 G.Dittenberger, *Sylloge Inscriptionum Graecarum*, 3rd ed., 801D
6 *Acts*, XXVIII, 30
7 *Romans*, XV, 24
8 This was deduced from I Clement, 5 (c. AD 96), Ignatius, *Ad Rom.* 4, etc.
9 E.g. Bishop Dionysius of Corinth to Bishop (Pope) Soter at Rome, Eusebius, *Ecclesiae Historia*, II, 25 (c. AD 170)). But Eusebius, *ibid.*, III, 4, seems to have believed that Peter outlived Paul (and had arrived in Rome before him).
10 Tacitus, *Annals*, XIII, 32, 3
11 Josephus, *Contra Apionem*, II, 165
12 Seneca, *De Superstitione*, fragment 42
13 *Philippians*, IV, 22
14 St John Chrysostom, *Homilies*, XLVI, 13. There is no particular reason to suppose that this was Acte.
15 *Acts*, XXVIII, 22
16 I Peter, IV, 7, 12, 13
17 *Romans*, XIII, 7; XII, 14
18 *Ibid.* XII, 1; cf. 2, 5

19 Tacitus, *Annals*, XV, 44, 6–7
20 Suetonius, *Nero*, 16
21 Tacitus, *Annals*, XV, 44, 8

CHAPTER 10

1 This was particularly timely because the year was the half centenary of the death and deification of Augustus, with whose cult the shrine was closely connected: it was regularly depicted on such anniversaries.
2 Tacitus, *Annals*, XV, 43, 1–4
3 *Ibid.* XV, 43, 5
4 Suetonius, *Nero*, 29 (trans. R. Graves)
5 Tacitus, *Annals*, XV, 42, 1
6 Petronius, *Satyricon*, 131 (trans. J. Sullivan).
7 Suetonius, *Nero*, 31, 1
8 *Ibid.* 31, 2
9 Tacitus, *Annals*, XV, 42, 4
10 Pliny *HN*, XXXV, 3. Other innovations of the day are described in XVI, 233 (tortoise-shell painted to look like wood), 195 (new sort of glass-making).
11 *Ibid.* XXXVII, 17
12 *Ibid.* XXXV, 120
13 Martial, *De Spectaculis*, 2
14 Pliny *HN*, XXXVI, 37
15 Seneca, *Naturales Quaestiones*, VI, 1, 2
16 E.g. the Temple of Isis: the rebuilding was financed by a six-year-old boy.
17 The theme recurs on a mixing bowl found at Hildesheim. The museum at Aquileia has a pedestal from a statuette of Hercules which seems to have been dedicated to Apollo by Nero himself.
18 Cf. Petronius, *Satyricon*, 89 (trans. W. Arrowsmith)
19 Pliny *HN*, XXXV, 112
20 *Ibid.* XXXV, 52
21 *Ibid.* XXXVI, 36, 184
22 Tacitus, *Annals*, XVI, 18, 1–4
23 Petronius, *Satyricon*, 93 (trans. J. Sullivan)
24 Tacitus, *Annals*, XV, 37, 1–7
25 Pliny *HN*, XXXI, 40
26 *Corpus Inscriptionum Latinarum*, X, 6324
27 *Ibid.* 9004
28 Pliny *HN*, XXXVII, 65
29 *Ibid.* XXXVII, 17
30 Tacitus, *Histories*, I, 20. Galba demanded nine-tenths of these sums back.
31 E.g. Lucilius, *Anthologia Palatina*, IX, 572; XI, 132, 185, 254
32 Dio Cassius, LXI, 5, 4

CHAPTER 11

1 Seneca, *Epistulae Morales*, 114, 26
2 Pliny *HN*, XVIII, 35. An inscription from Ain-el-Djemila may refer to imperial estates formed from Nero's confiscations.
3 *Ephemeris Epigraphica*, IX, 1267
4 Cf. Seneca, *De Beneficiis*, IV, 39, 3; VII, 6, 3. The terminology adds to the confusion.
5 M. Grant, *Roman Imperial Money*, p.45
6 Suetonius, *Nero*, 51
7 Seneca, *Epistulae Morales*, 119, 24; Petronius, *Satyricon*, 27
8 In 66 according to Suetonius, *Nero*, 13 (the tercentenary of the first attested closure): but he must be referring to a second closure by Nero, since one at least of the coins is of 64/5.
9 For the Asian issues see M. Grant, *From Imperium to Auctoritas*, p.465. Nero's descent from Germanicus was also stressed by a coin emphasizing his retention of his grandfather's name: AVGVSTVS GERMANICVS.
10 Nero was also equated with Jupiter, by Calpurnius Siculus, *Eclogues*, IV, 142, and on coins of Dioshieron in Lydia. The towns of Cyme and Synaus describe him in his lifetime as a god (*theos*). The official coinage (issued outside Rome) more judiciously and ambiguously dedicated a reverse type 'to the Genius of the emperor' (GENIO AVGVSTI).

CHAPTER 12

1 Suetonius, *Nero*, 20, 1
2 *Ibid.* 20, 2 (trans. R. Graves, but adopting E. K. Borthwick's amendment *suffritinniturum*). Nero is consciously comparing himself with Pindar.
3 Tacitus, *Annals*, XVI, 4, 1–2. Suetonius, *Nero*, 21, 1, states that he anticipated the prescribed date for the second Neronian Games: some believe they were held in 64.
4 Suetonius, *Vitellius*, 4
5 Suetonius, *Nero*, 21, 1–2 (trans. R. Graves, amended)
6 *Ibid.* 23, 2 (trans. J. C. Rolfe)
7 Tacitus, *Annals*, XVI, 5, 1–4
8 A curse in Egypt also, according to its governor Ti. Julius Alexander, *Inscriptiones Graecae ad Res Romanas Pertinentes*, I, 1263

9 Seneca, *De Tranquillitate*, 12

10 Suetonius, *Vita Lucani*

11 Scholiast on Juvenal, *Satires*, V, 109. He is believed to be the subject of the eulogistic *Laus Pisonis*: 261 lines by an unknown young poet.

12 Cf. Plutarch, *De Garrulitate*, 505C; and see below for Dio Cassius.

13 Tacitus, *Annals*, XV, 60, 5

14 *Ibid.* XV, 67, 2–3

15 Statius, *Silvae*, II, 7, 118f.

16 Suetonius, *Nero*, 35, 4, states that she refused to marry the emperor after Poppaea's death.

17 Tacitus, *Annals*, XV, 72, 4

18 SECVRITAS AVGVSTI was perhaps ambiguous, since it could also mean the Security *provided by* the emperor, like the LIBERTAS AVGVSTI of Vitellius.

19 M.Grant, *Essays in Roman Coinage presented to H.Mattingly*, p.98 and Pl.IV, 1

20 The date of the marriage is fixed by coinage issued in the name of Man. Acilius Aviola, governor of Asia 65–6, for this includes coins mentioning first Poppaea and then Statilia Messalina.

21 Plutarch, *Praecepta Reipublicae Gerendae*, 810A

22 M.Grant, *Roman Imperial Money*, pp.30, 168, 173f.

23 Seneca, *De Tranquillitate Animi*, 14, 4–9

24 Musonius Rufus exiled to Gyaros, Flavius Philostratus, *Vita Apollonii*, 7, 16

25 The saga was probably responsible for the emphasis by Aurelius Victor, *De Caesaribus*, V, 2, on the excellence of Nero's 'five years' (probably meaning the first five years of his reign) – for this was the period when Thrasea had collaborated with the emperor.

26 If the cases were closely linked, it seems strange that Demetrius the Cynic, who was Thrasea's philosophical adviser, later defended in court Egnatius Celer, the elderly Syrian Stoic who was alleged to have betrayed Barea; Tacitus, *Histories*, IV, 40, 5.

27 Tacitus, *Agricola*, 42, 5

CHAPTER 13

1 Suetonius, *Nero*, 13, 1–2 (trans. R. Graves)

2 Dio Cassius, LXIII, 5 (trans. M.P. Charlesworth)

3 Samus and Severus, the sons of Venicarius

4 Dio Cassius, LXIII, 15, 1

5 Pseudo-Lucian (? Philostratus), *Nero*, 3

6 This is a more probable date than 28 November, 66

7 G.Dittenberger, *Sylloge Inscriptionum Graecarum*, 3rd ed. 814

8 *Ibid.* (trans. M.P.Charlesworth)

9 *Catalogue of Greek Coins in the British Museum* (Thessaly to Aetolia), no.85

10 Dio Cassius, LXIII, 21

CHAPTER 14

1 Probably not the Albani, as in Tacitus, *Histories*, I,6. The Alani are first mentioned in Lucan, *Bellum Civile*, VIII, 223; X, 454. They broke through the pass in *c*.72, Josephus, *Bellum Judaicum*, VII, 244, 6.

2 Mela, III, 38: known by the time of Caligula or Claudius

3 Seneca, *Epistulae Morales*, 91, 94, 119; Lucan, *op. cit.* X, 26–28

4 Lugdunum had contributed four million sesterces to Rome after the Great Fire, and this was returned to them after Lugdunum was gravely damaged by fire in 65.

5 Cf. Pliny *HN*, XX, 160, *adsertor a Nerone libertatis*

6 Suetonius, *Galba*, 9

7 Pliny the younger, *Epistulae*, VI, 10, 4; IX, 19, 1

8 Plutarch, *Galba*, 6, 3

9 Tacitus, *Histories*, I, 73 (Clodius Macer). He issued coinage of his own, ostensibly as delegate of the Senate, but probably not until after Nero's death.

10 Suetonius, *Nero*, 43 (trans. R.Graves)

11 This is the view of Josephus, *Bellum Judaicum*, IV, 9, 2

12 Plutarch, *Otho*, 2

13 Plutarch, *Galba*, 2

14 Suetonius, *Nero*, 47

15 For his loyalty, cf. Tacitus, *Histories*, I, 6, 2, *pace* Zonaras, XI, 13. According to another view, what Nero now heard of was the move to make Verginius Rufus emperor.

16 Though it is perhaps suspicious that Alexander was issuing an edict in Galba's name less than a month after Nero's death: G.Dittenberger, *Inscriptiones Graecae ad Res Romanas Pertinentes*, I, 1263.

17 They are identified by *Epitome de Caesaribus*, V, 7, as Phaon, Epaphroditus, Sporus and Neophytus.

18 Referring to the drink of snow-cooled water he invented (the *decocta Neronis*).

19 Such condemnation of an emperor was unprecedented, Tacitus, *Histories*, I, 16.

20 Suetonius, *Nero*, 47–50. The first three paragraphs are from a translation by G.B.Townend, though I have preferred another version of Nero's cry about his artistic gifts ('What a loss to the Royal Academy!' was once suggested). The rest is adapted from R.Graves' translation (but modified, e.g. at the end). Nero's quotation ("Hark to the sound . . .") is from the *Iliad*, X, 535.

By the end of 69 Galba, Otho and Vitellius had all reigned and were all dead. Sporus was taken over first by Nymphidius and then by Otho, and killed himself when forced by Vitellius to act the part of a ravished maiden on the stage. Nymphidius made trouble against Galba but was killed by his own praetorians. Galba had Helius, Patrobius, and Locusta led through the streets and executed. Both pro- and anti-Neronians wanted the blood of Tigellinus, who committed suicide at Sinuessa by order of Otho, 'in an atmosphere of lechery, kissing, and nauseous hesitations', Tacitus, *Histories*, I, 72. *Ibid.*, 73, Otho refused to execute Calvia Crispinilla, who survived and died exceptionally rich. He contemplated marriage with Statilia Messalina, who retained a brilliant position under Vespasian and his sons.

21 Nero had recently dismissed the son of one of his nurses, Caecina Tuscus, from the governorship of Egypt for using a bath that had been made for Nero's first projected visit.

1 The Legend of Nero

1 Tacitus, *Histories*, I, 16
2 Suetonius, *Otho*, 7
3 Suetonius, *Vitellius*, 11
4 Tacitus, *Histories*, II, 8, 1, seems to imply that there were at least three pseudo-Neros before 96. *Oracula Sibyllina*, IV (*c*.80) and V (second century) and VIII are all related to the flight to, or return from, the east.
5 Dio Chrysostom, *Orationes*, XXI, 10
6 Plutarch, *De Sera Numinis Vindicta*, 567F
7 *Revelation*, XIII, 8
8 M.Grant, *Roman History from Coins*, Pl.9, no.6 ('contorniate')
9 E.g. Bibliothèque Nationale, Paris
10 Augustine, *De Civitate Dei*, XX, 19

2 Sources of Information

1 Dio Cassius, LIII, 19; cf. LXI, 18, 5
2 Petronius, fragment 28 (trans. J. Sullivan)
3 Tacitus, *Histories*, I, 1 (trans. K.Wellesley)
4 Josephus, *Antiquitates Judaicae*, XX, 154
5 Tacitus, *Annals*, XIII, 20, 3; XIV, 2, 1; cf. references in *Histories*
6 Tacitus, *Annals*, XV, 61, 6; cf. XIII, 20, 2f., XIV, 2, 3
7 *Ibid.* XV, 16, 1
8 *Ibid.* IV, 53
9 *Ibid.* XIII, 14, 3
10 *Acta Fratrum Arvalium*, ed. G.Henzen (1874) and A.Pasoli (1950)

3 Sums of Money

1 B.Radice, *The Letters of the Younger Pliny*, Penguin, 1963, pp.309f.
2 M.Grant, *Julius Caesar*, 1969, p.11

List of Emperors

BC	AD	
31 –	14	Augustus

AD		
14 –	37	Tiberius
37 –	41	Caligula (Gaius)
41 –	54	Claudius
54 –	68	Nero
68 –	69	Galba
	69	Otho
	69	Vitellius
69 –	79	Vespasian
79 –	81	Titus
81 –	96	Domitian
96 –	98	Nerva
98 –	117	Trajan
117 –	138	Hadrian

Further Reading

1 ANCIENT SOURCES

The three principal literary sources are available in the following translations: Tacitus, *Annals*, trans. M.Grant, Penguin Classics, revised ed. 1970; Suetonius, *Life of Nero*, trans. J.C.Rolfe in Loeb edition of *The Caesars*, Heinemann–Harvard, 1914, and trans. R.Graves, Penguin Classics, 1957; Dio Cassius, trans. E.Cary, Loeb edition, Vol. VIII, 1925.

For the main contemporary sources, see above, Appendix 2.

A selection of inscriptions and coins is published by E.M.Smallwood, *Documents Illustrating the Principates of Gaius, Claudius and Nero*, 1967; cf. M.P.Charlesworth, *Documents Illustrating the Reigns of Claudius and Nero*, 1939. See also Appendix 2.

Except in special cases, my notes have not given specific references to the official coins of the Roman state, which are generally to be found in H.Mattingly, *Coins of the Roman Empire in the British Museum*, Vol. I, 1923, cf. M.Grant, *Roman History from Coins*, revised ed. 1968, Ch. 2 and Plates 8–10. Many coinages of towns in the provinces and of provincial authorities are published in the various British Museum Catalogues, and in E.A. Sydenham, *The Coinage of Nero*, 1920.

2 MODERN SOURCES

Balsdon, J.P.V.D., *Life and Leisure in Ancient Rome*, Bodley Head, 1969.

Beaujeu, J., *L'Incendie de Rome en 64 et les Chrétiens* (Collection Latomus, Vol. XLIX), Brussels, 1960.

Millar, F., *A Study of Dio Cassius*, Oxford University Press, 1964.

Momigliano, A., in *Cambridge Ancient History*, Vol. X (Chapter 21: Nero), Cambridge University Press, 1934.

Pascal, C., *Nerone nella storia aneddotica e nella leggenda*, Milan, 1923.

Sevenster, J.N., *Paul and Seneca*, Leiden, 1961.

Smallwood, E.M., *Documents Illustrating the Principates of Gaius, Claudius and Nero*, Cambridge University Press, 1967.

Bishop, J.H., *Nero: The Man and the Legend*, Robert Hale, 1964.

Boethius, A., *The Golden House of Nero*, Ann Arbor and Cresset Press, 1961.

Campbell, R., *Seneca: Letters from a Stoic*, Penguin, 1969.

Charles-Picard, G., *Augustus and Nero: the Secret of Empire*, Phoenix House, 1966.

Corte, F.della, *Suetonio: eques Romanus*, 2nd ed., Florence, 1967.

Dorey, T.A. (ed.), *Tacitus*, Routledge and Kegan Paul (Studies in Latin Literature and its Influence), 1969.

Dudley, D.R., *The World of Tacitus*, Secker and Warburg, 1968.

Dudley, D.R. and Webster, G., *The Rebellion of Boudicca*, Routledge and Kegan Paul, 1962.

Friedländer, L., *Darstellungen aus der Sittengeschichte Roms*, 9th ed., Leipzig, 1920; 7th ed. translated as *Roman Life and Manners under the Early Empire*, Routledge, 1908–13, reprint 1965.

Grant, M., *Roman History from Coins*, 2nd ed., Cambridge University Press, 1968.

Grant, M., *The Ancient Historians*, Weidenfeld and Nicolson, and Scribners, New York, 1970.

Henderson, B.W., *The Life and Principate of the Emperor Nero*, Methuen, 1903.

Hohl, E., in Pauly-Wissowa-Kroll, *Realenzyclopädie der kl. Altertumswissenschaft*, Supplementband III, 350–394, s.v.Domitius (Nero), 1918.

Kiefer, O., *Sexual Life in Ancient Rome*, Routledge, 1934.

Levi, M.A., *Nerone e i suoi tempi*, Milan, 1949.

MacDowall, D.W., *The Western Coinages of Nero* (American Numismatic Society), New York, 1970.

Sullivan, J., *The Satyricon of Petronius*, Faber and Faber, 1968.

Syme, R., *Tacitus*, Oxford University Press, 1958; *Ten Studies in Tacitus*, 1970.

Thackeray, H.St.J., *Josephus the Man and the Historian*, New York, repr. 1967.

Waltz, ., *La Vie Politique de Sénèque*, Paris, 1909.

Warmington, B.H., *Nero: Reality and Legend*, Chatto and Windus, 1969.

Genealogical Tables

THE FAMILY OF NERO

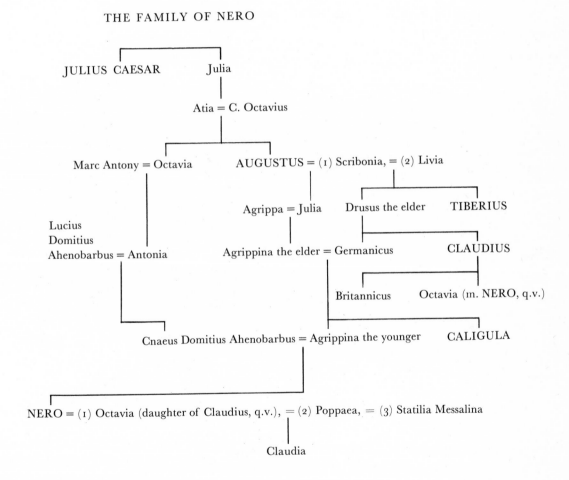

THE VICTIMS OF NERO'S REIGN

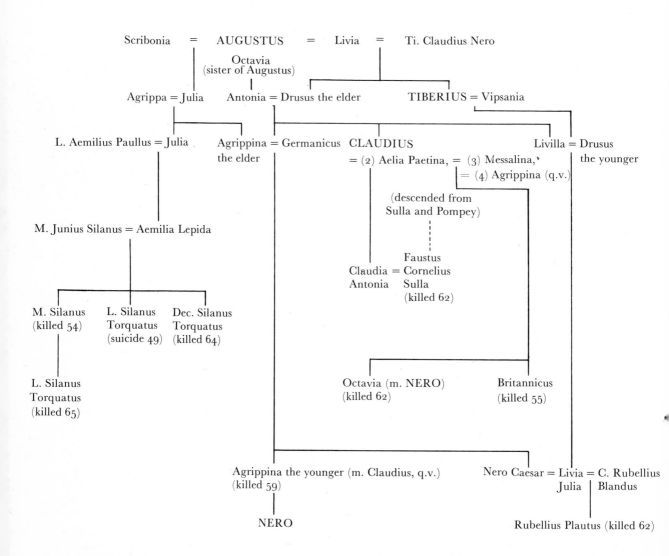

Index